Common
Human Needs

Common Human Needs

Charlotte Towle

Revised Edition

National Association of Social Workers, Inc. • Silver Spring, MD 20910

Suzanne Dworak-Peck, *President* • Mark G. Battle, *Executive Director*

The language of *Common Human Needs*, first published in 1945, may appear biased compared with standard usage today. In the interest of accurate and unbiased language, current policy of the National Association of Social Workers, Inc. (NASW) publications program is to subscribe to a belief in the importance of avoiding language that might imply sexual, ethnic, or other kinds of discriminators, stereotyping, or bias. NASW is committed to the fair and equal treatment of individuals and groups. —ED.

© 1987 by the National Association of Social Workers, Inc.

Earlier edition © 1965. Original publication date 1945.
Revised edition 1952, published by the American
Association of Social Workers. Revised edition 1957,
published by the National Association of Social Workers, Inc.
Revised edition, 1965.

Revised edition, 1987
Cover and interior design by Ellen C. Dawson

Library of Congress Cataloging-in-Publication Data

Towle, Charlotte.
  Common human needs.

  Bibliography: p.
  1. Public welfare—United States.   2. Social
service—United States.   3. Needs assessment—Handbooks,
manuals, etc.   I. Title. [DNLM: 1. Social Welfare.
2. Social Work.   HV 85 T742c]
HV91.T6 1987   361.3'2   87-22016
ISBN 0-87101-154-9

Printed in the United States of America

Contents

Preface

It is appropriate that the National Association of Social Workers (NASW) publish a revised edition of *Common Human Needs* in 1987. This year is the 30th anniversary of the first edition published by the association. In 1957, NASW, which had been in existence as an amalgamated association for only two years, issued a revised edition of the widely used pamphlet first published by the Federal Security Agency in 1945 and reissued by the American Association of Social Workers when the government banned it in 1951.

The republication of *Common Human Needs* reminds social workers of the values of our profession and of the work that faces us in the public policy arena. In her foreword to the 1987 edition, Jacqueline Atkins describes how special interest groups used the book to attack proponents of national health insurance. Today, the controversy over national health insurance still rages, and it is incumbent on us to advocate for a health insurance package that will meet the needs of those it is intended to serve.

Common Human Needs was written to provide training for public assistance workers who had the difficult task of administering financial aid to families in economic distress. Today, social workers in public agencies face an even more difficult task because the emphasis has changed from human rights and human needs to economic self-reliance. Social workers must pay close attention to the many welfare reform proposals now before Congress to ensure that common human needs are not lost in a push to reduce federal and state expenditures.

Even the most experienced practitioner will benefit from frequent rereading of *Common Human Needs*. No writer since Charlotte Towle has described the stages of life, the basic human motivations, the needs and desires of people with such profound simplicity and concern.

SUZANNE DWORAK-PECK, *President*
MARK G. BATTLE, *Executive Director*
National Association of Social Workers, Inc.

August 1987

Foreword to the 1987 edition

Common human needs: looking backward

"Viciously" and "malevolently un-American" is how Elmer L. Henderson, president of the American Medical Association (AMA), characterized *Common Human Needs* in 1951. The growing political conservatism in the United States throughout the 1940s that culminated in the McCarthy era of the early 1950s provided fertile ground for the seeds of dissension that flourished around the book. This attack, at the end of many that had occurred in the years following first publication in 1945, coupled with the political climate and a fear of any use of the term *socialized*, finally drove the government to rescind publication and marked the closure for continuation of the volume under government auspices.

Common Human Needs, originally written at the request of the Bureau of Public Assistance, a subunit of the Federal Security Agency (FSA) (forerunner of today's Department of Health and Human Services), recognized the principle of public assistance services as a right, the need for public assistance workers to have a solid understanding of the common human needs that govern behavior, and the role of government in meeting those needs. An extraordinary outpouring of support for the book and its precepts by the social work community and related professionals, however, could not stem the flow of criticism that was leveled at it from local chambers of commerce to members of Congress—*Common Human Needs* became one of the victims of a negative public attitude that viewed public assistance as a major step on the road leading ultimately to the socialized state. The book also was used as a major tool in a concerted crusade orchestrated by AMA that was intended to prevent the federal government from implementing a national compulsory health insurance program, or, in the AMA view, "socialized medicine." The events leading to the government's "book-burning" action and the subsequent republication of the book by the American Association of Social Workers (AASW) [later the National Association of Social Workers (NASW)] are well worth reviewing today as *Common Human Needs* moves into its fourth edition and its fifth decade in print and because some similar conservative attitudes and trends can be seen in welfare issues today.

The early years

The landmark Social Security Act of 1935 and other federal public assistance legislation passed during the 1930s and 1940s created new opportunities and new problems for social workers. Workers often found themselves juggling the disparate objectives of protecting the entitlements of assistance recipients (an objective that frequently met with public resistance), protecting the interests of the taxpayers, and determining whether recipients truly met assistance eligibility requirements. Additionally, few written materials existed that offered guidance in any of these areas.[1] Although workers in public assistance programs were trained on a state and not the federal level, Jane Hoey, then head of the Bureau of Public Assistance, recognized the need for high-quality materials that could help to provide guidelines and interpretations for workers to follow in the varied and difficult situations that they faced daily. Thus, she established a program under which the bureau would develop and disseminate materials that addressed specific public assistance concerns or issues and could be used by state supervisors and others in training workers in public assistance programs.

Under the program established by Hoey, Charlotte Towle, a highly regarded social work professor at the University of Chicago School of Social Service Administration, was approached to undertake the development of a pamphlet that would aid public assistance workers in fulfilling their duties. In 1944, when she agreed to develop the pamphlet, she had little idea of the furor that would occur in the six years following its publication, or of the use that would be made of its content in attacks on Oscar Ewing, head of FSA from 1947 to 1952, on FSA itself, and on the efforts of the Truman Administration to launch a program of compulsory health insurance.

The first draft of the pamphlet was completed in only six weeks, and an intensive round of reviews and revisions marked the following eight months. A number of people within the bureau read the manuscript, and although some expressed concern that Towle did not emphasize enough the law as a meeting place for worker and client and delivery of service, the reviewers were excited about the potential of the publication for training public assistance workers; none faulted the sections that later would cause so much controversy.[2]

The pamphlet was published in fall 1945 and was distributed immediately to public assistance agencies around the country. A covering memorandum that accompanied this first distribution outlined some of the ways in which the book could be used most effectively, noting that it "might be used as a basis for discussion of the purpose and philosophy of public assistance while reviewing existing policies of the agency...to determine whether agency practice is achieving the social purposes for which the program was established."[3] The publication was received enthusiastically by the social welfare community and quickly gained a readership far beyond that originally envisioned in the public assistance field. This receptive state of affairs in the profession did not carry over into the public sector, however, and by 1947, only two years after its publication, the attacks on *Common Human Needs* began.

Years of criticism

In 1947, a major review of the public welfare program in Baltimore was underway, and a great deal of concern had been expressed—particularly by the business community—about possible inefficiency and irresponsibility within the welfare system, perceptions that were common among many members of the American public. Although the Baltimore Commission on Governmental Efficiency and Economy report identified a number of issues that undoubtedly needed attention, many of its findings and recommendations were blown out of proportion in the newspaper articles published following its release; what had begun as a local controversy soon escalated to a political football receiving national prominence.[4] Blame for a weak system that kept receivers of public assistance dependent rather than becoming self-reliant was placed on the Bureau of Public Assistance, and two of its publications were charged specifically with encouraging caseworkers to follow guidelines and practices that would only lead to welfare abuse. The two publications cited were *Common Human Needs* by Towle and *The Nature of Service in Public Administration* by Grace Marcus; both books had been published under the auspices of the bureau as part of the program to provide information helpful to public assistance workers.[5] In the case of both books, material frequently was quoted out of context, with little understanding of the underlying intent of the social security legislation or the public assistance programs. It was at this time that the sentence containing the phrase that later virtually condemned Towle's book began to be extensively quoted: "Social security and public assistance programs are a basic essential for attainment of the socialized state envisaged in democratic ideology, a way of life which so far has been realized only in slight measure."[6]

The articles that appeared nationally in the press and presentations in Congress focused attention on this statement over the next few months—particularly the term "socialized state"—"socialized" was interpreted as "socialistic," rather than in the sense of "socialization" as Towle had meant it.[7] Rep. Ralph Gwinn of New York reflected a particular strong conservative view of this material when he quoted from a speech presented by the president

of a businessmen's group in which reference was made to the offending statement in Towle's book: "I've known for years that the ultimate aim of the public
assistance and social security boys was national socialism—the Government
owning everything and everybody—but this is the first instance...where one
of the insiders admitted this objective in so many words."[8]

Yet as early as January 1948, a statement had been developed by the Social
Security Administration (SSA) that clearly stated agency policy and practice.
The statement highlighted the many misinterpretations that had been made
in the newspaper coverage and supported the material contained in the two
books. However, for reasons that now remain unclear, this statement was never
made public but only circulated internally.[9] Towle herself seemed to think
that a response interpreting her terms and intents would be nonproductive
and only prolong the controversy. In a letter to a friend, she noted that "personally I doubt that this group are [sic] exerting a very wide influence....I think
therefore that such productions as these represent a defense which we do not
need to be too concerned about. I may be wrong in this estimate.[10]

Unfortunately, Towle was wrong in her estimate of the amount of continued concern that the book would generate. Although the furor died down
to some extent by spring 1948 and the following two years were comparative-
ly quiet, the controversy surfaced again in 1950 with the publication of an
article in a national magazine that sought to show Ewing and FSA as great
promoters of socialism.[11] Once again, Towle's reference to a "socialized state"
was used as support for this accusation: "In its advisory manual, 'Common
Human Needs,' for training state personnel in distributing this [public]
assistance, [the Social Security Administration] makes clear that a socialized
state is the desired goal."[12]

Soon after this article appeared, Rep. Gwinn again criticized the public
assistance program, SSA, and *Common Human Needs* in a press release entitled "Be Socialized and Stop Worrying"; this piece later also appeared as
a book review of *Common Human Needs*.[13] Gwinn's blast brought a request
to FSA from the White House for a copy of the document in question. Ewing
complied, commenting that the document was not part of the FSA operating
policy, as had been claimed by some of its opponents, but was issued as staff
training material for use by state and local welfare agencies. He emphasized
that the book was meant to highlight the kinds of problems that public
assistance workers faced so that the determination of need could be made in
a manner that did not injure the recipient's self-respect, yet recognized the
worker's responsibility to his or her agency. He went on to note that

> this report was the subject of considerable newspaper comment a few years
> ago, and from time to time others...have taken phrases and sentences out
> of context with the result that the real meaning of the passages quoted has
> been obscured and distorted...a reasonable reading of the full text...is the best
> defense against the "charges" made; several newspapermen who asked for

pies of the document apparently decided not to write about it after they
ad read it more carefully.[14]

Ewing's response apparently satisfied the White House because there is
no further record of question about the book from that source. In answer to
yet another congressional attack on the wording in the book, this time from
Rep. James Patterson of Connecticut, Ewing went one step farther, noting that
the choice of words in Towle's book was "unfortunate" but also including
a note from the Deputy Commissioner of Social Security that gave an explanation of the interpretation intended:

> I recognize that the sentence quoted...can be misunderstood. That is because
> the word "socialize" has several meanings. However, a careful reading of the
> pamphlet should make it clear that the author was advocating quite the op-
> posite of a "socialized state" as that term is now used to mean a political or
> economic theory.
>
> It is unmistakably clear that the author...uses the word "socialize" in
> its primary and in its educational meaning, namely, "To render social; especial-
> ly, to train for social environment...."[15]

Although Patterson's letter to Ewing criticizing the book and requesting an
explanation of Towle's terminology was included in the *Congressional Record*,
Ewing's response was never published, and so the controversy continued over
the next few months, coming to a climax in spring 1951.

AMA enters the fray

Since a 1945 address on health care that Truman had delivered to Congress,
the traditionally conservative AMA had feared that the federal government
would formally propose the implementation of some form of compulsory
health insurance. Both Truman and Ewing were known to favor such a proposal, while AMA was adamantly against any move toward what that
organization termed "socialized medicine." The AMA opposition to this issue
had begun as early as the 1930s, when some members of Congress had attempted to introduce a proposal for health care assistance into federal legislation and were defeated. This opposition escalated dramatically shortly after
Truman's reelection when a bill that supported compulsory health insurance
was reintroduced in Congress.[16]

AMA hired a well-known California public relations firm to play a major
role in its battle against compulsory health insurance, and a massive national
public relations campaign, which concentrated on "the evils of federal interven-
tion in the practice of medicine," was soon underway.[17] The campaign concentrated on discrediting Ewing, partly because of his strong support for

compulsory health insurance, partly because jurisdiction for health issues fell under his agency, and partly because of a concern that an all-out attack on Truman was not feasible because of his popularity at the time. From 1948 on, Ewing was pressured in many different ways by the AMA campaign, and charges were made in more than one place that Ewing's true aim was to turn the United States into a "socialized state."[18]

Towle's terminology played directly into the hands of those out to discredit Ewing and his goals, and the earlier criticisms of and attacks on *Common Human Needs* were used with great effectiveness by devotees of the AMA cause. Nowhere were these criticisms used more notably than in the monthly column written by Elmer L. Henderson, AMA president, in the March 1951 issue of the *Journal of the American Medical Association*. In that column, he first commented on the positive public response to the AMA campaign against the so-called "socialistic legislation" that could result in compulsory health insurance; then, using Towle's book as a point of departure, he launched an attack on Ewing:

> I think you will be interested, therefore, in a bit of light, cast from Oscar Ewing's Federal Security Agency, which illuminates his true aims. The follow-ing directive appears on page 7 [sic], chapter 4, of a current pamphlet issued by Mr. Ewing's "Bureau of Public Assistance," titled "Common Human Needs," and subtitled "An Interpretation for the Staff in Public Assistance Agencies": "Social security and public assistance programs are a basic *essen-tial for attainment of the Socialized State* envisaged in democratic ideology, a way of life which so far has been realized only in slight measure."
>
> Mr. Ewing's directive...does emphasize...that socialism remains a basic tenet of the Administration program....[19]

Ewing protested to the editor of the AMA journal by telegram, calling attention to Henderson's reference to *Common Human Needs* as "current" and as "Ewing's directive." He scored the AMA for not verifying its facts, noting that the book had been published originally two years before his appointment, had never had "the remotest authority as directive," and was not at that time "currently" being distributed by FSA.[20]

Ewing, unfortunately, also had failed to check his facts carefully, and Henderson quickly took advantage of this failure, replying to Ewing that the public records indicated the book had been reprinted in 1949, when he was indeed head of FSA, and noting that "five copies were received in the mail here [at the AMA offices] last week, which indicates certain currency still," and that

> in case it was without your knowledge that your office was reprinting and distributing such un-American directives during your tenure, you may wish to issue a public statement disclaiming responsibility for the material. If so, we shall certainly be glad to be helpful in giving such a statement further distribution....[21]

In that same telegram, Henderson further suggested that Ewing might wish to make a formal disavowal to Congress of the principles expressed in *Common Human Needs* because it was "a grave misuse of taxpayers' money to disseminate wholly un-American philosophies."

In Ewing's reply, again to the editor of the journal rather than to Henderson, he noted somewhat apologetically that FSA had made only one distribution of the book—in 1945—but that he had learned that occasional copies had been mailed out since then in response to specific requests and that the Government Printing Office had reprinted the document when supplies were depleted. Ewing then accused Henderson of continuing to make misleading statements; he refused to be held accountable for actions taken by the agency, its employees, or the Government Printing Office before he became administrator. Finally, he concluded, "The statement to which you refer is as objectionable to me as it can possibly be to Dr. Henderson, and his attempt to make me responsible for it is a blow below the belt for which you and he should apologize."[22]

Henderson, however, had the last word in this telegram exchange:

> ...the pamphlet carrying this viciously un-American pronouncement is being distributed currently under the imprint of your office, and carrying the printing date of 1949 when you were in charge there....
>
> You state...that the pronouncement concerning the socialized state is wholly objectionable to you...the reasonable manner in which to clarify your own position would not be in telegrams...but first by asking the Government Printing Office to cease reprinting and distributing the material attributed to your office.[23]

He then went on to suggest that Ewing's staff also be instructed to stop distribution of the book, reiterated his earlier suggestion that Ewing might wish to make a public statement on his position to Congress, and, in closing, noted that "we do appreciate your difficult position and are gratified to be advised that such a malevolently un-American pronouncement is not subscribed to by you."

During this exchange, Ewing gave orders to the Superintendent of Documents to destroy all copies of *Common Human Needs* that were still in stock, as well as the plates for the book.[24] Considering the strength he had shown in facing down other attacks, it is unclear why Ewing suddenly gave in on this particular confrontation. It can only be surmised that the accumulated public complaints over the six-year period since first publication of the book and continued Congressional pressure made it politically expedient for him to submit to an issue that he himself seemed to view with extreme discomfort. The public attacks on his political views were becoming increasingly personal, and he seemed to have reached a point where he felt that the language in the book, however innocent its original intent, was no longer defensible nor worth the effort of defending without leaving himself open to yet more censure from his conservative antagonists. In answering criticism from those who objected to his action in destroying the book, Ewing stated that the publication had been an ongoing source of embarrassment to FSA (and to him) and that he found it revolting that he and FSA could be accused of advocating a socialistic form of government on the basis of a few misinterpreted phrases found in the book. And, finally, that

> it was to protect these programs [in the Social Security Administration] from any such misinterpretation, as well as to dissociate myself as completely as possible from the foregoing construction put on Miss Towle's language, that I took such steps as I deemed necessary to make sure that there was no further distribution of this publication under the sponsorship of the Federal Security Agency....[25]

He also may have worried that the acrimony engendered by the ongoing debate was leaving him in a vulnerable position for carrying out his other work; in a speech given shortly after his decision to destroy the book, he noted that "when one salient gets too far out ahead, you may have to withdraw in order to protect the rest of the front."[26]

The road to republication

Throughout the period of greatest controversy and acrimonious interchange between Ewing and AMA and its supporters, the social work community as well as many in related professions poured forth strong statements of support for Towle and her work, citing its usefulness to workers in public assistance programs and the valuable contribution it had made to the professional literature in general. In addition to AASW and its state and local chapters, the American Association of Medical Social Workers, the American Association of Psychiatric Social Workers, the American Association of Schools of Social Work, the American Psychological Association (APA), the American Civil Liberties Union (Chicago Division), the National Association of Jewish Center Workers, numerous faculty and student groups for schools of social work throughout the country, and many individual social workers wrote to Ewing and to President Truman protesting the decision to withdraw the book and destroy the plates (a resolution from the American Association of Schools of Social Work called that action "indefensible" and an "arbitrary and unwarranted act") and upholding the value of its content for training social workers.[27] Some, including Dean Helen Wright of the University of Chicago School of Social Service Administration, drew parallels to the book burnings that had taken place in Nazi Germany and expressed concern about the possibility of future censorship of other materials; others questioned the need for withdrawing the book when a few simple revisions could have defused the bulk of the controversy.[28] In response to the issue of incorporating a few revisions, Ewing simply replied that he did not want to have the book revised and then republished because he felt that "this would merely continue the controversy in another form."[29]

Ewing further disclaimed any continuing responsibility for keeping *Common Human Needs* available to workers in the public assistance field; he stated that he had been informed that the University of Chicago was republishing the book and would make it available through its bookstore; therefore, it was unnecessary for the government to republish. Again, his information was inaccurate: although, when the Government Printing Office was temporarily out of stock in 1947, the university did indeed print a limited number of copies to meet an interim demand, there had been no plans to keep the book in print on any longer-term basis.

It was at this juncture that AASW decided to keep this important book available. As soon as it had become clear that Ewing had no intention of rescinding his decision and reissuing the book, Joseph Anderson and Benjamin Youngdahl, respectively executive secretary and AASW president, began discussions with Towle to ensure that the document stayed in print. Because the government had been the original publisher, the book had not been copyrighted; thus, Towle retained all rights to the manuscript. At the fall 1951 meeting of the National Board of Directors of AASW, a unanimous resolution was adopted recording the board's belief that the government action in withdrawing the book represented an "action so out of keeping with the general position of the Federal Security Agency in its advocacy and support of sound social welfare programs and effective administration and...a yielding to unjustified and unfounded criticism of the book." Furthermore, the resolution reflected the commitment of AASW to continued publication of the book that had become "a widely accepted exposition of basic social work concepts, practice and philosophy in relation to the common human needs of people."[30] A strong public statement of support from APA came to AASW for its decision to undertake this task; at its annual meeting in 1951, APA vociferously protested the "unwarranted Government censorship" that could "destroy intelligent thinking on which democracy rests" and further offered AASW assistance in making the book available again.[31]

Towle was delighted that the book was to be kept in print and readily agreed to have her professional association, AASW, handle its republication. Although she had been hurt personally by the negative attention her work had engendered over the years, she nevertheless had maintained a dignified professional silence throughout. Only after *Common Human Needs* had been repudiated by FSA did she express her feelings to Hoey and Ewing, noting her concern that some might take the action as a repudiation of social work itself rather than of the few "ambiguous" phrases in the book and that it could be seen as "horsetrading" one program for another; in her letters to them she asked, "Does the Federal Security Administration no longer contend for the aims of the Social Security Act?...If so, these are dark days indeed."[32] However, the knowledge that the book was not doomed to future obscurity helped to lighten the following days, and over the next few months she made minor revisions in the manuscript, primarily in those sections in which the term "socialized" had appeared. Both she and AASW executives agreed that "some effort should be made to safeguard against possible misinterpretation of the book as a protection to the state and local welfare departments who may use it in their staff training."[33]

The foreword to the 1945 edition, by Hoey, was deleted from the AASW edition as a sign of protest over the actions of the government in withdrawing the book, and specifically, over Hoey's perceived support of Ewing's decision to destroy a document developed originally at her suggestion. The new edition came off press in 1952, carrying a preface by Joseph Anderson. An initial decision to include a "fighting foreword" that would recognize the attacks on *Common Human Needs* as well as score the political climate under which such events could occur was later changed in favor of inclusion of a simple factual statement that would not continue to promote the air of contention then surrounding the book but rather support the value and usefulness of the principles of practice expressed in it.

Common Human Needs—1952 to 1987

In 1955, seven social work organizations, including AASW, merged to form NASW and began formal functioning in 1956. The new association, which, in addition to AASW, included others of the organizations who earlier had spoken out against the government's action on *Common Human Needs*, took over many of the publications of its predecessor groups and was delighted to find Towle's book within its purview. Work was begun on a second revised edition almost immediately, and Towle developed an expanded introduction for that edition that noted the changes in the Social Security Act and public assistance legislation since she had first written the book. A later request to Towle to consider updating and revising the entire book for a 1965 edition brought a reluctant refusal because she noted that "I regard this as my one and only piece of near great writing. It is the only one of my works I can re-read without some discomfort."[34] However, she did update the bibliography for that edition.

The 1987 edition reflects the changes made to the text in the 1952 edition (footnotes provide the original wording found in the 1945 edition) and also includes the updates Towle provided for the 1957 and 1965 editions. Although none of the earlier editions contained any record of the events leading up to the AASW/NASW ongoing publication of the book, an introduction by Helen Harris Perlman in the 1965 edition definitively placed *Common Human Needs* in the ranks of the social work classics, speaking glowingly of its lasting contribution to the profession and the continuing professional soundness of the basic social work concepts, practice, and philosophy that are expressed in the book.[35]

That Perlman was accurate in her assessment of the essential tenets of the book has been more justified in the intervening years. As *Common Human Needs* now goes into its first new edition in 22 years, it carries with it a venerable record of achievement: close to 160,000 copies printed (including those produced during its term as a government publication), translation into 11 languages (Arabic, Dutch, Flemish, French, German, Greek, Hebrew, Japanese, Korean, Spanish, and Turkish), a special 1973 British edition prepared by Dame Eileen Younghusband, and a major place on the "must" reading lists for the profession.[36] The influence of the book on the direction of social work and those in it has been significant; it clearly has deserved its stature as a "classic," and one that will long continue to be treasured for its historic contribution to professional growth and development as well as for the intrinsic— and still valid—principles of professional belief and practice that have helped to keep it alive against adversity and through the many years that have passed since it was written.

JACQUELINE M. ATKINS, *Former Director, Publications* *
National Association of Social Workers, Inc.

August 1987

Notes

1. *For a description of the material available in this area and early efforts to supply training aids, see* Wendy Beth Posner, "Charlotte Towle: A Biography," pp. 207–216. Unpublished Ph.D. dissertation, University of Chicago School of Social Service Administration, 1986. Available on microfilm (Ann Arbor, Mich.: University Microfilm International, 1987).

2. Ibid., p. 223.

3. Memorandum from Kathryn Goodwin, Acting Director, Bureau of Public Assistance, Federal Security Agency, to Regional Directors and Public Assistance Representatives, September 13, 1945. Papers of Oscar R. Ewing, "Documents Relating to Criticism of *Common Human Needs* 1945–1952," pp. 8–9. Courtesy of the Truman Library.

---

*For their willingness to share time, information, and material on Charlotte Towle and controversy surrounding *Common Human Needs* (and thereby making my task that much easier), I would like to give my sincere thanks to Wendy Beth Posner, Carol Meyer, Beatrice Saunders, Bernece Simon, Dorothy Lally, Sidney Berengarten, Alice Taylor Davis, Linda Beebe, and the staff of the Truman Library.

4. Posner, "Charlotte Towle," p. 226. *See also, for example, "Inefficiency Charged in Study of Baltimore Public Welfare System," Washington Star,* December 10, 1947, pp. A6; Howard Norton, "U.S. Deliberately Swells Relief Rolls, E. and E. Group Claims," *Baltimore Sun,* December 12, 1947, p. 34, 9; and "Order Aids to Swell Dole Lists," *Chicago Tribune,* December 16, 1947, Sec. 1., p. 1., 3.

5. Charlotte Towle, *Common Human Needs: An Interpretation for Staff in Public Assistance Agencies,* Public Assistance Report No. 8 (Washington, D.C.: U.S. Government Printing Office, 1945); and Grace Marcus, *The Nature of Service in Public Assistance Administration,* Public Assistance Report No. 10 (Washington, D.C.: U.S. Government Printing Office, 1947).

6. Towle, *Common Human Needs,* p. 57.

7. *In addition to the articles noted in footnote 4, see also* "Welfare Fog Traced to Federal Doctrine," *New York World Telegram,* December 27, 1947, p. 8; "FSA for Gentle Treatment of Relief Clients," *The New York Sun,* December 23, 1947, p. 1, 5; and "How to Induce the Needy to Take Relief Funds Told in FSA Bulletins," *The Washington Evening Star,* December 25, 1947, p. B6.

8. "Extension of Remarks of Hon. Ralph W. Gwinn," as quoted in *Congressional Record—Appendix,* February 2, 1948, pp. A602–603.

9. Memorandum from A. J. Altmeyer, Social Security Commissioner, Federal Security Agency, to Oscar R. Ewing, Administrator, Federal Security Agency, January 5, 1948. Papers of Ewing, "Documents Relating to Criticism of *Common Human Needs* 1945–1952," pp. 19–20. Courtesy of the Truman Library.

10. Charlotte Towle to Clarence Hille, personal communication, November 14, 1949. As quoted in Posner, "Charlotte Towle," p. 249.

11. Junius B. Wood, "Seed Beds of Socialism: No. 1, The Federal Security Agency," *Nation's Business* (August 1950), pp. 29–31, 64.

12. Ibid., p. 64.

13. Ralph W. Gwinn, "Your Congressman Reports," Release No. 180, October 19, 1950. *See also* Ralph W. Gwinn, "Current Reading," *Faith and Freedom,* January 1951, p. 13. Both documents found in papers of Ewing, "Documents Relating to Criticism of *Common Human Needs* 1945–1952," pp. 27–29. Courtesy of the Truman Library.

14. Oscar R. Ewing to David P. Lloyd, personal communication, November 30, 1950. Papers of Ewing, "Documents Relating to Criticism of *Common Human Needs* 1945–1952," pp. 30–31. Courtesy of the Truman Library.

15. Memorandum from William L. Mitchell to Oscar R. Ewing, December 15, 1950, attached to a letter sent from Ewing to the Hon. James T. Patterson, December 18, 1950. Papers of Ewing, "Documents Relating to Criticism of *Common Human Needs* 1945–1952," pp. 33–34. Courtesy of the Truman Library.

16. Posner, "Charlotte Towle," p. 231.

17. Ibid., p. 236. The husband-and-wife team of Clem Whitaker and Leone Baxter had a solid history in political public relations and were described as "the most dynamic single influence in California's politics" (*San Francisco Chronicle,* as quoted in Posner, "Charlotte Towle," p. 234). Carey McWilliams, in "Government by Whitaker and Baxter," *The Nation,* 172 (April 14, 1951), p. 346, noted that "Whitaker and Baxter has ushered in a new era in American politics—government by public relations."

18. *See, for example,* Wood, "Seed Beds of Socialism," pp. 29–31.

19. Elmer L. Henderson, "The President's Page," *Journal of the American Medical Association,* 145 (March 31, 1951), p. 988. Italics and capitalization as in Henderson's original editorial.

20. Telegram from Oscar R. Ewing to Editor, *Journal of the American Medical Association,* April 3, 1951. This and the three documents listed in footnotes 21–23 were entered in the *Congressional Record—Appendix,* May 1, 1951, pp. A2507–2508. Papers of Ewing, "Documents Relating to Criticism of *Common Human Needs* 1945–1952," pp. 37–38. Courtesy of the Truman Library.

21. Excerpted from telegram from Elmer L. Henderson to Oscar R. Ewing, April 10, 1951.

22. Excerpted from telegram from Oscar R. Ewing to Editor, *Journal of the American Medical Association,* April 11, 1951.

23. Excerpted from telegram from Elmer L. Henderson to Oscar R. Ewing, April 13, 1951.

24. Memorandum from Harold Dotterer, Director, Service Operations, Federal Security Agency, to Roy Easton, Superintendent of Documents, Government Printing Office, April 5, 1951. Papers of Ewing, "Documents Relating to Criticism of *Common Human Needs* 1945–1952," p. 39. Courtesy of the Truman Library.

25. Oscar R. Ewing to Katherine A. Kendall, Executive Secretary, American Association of Schools of Social Work, personal communication, July 12, 1951.

26. As quoted in a memorandum from Arlien Johnson, Dean, University of Southern California School of Social Work, to Helen Wright, Dean, University of Chicago School of Social Service Administration, as quoted in Posner, "Charlotte Towle," p. 251.

27. Lucy Freeman, "Ewing Condemned on Towle Action," *The New York Times,* May 18, 1951, p. 30.

28. Helen Wright to Ernest Witte, President, American Association of Social Workers, personal communication, April 19, 1951. *See also* Freeman, "Ewing Condemned on Towle Action," p. 30, where Wright is quoted as follows: "If the…Government sets an example of destroying publications because they contain one sentence which—out of context—can be and is misinterpreted by some people, where is this going to lead? It is not a very long step to the censoring of textbooks and other publications, such as was the practice in Nazi Germany…."

29. Oscar R. Ewing to Katherine A. Kendall, personal communication, April 13, 1951.

30. "Resolution on *Common Human Needs.*" Resolution presented and adopted by the National Board of Directors of the American Association of Social Workers at its meeting in New York City, October 18–20, 1951. The resolution is included in the *Appendixes.*

31. Lucy Freeman, "Psychologists Lay Censorship to U.S.," *New York Times,* September 6, 1951, p. 33.

32. Letters from Charlotte Towle to Oscar R. Ewing, May 22, 1951, and Jane Hoey, June 12, 1951. Ewing's response to Towle (June 25, 1951) disclaimed any intent to repudiate the basic philosophy of social work, but his alienation from the book is clear when he says, "I have more important things to do than to spend my time arguing about your use of language."

33. David French, Assistant Executive Secretary, American Association of Social Workers, to Charlotte Towle, personal communication, December 6, 1951.

34. Charlotte Towle to Bea Saunders, Publications Director, National Association of Social Workers, personal communication, October 11, 1963.

35. The 1965 edition reinserted the earlier preface by Jane Hoey as well as the acknowledgments from Towle. All original front matter, as well as the Joseph P. Anderson preface and the Helen Harris Perlman introduction, are included in the *Appendixes* in this edition.

36. The National Association of Social Workers, Inc., extended permission to the National Institute for Social Work Training for this "anglicized" edition, which made all references to U.S. services and regulations more general. Charlotte Towle herself had given Dame Eileen permission to do such a revision during Towle's tenure as a consultant to the London School of Economics in the early 1950s. Charlotte Towle, *Common Human Needs*, edition prepared by Dame Eileen Younghusband, National Institute Social Services Library No. 26 (London, England: George Allen & Unwin, 1973).

Introduction

This statement is based on the conviction that public assistance services achieve their broad social purpose only when those who administer them understand the significant principles essential to sound individualization in a program based on legal right.

This matter of the individual's right to assistance currently is feared by some people, to whom it connotes indiscriminate giving to any and every idler who chooses to be supported by those who toil. It is even decried by some as a threat to democracy. It is well to remember that the American conviction that the needy individual has a claim on society of the right to financial assistance had its beginnings for us in the passage of the English Poor Law in 1601. With the growth of our Anglo-American legal system, poor relief practices were instituted by our colonial and early American forefathers. Implicit in their concept of democracy as a way of life they were intent to attain was a faith in man, his worth, his possibilities, his ultimate dependability. Accordingly, there was concern that no man should lack the means to survival. It was the common belief that he was obligated to work but that, temporarily or permanently lacking capacity or opportunity to earn his livelihood, he had a right to assistance. To gain assistance he was obligated to establish his eligibility through submitting proof of current need, as defined in the law, which has involved submitting evidence of lack of capacity and/or opportunity to survive without assistance.

The community's conviction of man's right to survive has been sufficiently strong and unwavering that legal provisions have been extended rather than curtailed with the passage of time. Throughout the years, however, in extending this right local communities have shown fear that when man is accorded the opportunity to survive, he not only will come to feel entitled to depend on others for support but also to expect a way of life beyond a bare survival level. In this connection a dominant fear has been the fear that man would *feel* he had a right to assistance. Hence, incongruously, man must not feel entitled to that to which he is entitled by law. Accordingly, he must be treated as though in bad standing through placing "ignominious penalties" on him.[1] He must be publicized through paupers' lists, his movements restricted through settlement laws, his spending controlled through relief in kind and dictated by close supervision. Furthermore, his assistance grants must be kept below a level essential for well-being. In short, he must be set apart and above all feel properly humble and sufficiently unentitled to benefits that he will be motivated toward self-dependence by loss of status, loss of certain freedoms as implied above, and the pressure of unmet needs.

With the Great Depression of the 1930's, when all classes and conditions of men became applicants for assistance, local relief provisions—public and private— were unequal to the demands made on them. Those who had never expected to experience the "degradation" of economic dependency experienced it, sometimes without but often with a sense of loss of personal worth. As a great cross section of the population became victims of circumstance, a long-growing sense of man's interdependence mounted to culminate in the passage of the Social Security Act in 1935. Antedating this event, particularly since the end of World War I, many other developments destined the public assistance provisions of the Social Security Act to attempt to be something more than a repetition of the poor relief practices of pioneer and early industrial America. Notable among these were advances in the integration of the social, biological, and psychological sciences through which man's understanding of human needs, of human motivations, of the conditions of life essential for man's physical, intellectual, emotional, and spiritual development had extended and deepened.

The professions charged by society to educate, help, and heal people had become increasingly concerned with contributing to the development of the individual. As we had inched toward the interdependence implicit in a democracy, society's aim progressively had been to afford the individual opportunity for the development of his capacities. This was reflected in educational provisions and objectives that were increasingly directed toward patterning the young not merely to outwit one another, but to live socially useful lives. It had been reflected in medical practice, in trends toward the prevention of disease and the promotion of health. It had been reflected in the expansion of the social services under public as well as private auspices. The objectives of social work practice likewise had gone beyond emergent concern with the individual's survival to concern for his rehabilitation as well as for the provision of opportunities and conditions that would promote his development, thus hopefully decreasing those social ills that in the long run burden the taxpayer and threaten the common good.

The Social Security Act established a framework for the partnership of the federal government and the states in providing financial assistance to large groups of individuals who temporarily or permanently lack the means to livelihood. The act strengthens and extends the concepts and principles previously held with respect to the rights of the needy to assistance. It abides by the common belief that man is obligated to work, so that to obtain assistance he is obligated to establish his eligibility as defined by law through giving proof of lack of capacity or opportunity to work. Its new features are a more specific spelling out of conditions of eligibility; assurance of a confidential relationship between recipient and agency (abolition of paupers lists); the provision that payments made to needy eligible persons must be in the form of unrestricted money payments, not unrestricted in size but unrestricted in permitting the individual the right of an adult in our society to plan his expenditures of his money (abolition of relief in kind is implied); the requirement that aggrieved applicants and recipients must be given a fair hearing before the state agency.

The very nature of these statutory departures from traditional relief practices has implied marked change in attitudes on the part of those administering the act with concern to fulfill its intent. Notable attitudes are conviction about the provisions of the act, absence of fear of them, and faith in the ultimate dependability and worth of the recipients of public assistance services. Out of social, biological, and psychological knowledge and insights, administrative bodies have been concerned to institute policies and procedures that conserve human resources through safeguarding opportunities for self-development and through contributing to family and community life. Consequently, the federal administration has encouraged the states to extend adequate financial assistance. It has required that all applicants be afforded the services of public assistance staffs, who are committed to uphold the eligibility requirements as defined by law, but who also are committed to make known to the individual his rights under the law and to offer advice and guidance to him in establishing his eligibility. This has not implied helping the individual to circumvent the law. It has established a technical training service in the Bureau of Public Assistance to give regular service to states in promoting the training of staffs. It was in response to the urgent requests of supervisors and training consultants in state agencies for training materials that would widen and deepen the staff's understanding of individuals and that would serve to develop skill in administering services that this document was written. The federal administration, furthermore, has undertaken to encourage state staffs to evaluate their statutes and policies to determine their social import, with a view to making known their human consequences in order that the communities, through legal process, or the agencies, through administrative process, might effect the changes indicated.[2]

Although the concepts of explicit statement of eligibility requirements, confidentiality, unrestricted money payments, and right to fair hearing are included in the federal act, which was passed almost unanimously by both houses of Congress and has been continuously broadened and extended by congressional action since its original passage, these departures from the past still incur opposition. This is in part because traditional attitudes persist in the present. Specifically, among others, the concept that it is essential that the individual *feel* he is entitled to his rights under the law often is contested. Individuals by and large do not expect nor are they expected to educate themselves, heal themselves, conduct their legal affairs without counsel, or get along without benefit of clergy. Those who need financial help together with other social services that aim to rehabilitate, however, are expected by certain segments of the population to help themselves and to feel unentitled to help. For the most part, the services for which people seek aid in public assistance agencies represent a failure in their expectations of themselves and in the community's expectations of them. Consequently the "give" in this situation is taken with more humiliation, fear of social consequences, resentment, and resistance than ordinarily occurs in other professional services. Therefore, applicants for help and recipients of it ordinarily feel a potentially demoralizing degree of humiliation and obligation.

Public assistance staffs are concerned to diminish these feelings because, out of social work's long experience in helping people, it is known that the individual is motivated to self-dependence through the maintenance and restoration of his feelings of self-respect, that he strives to master the stresses of his life out of hope and confidence rather than out of despair and self-depreciation. Public assistance administrators regard it as highly important that the individual not only know his rights under the law, but also that he feel he has a right to the help to which legally he is entitled. When this sense of right is conveyed, the majortiy of recipients still will feel sufficiently obligated to do their part in regaining self-dependence. To feel excessively and shamefully obligated is to feel helpless, worthless, and resentful. Out of feelings of inadequacy one may give up striving. Out of resentment one may become dependent as a defense against fear or as retaliation against the helping hand that hurts one deeply. The experience of social work has established the professional conviction that when and if early relief practices fostered pauperization, it was insofar as individuals experienced fear, humiliation, and resentment through seeking help and, in addition, received inadequate assistance.

In our emphasis on the importance of public assistance for the restoration of self-dependence it must be remembered, however, that the Social Security Act was established for those who cannot attain this aim. It separates out for special consideration those categorical groups in which, by reason of age or the very nature of the handicaps, the members normally would not be in the labor market: children, the blind, the aged, the permanently and totally disabled. Some of the blind excepted, the others are more largely subjects for protection than for rehabilitation. Since all individuals who are normal in their physical, mental, and emotional development are bent on becoming self-supporting, agency services should assist them in attaining this objective whenever possible. In many instances when this is not possible or advisable, it is equally important that services be dedicated to the development of a state of mind and heart that promotes constructive living. An employed mother may, in maintaining her economic independence, fail to meet the needs of her children and thus create future dependents. A humiliated and embittered grandparent may be a disruptive force in family life when instead he might have had the heart to share responsibility and give affection. A bedridden father still may be a force for good or evil in the lives of his children, contingent on the nature of his experience as he undergoes dependency. The Social Security Act bespeaks this country's commitment to a set of values beyond the sole value of economic self-dependence. Depletion of the personality and pauperization of the spirit are evils to be avoided as well as economic pauperization. The administrators of the act are committed to the principle that man does not live by bread alone nor is he to be valued solely by his breadwinning capacity.

Public programs are administered by humans for humans. Therefore, among other orientations, some understanding of common human needs and some comprehension of basic principles of human behavior are essential. The general purpose of this discussion is threefold: to convey a limited content of knowledge of human behavior, with focus on normal responses to social and economic stress; to encourage consideration of the import of some of our statutory provisions and agency policies in the light of this understanding— not merely what we are doing for people but what we are doing to them is a question that should be uppermost in the minds of persons responsible for administering public assistance, and, within the framework of public assistance, to help supervisors and workers understand people better, so that they may administer assistance services with reference to right, to need, and to obligation. Insofar as the worker's understanding of human needs and motivations is deepened, he may be stimulated to evolve ways of helping that strengthen the individual.

From administrator to caseworker, we are administering a program in which many of the statutory provisions have been inherited from the past and in which agency policies are colored by outmoded conceptions of what is good for individuals and for society. If the institutions and agencies established to serve mankind are not to lose identity with people, becoming self-perpetuating and rigidly unsuited to human needs, then they must continuously have the breath of human life breathed into them. What is this breath of life? It is basic understanding of individuals, a growing comprehension of their common needs, their behavior motivations, and the factors and forces that shape men to be primitive or civilized in their strivings.

It is to be hoped also that this discussion will point the need for creative effort to make the most of our statutory provisions. Sometimes statutes intended to safeguard the individual's and the community's welfare have been interpreted in such a way as to defeat their purpose. Interpretations sometimes have been restrictive beyond the intent of the law. Understanding of the common needs of the individual and of the decisive import of individual well-being for the good of society may lead to the formulation of policies that more adequately interpret the law's intent, through leading to critical evaluation of the effect of legal provisions and policies on our services and on the people for whom our help is intended.

If this discussion gives greater significance to the relationship between public assistance programs and the growth of the individual, it may enable supervisors to help workers use the agency more constructively. Insofar as it contributes to an understanding of basic needs and problems that grow out of human relationships and to an appreciation of the various appropriate ways in which different people meet and deal with the same events and circumstances, it should help the worker to individualize the person in the process of establishing eligibility and to differentiate need for other services, even though he cannot individualize the eligibility requirements or the assistance standards beyond the limits of established policy. A worker with this understanding should be less inclined to impose services and to interfere with the recipient's right than one who has little comprehension of the meaning of the individual's response or of the significance of what he says when he applies for assistance.

Furthermore, if this presentation deepens the supervisor's understanding of human motives and principles of personality growth, it may contribute to his understanding of the worker's response to the impact of work that at times makes heavy emotional demands on the worker. This understanding may throw light on the worker's learning response and thus enable the supervisor to advise and guide him more patiently and objectively. In a discussion of qualities needed by workers in public programs, it has been said, "What is involved is not a detached or abstract interest, but an attitude and a feeling that can be the basis of a disciplined skill exercised in a setting of policy and organized procedure designed for human service."[3] "Liking and concern for people" that holds amid "disadvantageous circumstances" in which the individual may respond in baffling ways, ways different from the worker's conception of how he should respond, may represent in a few people an inherent capacity for understanding. By and large, however, a "quick and vivid interest" in people, together with a liking for them regardless of circumstance or response, derives in part from and can be greatly increased by understanding that is based on knowledge. The purpose of this presentation is to contribute in some small measure to that understanding.

CHARLOTTE TOWLE

Notes

1. Grace Abbott, *From Relief to Social Security. The American System of Poor Relief Backgrounds and Foregrounds* (Chicago: University of Chicago Press, 1941), pp. 6-11.

2. Since this document was originally written, amendments to the Social Security Act have added Aid to the Permanently and Totally Disabled and have otherwise broadened the base of operation and increased the amount of federal matching funds available to the states. The most extensive amendments were enacted in 1962, making possible the strengthening of public assistance programs in many ways: increased social services and expanded staff training programs with a larger federal financial contribution, community programs for training or retraining employable or potentially employable adults in the program of Aid to Families with Dependent Children, combination of all categories of public assistance for adults into a single administrative unit, provision for reserving income or earnings for future needs of dependent children without affecting the assistance grant, permanent provision of a 1961 temporary provision allowing federal participation in continued assistance to children removed from their families and placed in foster care, and a substantial increase in the child welfare services program.

3. Karl de Schweinitz, "Education for Social Security," *The Educational Record*, Vol. 25, No. 2 (April 1944), pp. 142-153.

PART ONE

Significance of public assistance for the individual and society

1

Place of public assistance in a democracy

The present war, which gives promise of victory to the allied armies on many battlefields, will be only nominally won there. This struggle, which is dedicated to the idea of the dignity of man and to the concept of his individual worth, will be won or lost in postwar days, insofar as certain basic problems in his social interrelationships are solved, locally, nationally, and internationally. Public assistance laws and other social legislation are the culmination of a democracy's conviction regarding its responsibility for human welfare. Such laws provide a way for us to work with individuals in meeting their needs. Those of us who participate in the administration of the Social Security Act through any of its programs are engaged in work of decisive importance. Day by day ours is the opportunity to carry forward and to make real the aims of democracy. Insofar as we comprehend the import of our work we will value our efforts in terms of long-run gains and perhaps be less discouraged by the frustrations of the present. Insofar as we glimpse the significance of the program in which each of us plays a part, we may approach our work more thoughtfully, more imaginatively, and with a more stirring conviction. Man has failed to solve problems in social relationships that seemingly, in the light of his ingenuity, should not have defeated him. What have been some of the obstacles that have prevented him from attaining ends now essential for his survival? What part may social security play in his preparation for the solution of social problems? From the answers to these considerations derive the ultimate meaning and value of our work.

We live in a period of scientific enlightenment and of great technical achievement which, if intelligently used, could render the life of all people more satisfactory than ever before. Only recently, however, we experienced a worldwide economic depression in which widespread want and fear became the base for a progressive curtailment of man's freedom. Today, as repeatedly throughout history, this basic want and fear have engendered hostile feelings that, in turn, have pitted man against man and prompted him to use his scientific enlightenment in a wholesale destruction of life and property that threatens not only the realization of his social goals but also his very survival. One encounters here a curious manifestation of human behavior. Through intellectual achievement man attains the heights from which he can glimpse that better life for all people for which he has been striving throughout the ages, only to fail to solve the problems that would entrench his gains and only to be forced to use those attainments against himself and his kind.

Students of human behavior who have sought the reason for this dilemma are in general agreement with the explanation given by Alexander, that man fails to solve the basic economic problems the solution of which would eliminate inevitable want and the most elemental fears from which stem some of his most hostile aggressions, not because these problems are beyond his intellectual scope—that is, his mental ingenuity—but because economic strivings have deep emotional determinants that involve human relationships in complex ways. He maintains that human relationships are primarily governed not by reason but by essentially irrational emotional forces, and that man's mastery of nature has proved a curse rather than a blessing in the hands of men ignorant of their own personalities and of human relationships. His conclusion is that the gap between the natural and the social sciences must be bridged: "The critical, empirical attitude of the natural sciences must now be extended to the study of personality and to the social sciences in order to achieve the same mastery of individual and social behavior which we have acquired over the forces of inanimate nature."[1]

The study of personality and the social sciences is certainly an essential step in acquiring mastery of individual and social behavior. Unlike the situation in the natural sciences, however, this mastery may not be attained through study alone. In fact, even the "critical, empirical attitude" essential to productive study can be attained only insofar as the individual's total personality growth makes it possible for him (1) to look at human behavior objectively, (2) to accept emotionally the insight gained, and (3) to utilize this understanding in the modification of his behavior from self-centered aims to social concerns. What are the factors and forces in life that may enable man to develop capacity for self-understanding and for using that understanding in attaining more constructive human relationships and helping others do likewise? What are the essential elements in the individual's life experience that may make him more susceptible to social aims—that is, less hostile, less anxious, and thereby less self-aggrandizing or less submissive? The decisive point here is that knowledge of personality may not enable him to behave more rationally if his experiences have been such as to create excessive or distorted needs that operate as a force compelling beyond the dictates of reason. We want for ourselves and for others the kind of experience that will promote personality growth toward attaining a greater capacity for rational behavior. We desire this so that we may permit ourselves to solve the problem of widespread want and so that we may become less fearful, less hostile, and freer to grant to others the freedoms that we want for ourselves. Social workers need to know something of common human needs, something of the motivations of human behavior, something of the factors and forces that shape personality and are significant in man's development.

Essential elements governing development

Consider, first, in a general way and not necessarily in the order of their importance, some of the essential elements in the individual's life that may make him less hostile, less anxious, and more inclined toward social goals. Obviously, the conditions conducive to maximum physical health are important from the standpoint of creating a citizenry physically powerful and efficient in contributing to the nation's wealth in time of peace and to its safety in time of war. We are interested also in physical health from the standpoint of personality development. The relationship between the nutrition of infants and their emotional growth is well established. The infant gets a sense of well-being that is equivalent to a sense of being loved insofar as he is comfortable, which means well fed. In a satisfactory feeding experience he enters into a positive relationship with the mother, and first relationships are believed to be strong determinants of response patterns in subsequent relationships. On the other hand, the malnourished infant is one who experiences a deep affectional starvation. Undernourished infants have been noted to be restless, irritable, hyperactive, or, in extreme cases, apathetic, and these symptoms begin at once to influence their total experience in relationships. For example, the hungry child feels deprived, uncomfortable, and becomes restless and irritable, crying and whining until the mother, provoked beyond human endurance, scolds, slaps, or in some way shows her irritation, thus reinforcing the infant's feeling of being unloved. Gradually, however, there may be secondary gains for him in the extra attention given in response to his wails, and so he finds this behavior useful. We may find, unless the cause is removed and the mother's response to the persistent symptoms quickly modified, a child who relates himself to life in an aggressive, demanding, protesting way. He may grow into a person who, throughout life, will be doomed to frustration because, though he may get the attention he urgently and annoyingly demands, the love he is seeking is withheld. For him who still seeks the mother's love in every relationship, the gift without the giver is peculiarly bare.

Physical welfare and personality development

It may seem a far cry from the malnourished infant of today to the dictator or asocial citizen of tomorrow. To child welfare workers and all those versed in the basic essentials of child development, however, there seems to be a logical cause-and-effect relationship. Likewise, illness and physical handicap may become decisive factors in the formation of personality. Quite frequently in delinquent children we find physical inadequacy—a physical defect or a crippling handicap—as part of the basis for the child's feeling of bitterness, hatred toward others, and his impulse to compensate and retaliate through antisocial actions. Just as the passing mood of any one of us may be created by a state of hunger, physical fatigue, or the condition of our general health, so persistent hunger, fatigue, and bodily suffering may shape the personality to their own ends. It has been said, "Man cannot reason with his ills for they know more than he does."

The import of this relationship for public assistance is obvious. The longstanding plea that assistance payments and other resources be adequate to ensure physical and mental health is valid. Nationwide programs of many kinds are indicated. Prenatal care, infant welfare services, health care, and a more adequate distribution of medical care—all are needed continuously not only for man's physical welfare but also for his psychological well-being. On the preventive side there is need also for better housing, stable and enduring provisions for employment, and minimum economic security. Tomorrow's world is thus contingent on today's provisions to conserve human resources.

Emotional growth and development of intellectual capacity

Another essential element in enabling the individual to grow toward greater freedom from irrational emotional forces is the opportunity for the maximum development of his intellectual capacities. In America this need has been considered more sympathetically than many other common needs. While the establishment of public school systems at first evoked some of the protests that public assistance programs have encountered, this resistance soon gave way and provisions for public education have been extended to higher levels, while the taxpayer takes it for granted that the opportunity for an education is every man's inalienable right! In an achievement-worshiping culture, learning has been respected as a means by which the great majority are unquestionably entitled to rise from poverty and ignorance to wealth and eminence. Theoretically, then, the American has met with less frustration in developing his mental abilities than have people of many other nations. Public school facilities from kindergarten to university have been there for his use. This is a great social resource for the development of human personality to constructive ends, and one we should safeguard with resources that assure maximum productive use of our educational systems. This requires provisions within the systems to make possible the kinds of training and education appropriate to the individual and the kinds of educational method most suitable to the development of citizens for a democracy. It also implies provisions in the community that make it possible for every individual to obtain, under conditions conducive to productive learning, the education essential for the full realization of his powers. This objective involves such measures as adequate enforcement of child-labor laws and removal of restrictions against minority groups. It involves also at least a minimum economic security.

It is incongruous with American tradition that the economic status of the parents, rather than the intelligence of the child, should set a ceiling on his educational opportunities. It may be argued that this limitation need not occur in view of our extensive facilities. Economic factors, however, do operate both against actual attendance at school and against the productive use of the educational opportunity during attendance. That the child who is ill fed, ill housed, ill clothed, and physically below par may not be in a receptive mental state is an idea to which the American public warms slowly. Perhaps it is in our tradition to believe that poverty and hardship not only need not be deterrents to progress but also may well stimulate endeavor. Perhaps it is in our tradition to give freely and without fear only that which seems to contribute directly to man's capacity for achievement. We give hesitantly and grudgingly—that is, fearfully—the nurturing services that would seem to foster dependence. *We fail to comprehend the interrelatedness of man's needs and the fact that frequently basic dependency needs must be met first in order that he may utilize opportunities for independence.* Accordingly, funds are appropriated for school lunches and school clinics less willingly than for schoolbooks. The cold, hungry, ragged schoolboy who wins scholarships and rises to fame is an American symbol, cherished by many a rugged individualist. Every social worker knows, however, that for every eminent American cited as a case in point there are innumerable unknown persons who might have made good use of educational opportunities under more advantageous circumstances. They know, too, that many of these same individuals are now a charge against public funds, on relief rolls, in mental hospitals, and in correctional or penal institutions.

Public assistance workers frequently have not realized the many implications for both the individual and society when educational opportunities are not commensurate with an individual's abilities. First, there is the loss to society of the richer contribution he might have made; second, the loss to the individual of a more satisfying and productive life work; third, the deep frustration that may be experienced when aspirations cannot be attained, a defeat that may lead to embittered rage or discouraged inertia. Thwarted mental powers seek destructive outlets. Deep personality disturbance and regressive behavior trends of many sorts may be induced when the mind is obstructed in attaining its full growth. As public assistance staffs gain conviction about the importance of educational opportunity in the development of the total personality, they will lend every effort to safeguard it, through using the agency's resources to the utmost in seeing that children have every possible provision to enable them not only to continue in school but also to make productive use of schooling. This endeavor implies adequate assistance so that children may go to school well fed and decently clad. It also implies prompt use of health and nutrition services and of scholarship opportunities. For some adolescents it may imply also wise counseling of child and family on part-time work in relation to educational goals. Interpretation to the family of the purpose of child-labor laws and the possible consequences of violation may be indicated.

There has been considerable discussion and some controversial thinking concerning the attitude workers should take toward higher education for young people in public assistance families. Should they be encouraged or discouraged to hope and plan to continue school as a preparation for college? Since when has it not been every American's privilege to hope and to plan beyond the limits of his life situation? This may have been one of our weaknesses, but let us not forget it also has been our great strength. The significant question here is: Why should public assistance children be set apart on the basis of economic factors? In a democracy, should not educational opportunities be provided on the basis of mental capacity rather than economic status?

Relationship with others has import for personality development

It is essential that we understand man's emotional nature as well as his physical and intellectual needs. This leads to recognition of a third important element in a life experience conducive to personality growth—the kind of relationships an individual experiences in the early years within the family and throughout his life in other groups. The early family relationships are generally conceded to be of primary importance, since they determine the basic personality patterns and influence in considerable measure the nature of his subsequent relationships. In the human personality there is a natural and inevitable impulse toward growth from the original state of dependence to a state of greater self-sufficiency and independence. It is generally agreed that the human personality grows, develops, and matures through relationships with others, and that there is an innate tendency to gravitate into relationships with others in the interests of survival. Man's social needs, that is, what he seeks in relationships throughout life, will vary with age, changing circumstances, and prior relationship experiences. What he seeks at different ages and how his personality is affected by these experiences will be considered in some detail in the following chapters. At this point it is important to note the interrelatedness of the various elements—physical, mental, and emotional—in the total life experience. In the last analysis we note the vital, perhaps even primary, importance of experience in human relationships.

For instance, a chronically sick child may elicit a response from his parents quite different from that proffered his brothers and sisters. Thus, in the same family he has a different environment and he may emerge from the home with attitudes and needs that continue to make a vastly different life experience for him in the long run. A mentally dull child born into a family where intellectual ability is highly valued may find his mental condition a much greater hardship throughout life than a similarly endowed child who grows up in a family where his limitations matter very little. Conversely, relationships may create conditions and circumstances that are decisive in the individual's development. A child who is reared in a home where there is marked marital friction and continual tension centering about him may grow up with deep emotional conflicts that are expressed in physical symptoms. These symptoms in turn create for him the problems of the physically handicapped, so that his further development is shaped by the physical condition as well as by the primary difficulty, the emotional conflict.[2] Or an emotionally disturbed child from such a family may have reacted with inability to function mentally so that his intelligence, although adequate, is negated; being uneducable, he goes forth into the world seemingly a mental defective, and his further development is influenced by his lack of education, his confused thinking, and his general inability to use his mental capacity.[3]

Spiritual needs of the individual must be recognized

But, literally, man does not live by bread alone. Demoralization and disintegration of the individual are prevented, in part, through opportunity to work and to take one's place in the community. But spiritual needs of the individual must also be recognized, understood, and respected. They must be seen as distinct needs and they must also be seen in relation to other human needs. This entails provisions that safeguard church attendance, the use of church resources, and, in human conduct problems, respect for the individual's religious convictions. Through the influence of religion the purpose of human life is better understood and a sense of ethical values achieved. With that understanding comes keener appreciation of the individual's relationship to his fellow man, his community, and his nation. The need for religious influences is especially acute in childhood and through adolescence, when the individual is likely to require definite guidance and supportive judgments to help him toward becoming an emotionally mature adult.[4]

Essentials of program administration

Conditions and circumstances dictate the actions of men. A decisive point here is that it is not merely the nature of these conditions and circumstances in themselves that dictates action but also the emotional import the conditions and circumstances have for the person. Poverty, unemployment, mental ineptitude, illness, physical handicaps will have varying meanings for different individuals, depending not only on the nature of the problem but also on the person's age, prior life experience and personality development, and the timing of the problem in relation to other events in his life.[5] As public assistance workers, we therefore are concerned not merely with administering programs that alleviate the adverse circumstances in the individual's situation, we also are concerned to render those services in such a way as to contribute to the individual's social development. This aim implies several considerations, notably:

1. Since the human personality grows largely through relationships with others, and since family relationships are of primary importance in the individual's growth, we are concerned that our agency programs safeguard the strengths of family life.

2. Since we deal with people in time of trouble, when they are "in the midst of emotions that come from the major catastrophes in life," it is important that we help them as they talk to us to express their emotions and that we try to understand the meaning their problems have for them with a twofold purpose: (a) That as they give expression to their feelings they may be relieved of pressures and tensions that have made the problem deeply disturbing. Thus, as they experience some change in feeling, they may be enabled better to bear the problem and cope with it more resourcefully and realistically. (b) Through understanding the person's feeling we, as representatives of an assistance agency, may through thus sharing his problem afford each individual a relationship that strengthens him. We may thus help him find or maintain a sense of adequacy in a difficult life period. This does not mean that public assistance workers enter a situation with the primary purpose of helping people with emotional difficulties. It does mean, however, that as people express discomfort relating to the problem that brings them to the agency, workers should understand how this measure may ease discomfort.[6]

Evaluate strengths and weaknesses

It is essential that supervisors in public assistance programs help workers to learn to evaluate strengths and weaknesses in family life. We want them to learn to keep uppermost in mind such questions as: What is this service doing to promote constructive relationships for the individuals within a given family? What is this or that agency policy or legal provision doing to strengthen or endanger family life? It is essential also—and the two are interrelated— that workers be helped to understand the emotional import of the individual's social problem to him, as indicated in his reaction to it, and that workers be helped to know how to utilize this understanding in rendering the agency's service, even though that service may be a limited one.

Importance of social reform measures

Public assistance administrators and supervisors also must help workers realize that efforts to meet human needs individual by individual cannot be the whole answer to the problem of social welfare. Within a well-ordered social and economic system there still will be need for social security programs and for other social services through which the interests of the child and his family are safeguarded in the special vicissitudes of life that will occur in spite of all preventive measures. The social work profession has the broad purpose of trying to make it possible for every individual to have the most productive life of which he is capable. In achieving this purpose it works within a framework of institutions in two ways: efforts that aim to reshape institutions that are failing to fulfill their function and creation of special services for groups whose needs are not met. Traditionally this second area of activity has been more peculiarly and especially the province of social work. As we look to the future, however, we see the increasing importance of social reform measures. The observations and experience gained through the creation of special services for individuals in need must, however, constitute the testimony for reshaping institutions in the interest of human welfare.

Administer programs with understanding

Insofar as public assistance programs afford individuals and families minimum economic security, they have the opportunity not only to contribute to the physical and mental welfare of mankind but also to make possible that greater emotional growth essential for man's contribution as a citizen of a democracy, the interdependent relationships that impose mutual rights and obligations between the individual and society. It is generally agreed that economic security tends to safeguard relationships and to make it possible, by and large, for them to be more stable, more enduring, and more giving. As man is given to, he gives to others. As we extend to the individual the rights to which he is entitled, not only is *what we give important but how* we give it. Our services must be rendered not only with reference to the need presented but also with reference to the recipient who presents the need. It is only as we relieve want with understanding of the human personality concerned that fear and hostility can subside. So that the full benefit of our provisions may be realized, we must administer our programs in the light of present-day insights into human personality. As we look to the future, two significant developments spell hope for our country: (1) the passage of the Social Security Act and other social measures, and (2) the rapid advance during the last half century in the scientific study of human personality that has resulted in a deeper understanding of human nature. In the extension, modification, and co-ordination of these two epochal developments much is at stake. Those who participate in the administration of the Social Security Act through any one of its far-reaching programs have the challenging opportunity to integrate and carry forward work of decisive import to democracy.[7]

Notes

1. Franz Alexander, MD, *Our Age of Unreason; A Study of the Irrational Forces in Social Life* (1st ed.; Philadelphia: J. B. Lippincott Co., 1942), p. 22.

2. Leon J. Saul, "The Place of Psychosomatic Knowledge in Case Work," *Proceedings of the National Conference of Social Work, 1941* (New York: Columbia University Press, 1941), pp. 280–294. *See also* Charlotte Towle, "The Social Content of Work for Crippled Children From the Standpoint of the Psychiatric Social Worker," *Crippled Child*, Vol. 15, No. 1 (June 1937), pp. 9–12.

3. For a discussion of the effects of adverse circumstance and emotional stress on mental development, *see* W. H. Burnham, *The Normal Mind* (New York: D. Appleton-Century Co., 1924), chap. 18; and Phyllis Blanchard, "The Interpretation of Psychological Tests in Clinical Work With Children," *Mental Hygiene*, Vol. 25, No. 1 (January 1941), pp. 58–75.

4. Jane M. Hoey, "Social Work Concepts and Methods in the Postwar World," *Proceedings of the National Conference of Social Work, 1944* (New York: Columbia University Press, 1944), pp. 35–47.

5. It is for this reason that the content of Chapters 3 and 4, in which common human needs at various stages in the normal development of the individual are discussed, is especially pertinent for public assistance workers.

6. For further discussion related to this point, see chapter 2, p. 15. The application of this concept is noted in the case of Miss S, p. 72.

7. On the subject of the place of social work in a democracy, *see* Alexander, *op. cit.*; Gordon Hamilton, *Theory and Practice of Social Casework* (1st ed.; New York: Columbia University Press, 1940), chaps. 1 and 2; and Charlotte Towle, "The Individual in Relation to Social Change," *Social Service Review*, Vol. 13, No. 1 (March 1939), pp. 1–31.

2

Basic motivations
and adaptations
in normal human behavior

P ublic assistance workers, like all social workers, need to know something of the motivations and adaptations in human behavior. These are many and their interplay complex. A few of them are so basic that some knowledge of them *is* essential, even though our function is not that of treating behavior difficulties in and of themselves. These motivations and adaptations serve all individuals throughout life in all kinds of situations. We encounter them in our clients and in our colleagues. We experience them ourselves in our professional as well as our personal lives. Recognition of them in ourselves as well as in others may help us to function more effectively, especially if we can see them as *normal* responses about which we need not be anxious and defensive or condemning.

Emotions determine our thinking and action

First, and highly important, is the realization that behavior is largely determined by the emotions. Emotions not only determine what we do but also exert a strong influence on all our thinking. This is most evident in prejudices and biases, which are examples of emotionally determined thinking. Many of us may not like this idea, for civilized man thinks of himself as superior to primitive man in that reason controls his behavior. This is one ideal of ourselves toward the realization of which we struggle throughout life and that eventually we may attain in some measure, insofar as we understand the emotional forces that govern us. We cannot exert any consistent control over forces we do not understand. In working with people, then, *we start with the assumption that how this person feels is going to determine in*

13

considerable measure what he thinks, how he acts, and what use he makes of an agency's service.

A mother cannot accept a wise plan

Mrs. D, who is receiving aid for her dependent children, was advised by the worker that the doctor recommended a "lean-to" for the father, who is bedridden with tuberculosis. The worker explained the reason and stressed the importance of safeguarding the health of the children. To the worker's surprise and concern, this seemingly intelligent and devoted mother refused to take this precautionary measure. When minor obstacles she raised were disposed of by the worker, she still resisted, and as a last defense against the worker's persuasive efforts was able only to say with much feeling, "I couldn't put him out of the house that way," and "What would the neighbors think?" Repeated efforts to reason with her on health grounds as well as repeated reassurance of the "rightness" of this action were futile.

Ensuing staff discussion raised the current controversy as to the right of the public assistance recipient to manage his own affairs in his own way. Can and should the agency resort to coercive measures? In retrospect it is clear that this case might not have reached the impasse that made this difficult decision necessary had the worker understood that Mrs. D's feelings were preventing her from utilizing medical thinking. If the worker had tried to understand the feelings that occasioned the comment that she could not put her husband out of the house and her anxious inquiry about the reactions of the neighbors, he might have avoided the repetitive persuasive attempts that only defeated his purpose.

Subsequent acquaintance with this family revealed that Mr. D had been the head of the house and that Mrs. D always had been dependent on him and on the approval and disapproval of others. Some acknowledgment of her feelings and interested inquiry as to the meaning of this experience for her might have revealed the family relationship patterns at an early date and thus have pointed up the importance of Mr. D's participation in a medical plan for himself. He was far from dead, as revealed later when he insisted on seeing the worker and on being included to a greater extent in family planning. Mrs. D could not decide on this medical measure because her disturbed emotions obstructed rational action. This decision may well have been frightening in that it demanded more responsibility than she was accustomed to carry in a relationship in which she had played a dependent part. Perhaps it was disturbing also because hostility in the past toward her husband by very reason of her dependence on him and his domination of her made her unable "to put him out of the house."[1] If the worker had given her opportunity to express more fully what she felt and if, with the physician's permission, he had included the father in the medical care plan, the question of violation of the recipient's rights might not have arisen.

A father fears operations

Mr. C, an incapacitated father of dependent children who is an intelligent person quite capable of understanding the doctor's explanations, was confronted with the frightening reality of a major operation. Reassuring information as to the hopeful outcome for recovery with the operation, together with warning information on the consequences of neglecting the condition, failed to persuade him. Perhaps some early experience was the basis for his fear of being operated on. Or perhaps fear of putting his life into the hands of another, stemming from basic mistrust of others, operated against a reasonable choice.

The extent of fears about operations will vary widely from individual to individual. Many persons, like Mr. C, are not receptive to the idea that their fears are irrational. In response to the doctor's and the worker's interpretation, Mr. C supported his position by citing instances when operations had failed, by recounting cases in which doctors had been wrong in their diagnoses, and he finally wishfully reassured himself that his condition was not so bad after all and that some other measures might be effective. At this point his feelings were fashioning his thinking and his thinking was defending his feelings. Why? Here we come to an important point about our feelings. *They tend to make us do that which is most satisfying, most comfortable, and apparently most safe. They tend to make us avoid that which is dissatisfying and uncomfortable, that which provokes anxiety or makes us feel unsafe.* Apparently Mr. C's fears of an operation were so great that he found it more comfortable to evade the issue than to meet it. Out of our broader knowledge and greater experience in observing beneficial effects of operations in certain conditions, we see him as unreasonable in that he chose the greater threat to life. He does not see himself as irrational because, in view of his lack of knowledge, adverse experience of operations, and fears engendered by the nature of operative procedure, he actually is making, for him, a natural choice. We encounter here an important principle in human behavior: *No matter how unusual an individual's behavior may seem to us it has its rational foundation, its logic. His behavior, like ours, is serving him some useful purpose in the maintenance of a kind of equilibrium, that is, a state of comfort in his life.*

As public assistance workers, we care for people and are concerned that they make the choices that are to their best interests, choices that safeguard life, ensure health, and create as much economic and emotional security as possible. With all due respect to the individual's right to manage his own affairs, many of us in dealing with Mr. C would be eager, even anxious, to give him an opportunity to take over our way of thinking about operations. Obviously, he cannot change his thinking until he changes his feeling. We are confronted then with his fears—they must be eased. Social workers can sometimes allay anxiety, but sometimes they cannot do so. Frequently we are perplexed as to how far to go in trying to understand fears, and we need help in recognizing the kinds of fear that may be within our scope. When we encounter prolonged anxieties or acute fears, no matter of what nature, there is frequently the possibility that erroneousility ideas, lack of knowledge, or adverse prior experience may be their cause. In the case of Mr. C, the physician attempted to correct erroneous information and to give new ideas in interpreting the operation and in providing reassuring facts as to the outcome.

Social workers frequently have found it helpful to elicit from the client the information he has about a situation that now threatens him; sometimes they have found it helpful to him when they inquire into his former experience with similar situations. The worker may thus help him relate as much of his fear as he can bring forth *readily*.[2] In this process several things can happen. The individual has had an opportunity to be relieved of disturbing feelings in the telling, to look at his own ideas and thus perhaps gain some perspective on them, to experience our understanding and to sense wherein our response differs from his in not being fearful or anxious. He has given us information that should serve as a guide to us in our interpretation. We may *then* attempt to correct misinformation, share with him our observation in other cases, give new ideas and a valid statement as to the chances he is taking or not taking in deciding on the threatening course of action. He *now* may be more receptive to this thinking, more inclined to identify himself with our thinking and feeling about his dilemma, because (1) he had an opportunity to express his version and his fears and (2) while we understood his feelings we did not feel the same way. He thus may gain perspective, see his own ideas for what they are worth, and, now feeling differently about the problem, may be able to deal with it differently. This reaction is likely to occur when disturbed feelings stem largely from ignorance, misinformation, or prior experience that has not been too shocking.

When the individual's fears stem from highly shocking experiences—for example, when through an operation the person has lost someone to whom he was very close and has remained emotionally tied—he may not be able to attain a rational attitude about operations without more help than described. Or when the operation activates other fears, the present fear may not be eased through the kind of help depicted here. For example, if as a child a person developed a strong sense of guilt over some sin of omission or commission so that he developed a chronic dread of impending punishment, an anticipatory dread that sooner or later great harm will befall him, then his seeming fear of the operation may be fear of punishment long awaited. When we give such an individual an opportunity to state his fears, probably all he can produce will be vague, general fears. He may even be unable to give any reason why he fears operations. His comments may be of the nature, "I don't know why— I've always feared them." Or he may place responsibility for his fears on someone else ("My mother feared them"). At any rate, when the person is not articulate about his fears and is not receptive to new ideas, we can suspect fears of a deeper nature that are beyond our reach. If, after giving expression to his thinking and feeling, he is unable to accept new thinking but instead must strongly defend himself against our interpretations, we can then know that we have done everything within our capacity to help him. We can see also the futility of repeated efforts to cope with the issue itself.

New ideas may produce a change in feeling

In public assistance programs we deal with many people at times when they feel they have failed. Feelings of humiliation and fears of the future induce unrealistic attitudes. At such a time, it may be especially difficult for them to ask for help and to make constructive use of it. Assistance given in the light of an understanding of the individual's feelings about his dilemma may have decisive import in his eventual rehabilitation. The following case is of interest in this connection.

Mr. B, unemployed, applied for assistance. His opening statement of need was accompanied by comments to the effect that he had no idea of the existence of such an agency as this until now. He felt it was disgraceful that he had permitted himself to seek "charity" and had hardly been able to enter the door when he arrived. Only the thought of his child spurred him on. He felt he must submit to any humiliation in order to save her suffering. He interrupted the worker's initial attempt at interpretation of the purpose of the agency and of his right to assistance as though he had not heard, to recount how his financial difficulty began, how formerly he could turn to his family for help in time of need just as formerly they could turn to him. The worker replied to this with a remark that in the general economic situation many individuals and families could no longer help one another. Mr. B refuted the worker's attempt to ease his discomfort, insisting staunchly that it was not the state of society but his own fault that he could not earn. The worker then directed his inquiry toward why Mr. B felt it was his fault. There followed, with much feeling, a self-blaming account of his several recent job failures after a long record of success. In the course of his recital he brought out that his wife had a right to expect him to support her and the child. Before their marriage she had been a business success and she had no comprehension of failure. Since their marriage she had depended completely on him and did not understand what was happening in the world. But neither did he believe that this trouble of his was owing to economic conditions in general. (Subsequent investigation showed that his wife was fully aware of the economic situation, that she was understanding of his situation, and that she too repeatedly had tried to reassure him by attributing his business failure to general economic conditions.)

We have here another example of how a person's emotions can influence his thinking. Because Mr. B *feels* he is to blame for his failure and cannot understand and accept it himself, he *thinks* others feel the same way about his problem. We see here that Mr. B's feelings about being unemployed and having to ask for help determine what he does in applying. They make him deny that he is asking for help for himself. They make him present his child as the person for whom help is requested. Obviously he finds the experience too painful to enter into fully, so unconsciously he justifies his request and pretends to himself and to the world that he is only here because of someone else. Since he has not yet fully entered into the experience, he is not yet ready to relate himself to the agency or to understand what he hears about the agency, nor is he ready to use the service as a *right*.

We do not fully understand his discomfort or why this experience causes him to blame himself, but it is glaringly clear that he has an inner need to place his failure in himself rather than in the social structure. Why? Assuming that he is tending to do what makes him more comfortable, we conclude that this *self-blame* or this assumption of *responsibility* eases his discomfort. If his reaction is purely self-blaming, it would seem that the present catastrophe makes him feel guilty and we could suspect that the present problem activates old disturbed and self-accusatory feelings about himself and may be more than a response to the present situation. In this instance, the self-blame would be self-punishment and would ease guilt, perhaps thus relieving him of the fear of worse punishment through further economic reverses. The final economic reverse that could come to him now would be rejection of his application for financial assistance. Therefore, fear of the outcome here may be eased by "admission of wrongdoing." If, on the other hand, his reaction is part of a characteristic tendency to assume full responsibility for his own affairs, then perhaps claiming the failure as his own eases anxiety, for he is accustomed to being able to cope with the world. It may be a more threatening idea to him to think that the social order is against him than to think there is something wrong with himself, for he could deal with his own ineptitudes more readily than with a changed world.

Subsequent developments show the meaning of his response. After placing the problem on himself and expressing considerable feeling about it, Mr. B spontaneously brought the conversation back to his application for assistance. There followed a careful review of his financial situation, during which he presented a plan for moving into the rent-free house of a relative. The worker encouraged him in this plan. As the agency's need for certain information was conveyed to Mr. B, he anxiously raised questions about the agency's investigations and records. He eagerly set about procuring evidence of eligibility and showed lessened discomfort on hearing of the agency's way of working, the confidential nature of its records, and so on. At one point he asked the worker whether he thought a man could take money and retain his self-respect.

Interpretation of his right to assistance and of financial help as a temporary boost that anyone might need at some point obviously relieved tension and elicited a comment to the effect that now he was going to be able to face "this thing....I couldn't see my way out."

There was initial resistance to having his home visited, since he had not had the courage to tell his wife he was coming to the agency and had hoped to keep knowledge of the agency contact from her. On his return visit to the office, he expressed willingness to have the home visited and great relief because his wife had been so pleased at his coming here. Instead of being angry and humiliated, she had been gratified at "his courage in applying for help." Shortly after assistance was given, Mr. B moved quickly to look for kinds of employment that formerly he had considered beneath him and managed to get a part-time job. His account at the time of application showed that for some months he had been drifting along, using his savings, and hoping against hope that "something good would turn up." Now he became more realistic and, in contrast to his original denial that the economic situation had changed, he was able to say that "in these times" it would be better to take anything.

It would seem from his response that Mr. B's disturbed feelings about his problem were those of the man who, accustomed to managing his own affairs, finds himself suddenly helpless. He still could not give up completely and so he eased his anxiety over his helplessness by insisting that he alone was responsible. He was able to make constructive use of his right to assistance not only because of the way his application was handled but also because his anxieties stemmed from his strengths and from the reality of his economic dilemma. Had his attitudes been more purely self-condemning because his present failure was bringing to the surface basic feelings of inadequacy, his response to the help given might have been quite different. Financial assistance might have eased some of his anxiety. He might, however, have continued to feel humiliated and inferior and, if so, would not have moved so quickly into resuming the management of his own affairs. He might instead have been more inclined to succumb to dependency and to pay his way through self-blame.

One cannot say conclusively that this or that aspect of a service contributed to the rehabilitation of an individual. A person's experience with an agency is made up of several elements all of which probably combine to help or obstruct him and without full knowledge it is not possible to say which are the most important.[3] It might be assumed that the following factors in Mr. B's agency experience were significant:

1. The opportunity to state his problem and to bring out his feeling about it. Note that the worker was helpful here in quickly focusing Mr. B's discussion on his feeling about failure when he found Mr. B unresponsive to his efforts to ease his discomfort through interpreting agency functions and right to assistance. There is an important principle here: *We cannot talk people out of their disturbed feelings. They get rid of them through expressing them and*

then, feeling relieved, they sometimes can listen to and use our reassuring interpretations.[4]

2. The timing of the second attempt at interpretation of agency function and its ways of working. Note that it comes after Mr. B has moved more fully into the agency experience and is exploring the possibility of help; the first interpretation of this sort was futile because it was badly timed. He still was justifying himself for being here and so, although physically present, he had not yet emotionally accepted making an application for assistance.

3. The timing of the second attempt at interpretation of his right to relief. It comes in direct response to the client's expressions of self-doubt.

4. In this agency the bulk of responsibility for gathering evidence to establish eligibility was placed on the client. The agency's demands and placing activity on Mr. B may have eased his discomfort over asking for help. He gives information and effort in order to have the right to be given to. An interdependent relationship with the agency occurs instead of a dependent one. Furthermore, anxiety over helplessness frequently is eased through such activity.

5. The actual financial help doubtless relieved Mr. B's profound anxiety over survival. When we feel helpless to survive, we may feel so deeply inadequate that activity formerly pursued in the management of our affairs collapses. With assurance of survival, we may take hold of life again and deal with it realistically. We see the shift with Mr. B from needing to distort reality, that is, from needing to assert that the world situation was not relevant to his problem, to admitting not only that it was but to planning accordingly.

In summary, it is obvious that emotional aspects of human behavior have certain import for social workers in a public assistance program even though it is not our function to treat the individual's behavior difficulties in and of themselves. We have learned that every social problem normally causes some emotional disturbance, and that these feelings inevitably are brought into the client's use of the agency service. Whether we are aware of it or not, we are dealing with the client's feelings about his problem in everything we say and do. As we help him experience a change in feeling, we may help him deal with his problems differently and think and feel differently about himself in relation to his problem. *Also, in the interpretations and information we give him, we may impart new ideas that may cause him to feel differently about his problem. Educators know, through experience, that a new intellectual orientation may influence feeling and hence action.* This will occur inevitably, provided:

1. The new ideas do not run counter to deep emotional convictions. Conversely, a new orientation that meets a person's emotional need may be seized on avidly and used to the utmost.

2. There is not a deep emotional need to think in the old ways because the ideas have been satisfying and useful or derive from a relationship in which

the individual still is closely tied and on which he depends for gratification or safety.

3. The new orientation does not come from an individual or authority whom the person mistrusts or toward whom he feels deeply hostile or resentful. Conversely, new concepts may be quickly influential when they are imparted in a relationship in which the recipient feels secure because he feels respected and adequate in the eyes of the donor. The nature of the relationship with the person imparting new thinking, or the status of this person in the feelings of the recipient, often is a decisive factor.

Interpretations of problems may change attitude

We have all experienced the influence of new thinking regardless of whether we have been aware of what happened to bring about a change in feeling and action either in ourselves or in someone else. When feelings of humiliation or anxiety are allayed through interpretation of agency function, through information on eligibility requirements, or through clarification of the agency's ways of working, this principle may well be in operation. Interpretations of the individual's problems that bring a change in his attitude toward them also illustrate this principle. One could cite many examples from the daily experience of a public assistance worker.

In a family receiving Aid to Dependent Children, the mother, Mrs. K, showed complicated attitudes about her husband's mental illness and confinement in a mental hospital. Periodically she would insist on bringing him home against medical advice. There was a long record of marital disharmony preceding his hospitalization, and finally one day she brought out her fear that she had been to blame for his mental illness. Explanation by the doctor and the social worker of the nature of his illness and of the fact that it had its origin prior to the marriage helped Mrs. K see that the illness, rather than being caused by marital discord, merely had contributed to it. This conclusion, to which she came spontaneously, greatly eased her remorse. She became less depressed and more co-operative in the matter of her husband's hospitalization. She could leave him there for his own good instead of needing to take him home to ease her own disturbed feelings. That this woman was immediately receptive to new thinking about mental disorder probably was owing to the following factors: (1) a lack of any deep need to blame herself—instead, in fact, an impulse to be rid of the uncomfortable feeling that she had been responsible, and (2) confidence in the medical authority of the doctor who imparted the information and trust in the social worker who understood her need for interpretation may have enabled her to accept the facts as something other than false reassurance.

So, in the interplay of mental and emotional forces, it can be seen that emotions may facilitate or obstruct the learning process. The social worker's devotion to the idea that every individual has a right to be self-determining does not rule out our valid concern with directing people's attention to the most desirable alternatives. Therefore, some understanding of the factor of emotions as they operate in determining the individual's response to our efforts may be helpful to us in our work with people.

Interplay of positive and negative feelings

As we focus on understanding emotions, we soon realize that both positive and negative feelings occur in close interplay. It would be much simpler to understand and help people if they always felt decidedly in favor of or definitely against a situation, a person, or a course of action. It is probable that they more often *simultaneously* feel two ways. Consequently, love and hate, attraction and repulsion, daring and fear, go hand in hand. As a result of this two-way pull, individuals may shift back and forth in their actions and decisions. Or at times, when both sets of feelings are equally strong, they may be indecisive or blocked in action.

Public assistance workers encounter people in time of trouble when their feelings are strong. Even though public assistance is their right, it is not uncommon for applicants to have ambivalent feelings about the experience. Therefore, at the very start of a relationship with a recipient we frequently sense a conflict in feelings about applying for help. *On the one hand*, the individual may feel relieved, even gratified, that there is an agency to which he can turn in time of need and an understanding worker on whom he can depend for competent guidance. *On the other hand*, he may resent and fear this agency. He may be fearful that his need will not be met or that, if it is met, he will be unduly obligated so that he will have to pay the exorbitant price of having the management of his affairs taken out of his hands. He may resent his predicament and feel hostile toward those with whom he must share it. His initial response may be one of dislike for the worker, in whose eyes he feels ashamed because he himself finds his situation humiliating. It is because of these complex feelings commonly experienced by public assistance recipients that helping each individual establish his eligibility is not a routine clerical task if it is performed helpfully.[5]

At such a time, when a worker fails to understand, feelings of humiliation and anxiety over status may readily be reinforced, thus contributing further to the person's sense of inadequacy. When the applicant feels inadequate, he is prone to become more dependent. Therefore, if we are to strengthen individuals at this decisive moment when commonly even the adequate person may feel somewhat helpless, it is important that the negative feelings about the experience be dissipated so that the positive ones may emerge. Only as the individual feels secure, has little resentment, and maintains or regains his self-respect will he be able to make constructive use of the agency.

Measures to affirm positive feelings

What means have we at our disposal with which to affirm the positive feelings for the agency experience and to disperse the negative ones? The following measures may be helpful in many instances:

1. Our response to the applicant can be courteous, kind, and interested. A well-kept and attractive office in which applicants are received courteously and appointments scheduled and kept promptly will give the person a sense of adequacy because it obviously matters to someone that he is well received. In contrast, an ill-kept, unattractive office, in which people wait indefinitely to be seen and are subject to casual, off-hand treatment, may only reinforce his worst feelings about himself. One large municipal clinic was operating against great odds in dealing with masses of people who were herded together, subjected to long delays, and discourteously treated by weary personnel. Social workers in agencies using this clinic learned that their clients referred to it as "the cattle pen" and that only under dire need for care could they be prevailed on to go there. What did it do to the recipients of this assistance to feel, *particularly when they were sick and too poor to go elsewhere,* that they had no more worth in the eyes of the world than to be treated in this fashion?

Here we encounter an important observation repeatedly made by experienced social workers: *In time of trouble, when people are emotionally disturbed, they tend to be more sensitive to the reactions of others, and consequently they may assign great meaning to what we say and do in helping them.* We have found that just ordinary kindness and seemingly casual relationships with a client to whom we have given only a bit of service at time of need is commented on in glowing terms long afterward. At such times we have been surprised to learn that what we did meant so much to the person. Likewise, a brusque manner, a hurried and inattentive response, abrupt questions timed to our pressure rather than to the applicant's readiness to answer them may take on values irrelevant or out of proportion to their intent. In such an instance, the individual may personalize our response and charge us with having been rejecting, indifferent, or suspicious when we were only busy and fatigued. When this occurs, his feelings of mistrust and resentment may well be strengthened. Insofar as he must have the assistance, he may not be free to express these negative feelings in a relationship in which he is so insecure. He may, therefore, repress them, and in accepting assistance with little feeling of a right to it, he may build up a strong sense of obligation with a resultant sense of inferiority. This, in turn, may lead to a dependent response in which he looks to us to manage his affairs. Placing his affairs in our hands may have dual gratification: he reassures himself thereby that he is accepted here, and he has an outlet thereby for his resentment. Demanding attitudes may mount as an expression of his continued need for reassurance and of his increasing hostility. Or, some applicants may express their mistrust and resentment through remaining singularly unfree to make known their needs and to use their right to all forms of assistance available to them.

2. If we public assistance workers have a deep conviction that every individual has a rightful claim on society for assistance in time of need, as defined by the Social Security Act, we will reach out to help the person establish eligibility with an attitude that expresses our confidence in his application. If, on the other hand, we do not believe this, or are divided within ourselves in our thinking and feeling about the provisions or the rights accorded the individual under the Social Security Act and in our attitudes toward those who must seek help, our conduct of the investigation probably will express mistrust. This is an important factor in the problem of *how* we may help the person express negative feelings about the agency experience, so that he may make more positive use of it. It is essential that the applicant feel that in our eyes he is eligible until proved ineligible. Instead, we have sometimes conveyed our feelings that he is ineligible until the final shred of evidence has proved beyond the shadow of a doubt that—surprisingly enough—he does have a valid claim. This attitude has the limitation of making the applicant feel unworthy. It puts him on the defensive, and in response to our mistrust he may become less trustworthy, that is, he may be driven into deceit out of a resentful need to prove us wrong. It may also discourage active participation on the part of the applicant in establishing eligibility because, feeling our lack of confidence in him, he may place the burden of investigation on us. Since eligibility must be re-established periodically, our attitude sets the pattern for the continuing relationship in all areas of service. An attitude of trust in the client's application does not imply relaxation of investigation. Instead it may well elicit a more revealing account of the applicant's situation.

When services in addition to financial assistance are indicated, a constructive or destructive relationship with the agency, arising from our initial attitude of confidence or mistrust, may determine his use of those services and how he feels about them. Services other than financial assistance for which he has applied have often been felt to be an infringement on right when the worker's whole attitude about the individual's initial and continued eligibility has been suspicious and mistrustful, and the investigatory process accordingly has seemed an intrusive and dominating inquiry. This important point merits emphasis and it is, therefore, stated conversely. When an individual has been helped to establish eligibility in such a way that he has a genuine feeling of his*right to assistance, all the services will appear as a right to which he is entitled and which he is free to accept or refuse. Finally, it must be emphasized that because helping the applicant file claim to assistance is the

---

*In the 1945 edition, this line read: "...he has a genuine feeling of *unobligated* right to assistance,..." —ED.

initial* function of public assistance service, the relationship thus established becomes the core of the continuing relationship, the content and nature of which will be further determined by the wishes of the applicant and the total scope of services undertaken by the agency.[6]

3. If, as public assistance administrators, we have genuine conviction as to the applicant's rightful claim on society in time of need, if our feelings about this principle are not divided, we will be inclined to think in terms of the applicant's needs and in the long run protect the taxpayer.[†] If, however, we are in conflict in our thinking about the individual's right to public assistance, we may fear the community's attitude toward our spending and, instead of assuming responsibility for interpretation of the applicant's need, we may ease our fears by silently conserving public funds at the recipient's immediate, and the community's eventual, cost. We may then give our services grudgingly, inadequately, short-sightedly. In such instances, the negative feeling of the applicant for the agency may mount to such an extent that the agency experience in the long run is destructive for him. It is demoralizing to be the recipient in a relationship in which one feels deprived and hostile.

4. Our conviction about the applicant's right will also influence the way in which we interpret his right to a fair hearing. This may be presented in such a way as to make him feel that he is unquestionably ineligible and that he has no right to make use of this resource. Or it may be presented so that we convey an evaluation of him as a person with sufficient judgment and trustworthiness to have an opinion that merits consideration. In the latter instance he will be inclined to use this right realistically, whereas in the former he may be driven to use it as an expression of his negative feeling for the agency. Or he may give up and submit in spite of his conviction that he has not had just treatment.

Two-way feelings influence public assistance workers

Finally, we might say that our conviction about the individual's right to public assistance will influence our use of legal provisions. Properly conceived and interpreted, our laws enable us to develop a public assistance program that will serve individuals adequately. We have learned from experience that adequate legislation is sometimes defeated by limited or restrictive interpretation of its scope and intent or, on the other hand, that inherently poor legislation

---

*In the earlier edition, this sentence read: "Finally, it must be emphasized that because helping the applicant *to get financial assistance* is the *primary* function of public assistance service...." —ED.

†The 1945 edition stated: "...we will be inclined to think *and feel* in terms of the applicant's needs and *be less protective of the taxpayer.*" —ED.

has been liberally interpreted to provide the basis for constructive service. Moreover, we know that restrictive practice may modify the beneficial effect of our best legislation. Our conviction about the individual's right to assistance will influence our policy-making and our use of existent policies. It is definitely known that some agency staffs either do not make the most of present provisions or use them more restrictively than is necessary. We thereby fail to make full use of the recipient's capacity for a positive response to the agency's service and to make full use of the agency's responsibility to the community. Interpretation of right to assistance, careful explanation of what evidence the applicant needs to assemble in order to establish eligibility, making sure that he understands the basis for the amount of the grant, clarification of the agency's procedures, interpretation of the right to a fair hearing—all these measures may increase the applicant's positive feeling for the agency in that they contribute to his security. He knows where he stands and is not left anxiously wondering about his status. Insofar as assistance payments are incommensurate with need and insofar as agency investigative procedures must be rigidly imposed, there may be some reinforcement of the original negative feelings that he brought to the application. It is important that he have the opportunity to express such feelings; this opportunity, in fact, constitutes the measure that is sometimes useful in helping the individual to have more understanding of any limitations of the service, and thereby results in less frustration for him when all his needs cannot be met. The discharge of negative feelings is not always helpful, however. Obviously, this measure may fail when there is great discrepancy between extent of need and adequacy of service. A worker's understanding of the recipient's needs may lead to a refinement of skill in easing disturbed feelings over a program's failure to meet those needs adequately, but this skill cannot compensate for inadequate provisions or for unsound policies.

This discussion of the emotions has been presented with the assumption that how a person feels will determine in considerable measure what he thinks, how he acts, and what use he makes of an agency's service. It has been possible to portray here only a few of the ways in which emotions have influenced the recipient's reaction to his problem and his use of our help. It has been possible only to suggest the implications of this principle for workers who also bring their emotions into this joint adventure of helping and being helped. Further discussion of this basic factor in human behavior inevitably will be interwoven throughout the subsequent pages, for it permeates every facet of life and, therefore, every aspect of our work with people.

Failure to accept responsibility

All people tend at times to ascribe their own thoughts, wishes, feelings, and faults to circumstances or to other persons. When thoughts, wishes, feelings, or acts are unacceptable to his conscience or produce anxiety as to what other people will think, an individual commonly places them outside himself because of the inward discomfort they cause. Thus, Mr. C attributed his action in coming to the agency to his concern for his child because admitting his own need of help caused him too much discomfort.

Guilt about a retarded child

Likewise, Mrs. M emphasized a minor head injury as the cause of her daughter's mental defect and defensively reiterated that there never had been any such abnormality in her family. Much later, when she was secure in her relationship with the worker, she spontaneously expressed a long-standing fear that her own irregular sex life prior to marriage had been a contributing factor. Earlier she had shown two-way feeling about placing the child in an institution—by expressing the wish for placement and asking the worker's advice about resources yet repeatedly retreating from taking any action. She seemed inwardly compelled to keep the child at home and to give her overprotective care. After bringing out her own imagined responsibility for the problem and receiving the worker's interpretation that feeble-mindedness occurs in many families without a known cause, and with the worker's help in obtaining medical examinations for herself, she was ready to think and act in terms of what would be best for the child. It is probable that several factors operated in her eventual decision in favor of placement: (1) the relationship with the worker, with whom she felt safe and, therefore, free to bring out fear of that which other people might condemn, (2) the worker's understanding response, in which there was no evidence of shock or condemnation on his part, (3) the information the worker was able to help her obtain about her own medical condition and about feeble-mindedness apparently relieved her feeling of blame. Gradually it came about that she did not have to keep the child to ease her own disturbed feeling but, instead, became able to face the child's needs.

Blame is placed outside oneself

In another family receiving ADC, Mrs. E, also apprehensive lest she be found wanting as an adequate parent, at first placed the total responsibility for her son's delinquent behavior on bad inheritance from his father and on his associates in the neighborhood. Only gradually, as the mother realized that the worker's interest in the boy's problem stemmed from a wish to help rather than from an impulse to check on and criticize her, could she begin to admit her long-standing ineptitude in dealing with the boy and her need for help in understanding him and in knowing how to deal with him more effectively.

It must not be assumed that this common tendency to place the cause of a difficulty outside oneself is always a projection of blame or responsibility owing to an uncomfortable conscience. Frequently, difficulties have their origin in circumstances and persons outside the control of the individual. It is for this reason, among others, that we generally accept the person's version of the problem and start working with him on it in terms of the professed facts. His reactions to the help extended may soon let us know whether he is being realistic in placing the problem outside himself.

WPA worker could not obtain employment

Mr. G, aged 43 when he reapplied for financial assistance in 1940, had a long record on public assistance rolls. Married at 29, he had come to this country from Scotland in 1926 and had brought his family over shortly thereafter. From 1926 until 1934 he had been self-maintaining, although the family had had a precarious struggle. Trained as a draftsman at a polytechnic institute in Scotland, he was unable to obtain that work in this country, so he had taken employment as a harnessmaker, repairing saddles for riding horses. In the Depression years this work became increasingly irregular, so he bought a taxicab to help provide for his family. He was not able to earn enough for his family as an independent "cabbie" and found it necessary in 1934 to apply for public relief. He continued to earn part of the total expenses of the family with his taxi during the time he received public assistance and after he was transferred to a work-relief project. From 1934 to 1940 the family had been continuously on general relief or work relief for partial support. During this time, Mr. G showed unusual stability and both he and his wife were noted as having ability to manage resourcefully on a meager income.

In 1940, Mr. G reapplied for financial assistance on being laid off WPA. At this time there were five children, the family was living in a rent-free apartment in return for janitor service, there were no debts, they had managed to maintain some insurance, and the children were well cared for and were attending school regularly. Mr. G had been exerting every effort to get work as a draftsman, for which he had received further training and experience under WPA. He recounted the numerous employment contacts he had made and was deeply discouraged at his failure to get a job in a defense plant, where there was now a growing demand for workers with this skill. He attributed his failure to employers' prejudice against WPA workers. Careful inquiry revealed that he had become so convinced that employers would not hire workers from WPA that in his recent applications he had withheld information on this connection, creating in his employment record a gap of a period of years that also operated against him. He said that he valued this experience highly and was convinced that he could do this work, but he felt so keenly that others looked down on WPA that he could not sell himself or persuade others that it had been a worthwhile experience.

At the close of the interview the worker offered to see the employment manager at the aeronautical plant where he had applied, to help him get a job. Mr. G eagerly accepted this help. The worker learned that the employer had reservations about Mr. G because his record showed no recent work and a long-standing record of irregular work. Interpretation of the man's feelings about his WPA experience and of WPA projects and a statement regarding Mr. G's good record on WPA won the employer's interest, not only in this man but also in WPA employees in general. He said that he had no idea the city took this kind of interest in people receiving relief and that he would be interested in giving such men a trial. Mr. G immediately took the job proffered, arranged to get supplementary training in the use of certain instruments, and quickly and happily terminated his contact with the agency.

In this case we encounter a man whose failure to obtain work was attributed to circumstances over which he had no control. The worker, out of his experience with other WPA employees, knew that there was some reality for his belief that some employers were prejudiced. By December 1940, it is probable that labor shortages were fast eliminating these prejudices and that Mr. G's inability to "sell himself" stemmed from disturbed feelings over past defeats. At this time, it is possible that there was a considerable tendency on Mr. G's part to ascribe his own feelings of inferiority to others and to believe that they thought his qualifications inferior because, through job rejections, he had come to feel that way *to some extent* himself. The decisive points here, however, are that these feelings had some basis in reality, that Mr. G did not feel *wholly* inferior in his qualifications, and that, in general, he was a responsible person who still was actively striving to manage his own affairs and was not given *in general* to placing blame and responsibility on others.

While in casework practice we are loath to take over responsibilities a client might carry himself, and while frequently we prefer to help him face his feelings so that he may view his situation more realistically and tackle his own employment problem himself, many of us would consider the worker's immediate supportive help wise in this instance for the following reasons: (1) Mr. G's emotional disturbance *seems localized in one area of his life situation,* that of getting a job; therefore, suitable employment could be relied on as the quickest and most effective treatment. (2) Mr. G has shown many strengths and no tendency to become dependent, as evidenced by the persistence of aspiration and self-activity throughout a long period of enforced economic dependency and adverse circumstance. We therefore can feel free to meet the fragmentary dependency need of the moment without fear of demoralizing him and with the assurance that he will make constructive use of our help. There is an important principle here, one of which we can well take note. *When an individual's impulses toward independence are strong and patterns of self-dependence are well entrenched, the resistance to becoming wholly dependent is also strong. It is as difficult to induce dependency, that is, to pauperize such a person, as it is to stimulate self-responsibility in a chronically dependent individual who is almost invariably mentally or physically ill.* (3) Insofar as the worker had grounds for believing that there was a basis in reality for Mr. G's assertion that employers were prejudiced, he might well seize on every such individual instance as an opportunity to overcome these prejudices in the interests of all public assistance recipients and of public assistance programs.

This tendency to place responsibility outside oneself is a common response of people when they first come to an agency. This may be owing to the strangeness of the experience and to lack of acquaintance with the worker. After they have tested out the worker's attitudes and feel safe, this tendency may subside. A sequence frequently is: (1) The individual, feeling uncomfortable over asking for help, may need to justify his request by attributing his dilemma to factors and forces beyond his control. Sometimes this is a valid statement of fact, but it is not always wholly valid. (2) Having established eligibility for assistance, he may then spontaneously begin to question his part in the problem and to reach out for help in managing his affairs in a way different from that he has used in the past. Or, in meeting certain demands of reality in the process of establishing eligibility, he may become aware of this tendency and be more realistic in assuming some responsibility for his difficulties. In the process of establishing eligibility, the tendency to disclaim responsibility for his problem frequently is not a vital issue. If he is eligible, he has a right to assistance regardless of personal responsibility for the problem.

The reality demands required in an objective discussion of the facts on which eligibility is based—that is, facts such as inability to work, death of wage earner, inability to obtain employment, lack of or unavailability of other financial resources, place of residence, and so on—will reveal any distortions that need clarification. When an applicant justifies his need for assistance in ways that have no bearing on his eligibility status, we have learned to go slowly in taking issue with the facts as he recounts them. We have also learned that it is not helpful to side with him against the persons or circumstances he blames. That is, we do not literally sympathize with him or make remarks that place us in agreement with his comments. If we were to do this, he might feel committed to continue the initial version of his problem because we have accepted it so completely. He might get the sense that we have accepted him because he is completely blameless and might infer that since we share his blame of others we would condemn him if he were to reveal his part in the problem. In continuing service, this matter of responsibility for the problem may become a vital issue if rehabilitation of the individual is our concern. It is often important that we do not deal with people in such a way as to increase their need to project responsibility if they are to continue to be active in the management of their affairs. Often, when the applicant's impulse to place his difficulties beyond his own control persists despite the efforts of a worker who has given the individual every reason to feel secure, it is owing to a well-established personality difficulty that is beyond the scope of the public assistance worker to modify.

Tendency to resist change

The individual's common tendency to resist change is another behavior manifestation of import to public assistance workers. It is a reaction with which we have been familiar all our lives. Sudden change-anxiety-resistance is a sequence that almost inevitably we have experienced and doubtless have observed in others. New customs, new ideas, new demands, new situations that call for different thinking and acting are commonly decried and struggled against. We repeatedly encounter people during catastrophes that bring sudden and sometimes great change in the individual's whole way of life. Some of the anxiety and some of the resistance to our helping efforts may, therefore, stem from the element of change in the person's life and may not mean that he literally does not want or gradually may not be able to use the help he momentarily rejects. He may have to adapt to new conditions slowly and in the process may revolt against the hand that would help him make this change.

This tendency to resist change Alexander terms "inertia"; he describes it as an energy-saving principle that, although creating problems for people and especially for social workers as they try to help people, has been a useful principle by and large throughout the individual's life. Rooted in our early automatic behavior, the persistence of this tendency to live by habit has meant that "when the best behavior in a given situation has been determined by experiment, and through repetition has become automatic, the mind is no longer required to function in that type of situation."[7] The advantage of automatic behavior is that it is effortless. Its disadvantage is that it is adapted to definite situations and is not easily modified when changed conditions require it. *As the individual masters his environment, as he gains maturity and independence to function on his own both physically and psychologically, automatic behavior plays a less important role and he meets changing circumstances more readily.* Dependence on others and fear of new situations go hand in hand. Therefore, the factors and forces in life that can be marshaled to give the individual basic emotional security will lead to less dependence on habitual ways of life and should increase the individual's capacity for greater flexibility in meeting new situations. In this connection, we have learned that sometimes a person cannot use his changed life situation in a responsible, resourceful fashion until certain basic dependency needs have been met through supportive help of one sort or another.

Dependent widow is discouraged about management

Mrs. L, a widow who had been receiving aid for her three dependent children ranging in age from 7 years to 6 months, sought the worker's help in finding a place for the children in order that she might go to work. As this request was considered with her, she showed marked anxiety about leaving the children lest they not receive good care and also lest her husband's people condemn her as an irresponsible and unloving mother. As the possibility of remaining at home with a plan for continuing the financial assistance was explored with her, she revealed that she was deeply discouraged over managing the two older boys. Their father had spent so much time with them and he had been such a help in disciplining them. They missed him and had not been the same since his death. She had had difficulty managing the money—her husband did the major part of the family purchasing and planning and she had been lost and confused in trying to make ends meet. She felt lost even in meal planning, as she always planned around his likes and dislikes. She had been depressed and lonely and her moods affected the children. Her husband was a sociable man who liked a good time. He would pile them all into the car and off they would go for picnics or to visit friends he had made at the plant. Now they had no car and she had lost touch with his friends. On this occasion, the worker proffered the agency's help in budget planning and advising her on child care, and also offered to help her find certain community resources she might find useful in rearing her family on a smaller income than they had formerly had. Mrs. L was appreciative of the worker's interest and in the subsequent months made eager and productive use of the supportive help given.

One notes that, prior to this time, the agency's service, beyond the money payment, was not recorded as having been conveyed to this mother. This lack raises many questions. One can appreciate that the worker may have been hesitant at the start about seeming to take over management of this woman's affairs. In connection with unrestricted money payments, it is important that a recipient be left free to plan and spend as he wills. In carrying out this principle to the letter of the law, we need not withhold help that the individual either seeks or readily accepts when offered. Perhaps, in the long run, there were certain values for this woman in attempting to struggle along on her own. It might be maintained that experiencing a deep need for help following the loss of one on whom she was very dependent would incline her to more eager, productive, and less resentful use of help when it came in response to her expressed need. One wonders, however, whether she might not have been helped earlier to meet the great change that was suddenly imposed on her.

Perhaps this case again points up the need for learning the relationship patterns that previously have existed in a family. Had we known the dependent role played by this mother, we might have proffered casework services earlier. Perhaps she could not have used them. Early observations in the record are to the effect that she seemed vague and unresponsive, and it is possible that she was absorbed in her grief and too confused to participate in planning until she turned to the worker with a decisive issue. Did the vagueness and unresponsiveness mean that she was *then* unable to use help, or did it mean that she was too crushed to articulate her need for it? We know that when deeply hurt, as sometimes when acutely ill, the individual withdraws from asking for the aid he both needs and can use. While there might be a difference in point of view on this in the field of practice, some of us would feel better satisfied had the worker tested out the woman's capacity to use help at an early date. A flexible readiness to be guided by the nature of the client's response would have been the worker's safeguard against forcing services on her. It is clear that we took pains to leave her free to be self-determining, an opportunity she could not use productively until her problem was shared and she was given certain supportive help in taking over a new way of life.

Regression to earlier satisfactory behavior

Closely related to this tendency to resist change is the behavior adaptation known as regression. As the individual gradually proceeds from the complete dependency of infancy and early childhood, his progress is smooth and uninterrupted by phases of regression *only insofar as the demands of his external world are appropriately timed to his physical and psychological readiness to master his environment. Since throughout the course of life the individual's life experiences seldom are so timed, fragmentary regressions are usual.* If graphically described, the growth process from infancy to maturity would show marked movement forward with slight movement backward from time to time. *It is only natural when life becomes markedly difficult that there is a tendency to return to earlier satisfactory life periods.* Each period in which the child makes a good adjustment can serve as a phase to which he may return later in life. If obstacles continue to prevent forward movement, these periods at which his responses are "frozen" may serve as a point of fixation. Regression, however, *need not be permanent* if the individual can be strengthened to meet the demands of life and/or excessive environmental frustrations can be cased.

This is a decisive point, one that gives significance to much of our work with people. We are all familiar with manifestations of regressive behavior, although we may not have known them by this name and we may not have been aware of the purpose of this behavior. For example, an infant reaches out to take his first steps, and before he has gained any security in this great venture he has a bad fall. Temporarily he retreats to crawling and may even wish to be carried again. As his confidence is restored through the comfort thereby received, he gains courage to set forth again. A young child has just begun to experience periods of separation from his mother but still has some anxiety about leaving her. A baby arrives to take the place he is not yet ready to give up or even to share. He seeks a return to his infancy through behavior that conscripts the mother's concern and attention in symptoms such as bed wetting, soiling, thumb sucking, crying, whining, and the like. An adolescent moves out into his initial relationship with a member of the opposite sex. He experiences defeat and retreats at least temporarily to his own sex, and becomes absorbed again in the interests and activities of a younger group. A man struggles against odds to maintain a place as wage earner, head of his family, and strives to meet the demands of his dependent children. He experiences prolonged frustration through unemployment, which brings a feeling of loss of status in the eyes of the world and of unworthiness in the eyes of his wife and children. So he returns to a life period of being the irresponsible boy who goes out with the gang and gets drunk, demands mothering from his wife, and competes with his children for first place in her concern and attention. The elderly person becomes physically inadequate, unable to continue his work, and no longer needed by his children. He suffers relationship losses through the death of those who mean much to him. The present becomes inordinately painful and the future is threatening, so he is driven to the past as an escape both from the present and the future. One may see much childish behavior.[8]

Regression to the past, generally to a state of childish dependence, is always forced on the individual by frustrating circumstances and by frustration in the human contacts of life. In the adult, except in outright mental illness, it is never complete, for it is met by the contrary desire to remain adult. In the case of Mr. G, for example, we saw a fragmentary regression in his inability to handle his affairs alone in the matter of getting a job. We saw Mrs. L on the verge of flight from the responsibilities of motherhood at a point when they had become overwhelming. Her actual capacity for self-dependence, revealed in her subsequent response to the help given, was greater than might have been expected from the impression given in the interview recorded earlier. On the verge of turning back from adult responsibilities, her desire to remain adult was expressed in her concern for the welfare of the children and in her anticipation of criticism from her husband's people.

We see people in time of trouble when the pressures of life have not necessarily been timed to their readiness to deal with them and, therefore, regressive impulses are at least temporarily in the foreground. Furthermore, there are elements in the public assistance setting that may provoke or reinforce regressive tendencies. For example, the very fact that people must account for their money may put them in what they feel to be the child's position. Each time family requirements are reviewed, this experience may be repeated by a worker who is prone to detailed and irrelevant inquiry. Or the worker who from the start has failed to build up partnership in establishing eligibility will find a childlike recipient who is able only to answer his inquiries and may not assume full responsibility for presenting the facts of his situation.

In general, public assistance programs can help individuals in relation to this conflict in several ways: (1) through contributing to the individual's chances of survival in a competitive social system in which the responsibilities of adulthood are heightened or at times abruptly taken away, (2) through rendering services that meet dependency needs in such a way as not to undermine the adult impulses, (3) through affording opportunities for growth and through removing obstacles to growth—all services that safeguard or strengthen man's physical, mental, and emotional welfare can well reinforce the adult impulses, (4) in the midst of an overwhelming present, the individual may need supportive help in looking to and in planning for the future. When he has an untenable present and no outlook to the future, his only recourse is to the past. Since the adaptive mechanism of regression has different treatment import at different ages, more specific discussion of how we may use our understanding of its meaning will occur elsewhere.

Inevitable impulse toward progression

There is evidence in human behavior that, in contrast to the tendency toward resistance to change and regression to the past, there is also a strong and *inevitable impulse toward progression. There is movement into new experience, giving of self to creative activity, giving of energy to work that serves a purpose beyond the objective of mere survival, giving of self in relationships that contribute to and gratify others as well as serve the purpose of self-gratification.* Just as the physical organism when it reaches it limits of growth tends to reproduce itself, so the human personality in the process of maturing begins to reach out beyond itself. Alexander considers the impulse to expand beyond the limits of self to be basic. It is his impression that this occurs when a point of saturation is reached. He comments:

> Sexuality proper is the expression of the surplus energy of the mature organism as a whole. As a container filled with water overflows, so the mature organism cannot any longer add to its own completion, and the tendency toward personal growth gives place to reproduction, which is nothing but growth beyond the limits of the individual person. . . .
>
> Sexual desire and love, and the desire and care for children are not the only indications of maturity. The creative tendencies of other sorts contributing to the interests of society at large are parallel expressions of this surplus energy. The whole range from totem poles to modern sculpture, music, and painting, as well as the discoveries of science, are products of this creative activity. Most economic activities are similarly motivated—though utilitarian factors cooperate—as can be seen in the peasant's attitude toward the soil or the artisan's toward his handicraft, or the industrialist toward his plant.[9]

He comments further that the creative urge differs from the utilitarian one of automatic behavior and the regressive tendency in that it is not seeking saving of energy. Instead, it prompts the expenditure of energy that is no longer needed for the selfish purposes of the growing organism that has reached its limit of personal growth. The emphasis in all creative activities shifts from self-centered aims to outside objects.

This growth principle has considerable import for public assistance workers in their efforts to understand and to help people. It means briefly that, insofar as the individual's physical, mental, and emotional needs are adequately met during the early years of life, he will move spontaneously in the direction of growth, reaching out from self-centered absorption in an infantile sort of existence to more social concerns of maturity. It means also that if his needs during childhood have been met in decent measure, he will carry into adult years considerable stamina to resist regression. Obstacles to continued growth will have varying values. They may be frustrating and thereby provoke irritation or rage. The decisive point here is that he will struggle to keep intact his identity as an adult and will find discomfort as well as gratification in his momentary regressive responses. Throughout the years, social workers have observed much to prove the validity of this principle. More recently, we have seen innumerable individuals who were seemingly demoralized during the Depression years weather that period of prolonged adversity with a surprising resilience and with a capacity to bury the past and move on. *Man normally desires a life beyond the narrow confines of an infantile self. He wants to learn, he wants to marry and to establish a family, he wants to work, he wants a participating and contributing part in the life of the community. He is deeply frustrated when he is denied the requisite opportunities for this fuller life.*

The social work profession deals with people who are experiencing some breakdown in their capacity to cope unaided with their own affairs. This breakdown may be owing primarily to external forces beyond the control of the person, or it may be owing partly, largely, or entirely to factors within the person—that is, he may have created his social dilemma. Whether the social problem is predominantly of external or of internal origin, the growth forces that carry the individual beyond absorption in himself to creative activity and to living in constructive relationships with others may well have been obstructed, so that regressive solutions frequently are being sought or may have become well entrenched. Experience has shown the individual's resistance to suddenly imposed change as well as his recourse to earlier satisfactory modes of behavior. In many of our contacts with people in all walks of life we have perceived that lack of "surplus energy" to give beyond the limits of individual need—a lack engendered by a meager life that has afforded more deprivation, frustration, and hostility than gratification, realization, and love, both in relationships and in circumstantial forces. We know all too well that the meager life guarantees the ascendancy of man's infantile self and that it does not develop individuals mentally and emotionally constituted to carry forward constructively the aims of a democracy.

When we see the relationship between social security provisions, of which public assistance is an integral part, and the growth of the individual, perhaps we are both discouraged and encouraged. Perhaps we are enabled to look beyond some of the discouraging limitations that beset us in our daily struggle to help people. Perhaps we are challenged also to obtain for people more nearly adequate assurance of their right not merely to survive but to live in a fuller sense of the word. The attainment of such a world implies support of social and economic measures that are outside the scope of public assistance. Whatever the limitation in our present programs, we can take heart in our labors in the realization that we are pioneers in the effort to make real man's claim of right on society.

Notes

1. Mildred E. Osborn, "Are the Fathers Forgotton?" *The Family*, Vol. 22, No. 9 (January 1942), pp. 295–303.

2. For discussion of the use of interpretation and authority and reality, *see* Gordon Hamilton, *Theory and Practice of Social Casework* (1st ed.; New York: Columbia University Press, 1940), pp. 209–230.

3. *See* Dorothy Bird Daly, *Casework Practice in Public Assistance Administration* (Chicago: American Public Welfare Association, 1942), chap. 2.

4. For a full discussion of application and intake, *see* Hamilton, *op. cit.*, chap. 4; of interviewing, *see* Hamilton, *ibid.*, chap. 5, and Annette Garrett, *Interviewing: Its Principles and Methods* (New York: Family Service Association of America, 1942).

5. *See* Grace F. Marcus, "Changes in the Theory of Relief Giving," *Proceedings of the National Conference of Social Work, 1941* (New York: Columbia University Press, 1941), pp. 267–279.

6. For an example of effective work in establishing constructive relationship in initial handling of eligibility, *see* the case of Mr. B, pp. 17–21.

7. Franz Alexander, MD, *Our Age of Unreason; A Study of the Irrational Forces in Social Life* (1st ed.; Philadelphia: J.B. Lippincott Co., 1942), pp. 144–148.

8. The grossly childish behavior we know as the state of senility frequently stems from organic brain change in the aging process. The extent to which frustrating life circumstances are a factor in these cases may be obscured by an organic condition. Childish behavior may occur, however, entirely in response to frustration.

9. Alexander, *op. cit.*, pp. 206–208.

PART TWO

Common human needs in relation to the provision of public assistance

As individuals apply for public assistance they may bring, in addition to economic needs, many other needs. In a money economy, money means different things to different people, and its import for the individual will determine the meaning for him of his right to assistance. More often than not he will feel, in addition to discomfort produced by actual want, some discomfort in applying for and in receiving assistance. Furthermore, the public assistance worker's feelings about economic dependency will influence his ways of helping and thereby determine the values of public assistance for the recipient. The individual's needs and their emotional value for him, in relation to services rendered and attitudes encountered as he experiences public assistance, are decisive in determining constructive or destructive use of the experience.

What, then, are the common human needs and feelings to which public assistance programs should be oriented? In general, we have noted the need to be well fed, properly clothed, and adequately housed as a basis for both physical and mental health. We have remarked also the need for educational, recreational, and religious opportunities under conditions conducive to the furtherance of physical, mental, and spiritual growth. The need for satisfying human relationships as a basis for physical, mental, and spiritual well-being has been mentioned. Since all our needs have varying import at different ages under differing circumstances, it is essential that we consider them more specifically. As a general background for public assistance workers, certain universal needs will therefore be presented and their relative importance at different age levels and under varying life conditions commented on. In order that normal development of the individual may be safeguarded as assistance is provided, the following chapters will cover their particular significance in the context of the public assistance experience.

3

Infancy and childhood

The most basic impulse in any organism is the impulse to survive. The need to feel secure—that is, safe as an assurance of survival—is fundamental. *Fear emerges quickly when survival is threatened.* The human being has a long period of physical inability to survive without the care of others. Normally, therefore, at the start of life he is acutely fearful and may become chronically anxious if he cannot depend on others. He is born with certain equipment that is essential for maintaining life, that is, the suckling reflex and such functions as digestion, absorption, respiration, and circulation. Initially his only inherent sources of security are vested in these bodily processes, and this explains why regular feeding, regular elimination, and good physical health are important in terms of his early feelings of security. This is why the infant readily turns to sucking his thumb as solace when fatigued or discomfited and why a baby who has had respiratory difficulties, gastric disturbances, or the like may early develop anxieties as expressed in restlessness, "nervousness," undue fearfulness, and so on after the subsidence of the acute illness.

The infant is equipped also with a capacity to learn, and this capacity has been described as "a fundamental biological function of every living organism and...indispensable to life." On the subject of adaptive behavior of the infant, Alexander writes:

> It has to learn by practice...almost all its functions in relation to its environment, for it inherits ready-made only its internal vegetative functions and the suckling reflex. It must learn muscular coordination: how to use its hands and feet, how to walk and keep its equilibrium, to focus its eyes, to speak and to establish and maintain associations with other human beings....

The infant is dependent upon the parents, but through learning acquires certain faculties in the exercise of which he can dispense with this dependence.[1]

41

The infant needs love, care, and a chance to learn

The infant, then, has three sources of security that enable him to feel safe and, therefore, to experience a satisfying relationship with others: (1) consistent physical care and conditions conducive to good health requisite to a feeling of well-being, (2) uninterrupted opportunity to learn and reassuring encouragement to persist in learning through sympathetic attention to his hurts when his first learning efforts endanger his safety, (3) relationships in which he is loved. Since actually the infant cannot survive alone in spite of learning efforts and since he early gets the sense that his physical well-being is provided by others and will continue to be provided insofar as he is loved, in the last analysis, then, "the child's security depends wholly *on being loved and cared for* by adults so that the wish to be cared for is *the central issue of his life.*"

Denial of opportunity to learn may cause emotional disturbance

There are many significant implications in these sources of security, notably that the impulse to learn is basic and related to the impulse for survival. *Therefore, learning eases anxiety, and consequently the denial of opportunity to learn or frustration in learning may produce emotional disturbance.* The infant's complete helplessness and the child's inability to get along without considerable reliance on others make the ministrations of others necessary and gratifying in terms of feeling secure. Awareness of infantile gratifications in dependency led in the early days of the use of psychological insights to the assumption that universally the human gets greater gratification from being dependent than from becoming independent; there was a phase in child rearing when it was thought that the child needed to be encouraged to learn, that he needed to be pushed into learning experiences, and that we should be wary of giving him much gratification in his infantile dependency lest he enjoy it too much and be loath to relinquish it for efforts in his own behalf. *Today the impulse to learn—that is, the impulse to gain self-sufficiency in order to feel safe—is recognized as a positive innate tendency.*

The infant early reaches out for the spoon to feed himself. If permitted to experiment, he shows great gratification in his clumsy efforts and has a wonderful time hitting and missing his mouth and smearing himself with food. More usually, the busy mother who must conserve food, laundry, time, and energy deprives him of this opportunity. Note, however, that when she takes the spoon he often resists and even yells with rage. Observe the young child's eager and persistent interest in learning to know the world about him— he reaches, he climbs, he touches, he feels, he grabs at everything within range. In the complexity of a civilized household he falls, he gets burned, he gets slapped to the tune of a continual "NO, NO—Don't touch—Stop that!" It is small wonder, then, that he early finds that learning is dangerous, that adults prefer to control him rather than permit him to manage his own life, and perhaps it is because learning is early fraught with so much restriction and disapproval that the enjoyment of helplessness seems to become the primary gratification in the lives of some children.

That the impulse to learn survives against so much discouragement is an argument for its strength and primacy.[2] Why does it persist? Probably because *in the last analysis there is no real security, no deep assurance of survival in being wholly dependent on others. If one's security rests largely outside oneself one is forever uncertain.* This is a decisive point and one that has import beyond the years of infancy and childhood. It has special import for social workers. We deal largely with individuals at a time of enforced dependency or at a time when adverse circumstance has strengthened the impulses toward dependency, thus at the same time provoking anxiety about and resistance to the loss of self-dependence.

The child must have love as well as care

For the central issue of the child's life, the wish to be loved and to be cared for, the noteworthy point is that *he must have love as well as care* in order to feel secure and to develop a socialized self. Being completely dependent on adults for his survival, he fears loss of care and can only be assured of its continuance insofar as he is loved. This is one of the reasons why some children remain deeply insecure and anxious even though given excessive protective care. And strangely enough, these highly protective parents frequently overprotect their children because, not loving them enough to give unbegrudgingly, they need to deny their irritation and mask their wish to reject—that is, to neglect the children—through enacting a role of great devotion. The children, however, sensing the lack of love, remain unsatisfied and insecure and manifest their resultant anxiety in behavior disturbances of varied sorts. Commonly encountered in these situations is a restless, demanding, attention-getting child who seems insatiable in his need to be cared for. Even though the gift without the giver is bare, he needs eternally to be given attention as an assurance that he is loved.[3] His life may become an endless restless quest.

Commonly also, these children, not having been loved sufficiently, grow into adults who have meager capacity to love others. One cannot give out of a vacuum; instead, one gives from a surplus. As unloved children become parents, they may repeat the pattern of their own parents. Frequently in their lives outside the family circle they are hostile, self-aggrandizing individuals who cannot relate themselves constructively to others and in positions of leadership may be driven by their irrational emotional needs into dictatorial measures. Or these children may solve their anxiety by becoming abjectly dependent, and their behavior may be more submissive than aggressive, more self-condemning than openly hostile. The response patterns to the insecurity created by lack of love are varied; these two kinds of response are cited merely to establish the point that *when the child's need for love is frustrated in one way or another—that is, when parents either show their lack of love through overt neglect or disguise it through overprotection—the chances for the attainment of rational attitudes and mature development are greatly diminished.*

Denial of love and care creates insecurity

In summary, then, we see that at the start of life all human beings need to be loved and cared for and to have an opportunity to learn in order to become increasingly less dependent on others. Dependence on others for love and care is the primary need, and insofar as this need is met freely the child reaches out spontaneously to learn to master his environment and is sustained in the failures and hurts that learning inevitably brings. This is a decisive point for all social workers in helping people, for it has import throughout the individual's life, and it is particularly significant for public assistance workers because we deal with people at a time of defeat in the mastery of life's circumstances. In infancy and early childhood, denial of love and care creates deep insecurity as to the chances of survival and produces both anxiety and resentment. Frustration in opportunity to learn likewise is a threat to the impulse for survival and produces the same feelings, so that either or both lacks in the child's family life may well lead to behavior disturbances.[4]

Administrators and supervisors will want to convey to workers the decisive importance of adequate financial assistance in order that the physical welfare of the infant may be safeguarded. Economic security is important also from the standpoint that the mother, if anxious and harassed, transmits her disturbed feelings to the infant, perhaps to an even greater extent than when the child is older. The importance of the mother's care and, in the case of a mother who seeks advice in relation to working, the need for an adequate mother substitute who will give the infant or young child not only consistent care but also affectionate response, are obvious. A careful appraisal of the nature of the mother's relationship with the young child is needed in counseling her as to whether she is wise to work outside the home. The significant points here are: Is there an adequate substitute for the mother? Will the added economic security the family gains through the mother's working enable her to be a more calm and giving mother while with the child? Is her present attitude toward child care such that one questions her ability to afford the child a constructive relationship so that a mother substitute might be preferable?

The schoolchild needs opportunities for creativity and attainment of skills

If his needs have been met during his earlier life so that his development is normal, the school-age child is less dependent, both physically and emotionally, on the adults in his environment than he was at an earlier age. At this point he experiences the first major separation from the security of the home and dependence on the parents, especially on the mother. In the early stages of this period he may seek to replace the parents with the schoolteacher and other parent substitutes, sometimes older children. In the interests of survival, the need to develop greater self-sufficiency emerges, perhaps to relieve anxiety caused by dependence on parent persons. He seeks security through close association with his own kind, children of the same age and sex, and tends to live in a group or gang that replaces the family to some extent. The group at this age denies both its dependence on parent persons and its attraction to the opposite sex. Symptomatic of these denials, one notes hostility toward the "teacher's pet," the mother-dependent child, and aversion to petting and coddling except at a time of stress when there may be a momentary regression into the mother's arms. The noteworthy point about this age is that the child now spends the energy formerly used in his struggle for adaptation within the family in increasing his knowledge and acquiring physical strength and prowess. There is great gratification in creative activity and in games through which he develops skills and in the acquisition of knowledge through which he can come to be more self-sufficient. This is a period of preparation for the emancipation from parents that begins to take place in adolescence.

Schoolchild still needs his parents

Because of the child's strong denial, at this age, of dependency and because of his rejection of the opposite sex, we may assume a degree of self-sufficiency that is not there. He still needs his parents and at times of stress needs the mother very much. This is the age when the child wants to go out to play rather than to stay at home, but on returning is reassured to find the mother there at least some of the time. An empty house occasioned by the mother's working, parents who are anxious and disturbed over the economic situation, an umemployed father who is depressed and defeated by a too-competitive world, do not give these children the base of security that they still need to sustain them in their struggle to make their place in the group.

In this period, the child whose dependency needs are not being met and have not been met in the earlier years may cling to the parents and be fearful of the give-and-take of the group. If he moves out into the group, his fears may make him the brunt of other children's aggressions or his hostilities may bring him into open conflict and win so much opposition that he is driven back into dependence on adults and into playing with younger children. If at this age he does not have adequate opportunity for developing his mental and physical potentialities, if he does not have opportunities for creative activity, he may readily resort to destructive activities. In either instance, whether he solves his problem through choice of unwholesome activity that gets him into trouble or through clinging to the ways of his earlier years, he is not developing the resources for mastering his environment that are the basis for the inner security essential to stability in adult life.

If the child's previous experience has met his needs, his early school years are a period during which there are relatively few problems. He is an easy person, provided he has the opportunity for lots of play and plenty of chance for pursuit of intellectual and physical interests that will stimulate growth and give him that feeling of adequacy and self-sufficiency for which he is striving. At this period, difficulties are avoided if emotionally demanding relationships are not forced on him, such as too much maternal affection centering on the boy or too much paternal affection centering on the girl. Too much parental control and repression are also inadvisable. Children living in crowded cities often have a more difficult time than those living in the country or in small communities where the mischievous activity normal to this age is less likely to get the child into trouble. The more repressive the environment at this period, the more chance of disturbing the child.[5]

Through the very fact of poor economic circumstances, school-age children in public assistance families may lack the opportunities essential for development. They may lack the stabilizing care of parents who are not too driven by the pressures of life to meet the dependency needs of their children. Instead, these overburdened parents may be inclined to slough them off now that they are becoming physically competent to fend for themselves. Supervisors need to help the worker understand the potentialities of this age period. Planning with parents should be based on an understanding of the needs of the child—both those that may be met within the home and those that may be met by the parents through effective use of community resources. When mothers seek help in deciding whether they will work and leave children of this age relatively unsupervised, there should be careful appraisal of the child's self-sufficiency, the mother's capacity to meet his need if she says home, and community resources that may be used in the interests of his development. In their work with the community, workers with understanding of children's needs will more convincingly present the importance of adequate assistance. When insufficient agency funds or restrictive community attitudes are factors in forcing mothers whose children need their major attention to seek employment, this interpretation is especially significant.

The adolescent is all ages in one

Adolescence has been described as a period in which all the earlier needs and phases of life are relived in some measure and in which certain early conflicts—those of dependency and authority and those pertaining to sex—are revived and lived through in the process of a general reorganization of the personality. The child will have a difficult adolescence, therefore, if he had a difficult early life experience that prevented him from being emotionally free to develop his self-dependence to the utmost. Furthermore, his capacity for sublimation of the now active sexual impulses is attained through the acquisition of knowledge, skill, and strength. *Also, if the child has known more deprivation than gratification in relationships so that he has had to invest his love largely or wholly in himself and is basically self-aggrandizing and fearful in relation to others, he will have an especially difficult time at adolescence.*[6]

The adolescent must be allowed childish behavior in times of stress

For the child whose earlier years have been essentially normal, adolescence still is a period of some conflict in which there will be discomfort for him as well as for those who live with him. It is a time when he reaches out to find self-realization in more adult ways and as a natural protective impulse resorts comfortably to the gratification of childhood when he finds the adult role too frustrating or too threatening. That is, when his efforts at self-dependency fail or become too difficult, he may revert momentarily to episodes of childish behavior and resort to the interests and activities of childhood. *It is important that this child-adult, that is, the adolescent, be permitted his childish ways at moments of tension, and it is a wise parent or social worker who encourages the adult impulses and eases the anxieties that the reality demands of the adult world momentarily engender, while at the same time permitting him recourse to childish ways when he needs protection from that world in which he has not yet found a secure place.*

These fragmentary regressions may serve a twofold purpose: (1) they permit him to meet needs formerly unmet and to work through earlier conflicts, and (2) they enable him to use the old familiar ways as a needed balm, solace, and protection at moments of hurt or defeat when he has found the adult world too much for him. Often adults fail to realize the usefulness of the old childish ways and are condemning and punitive out of their fear that the child is not developing properly and their concern that seemingly he is never going to grow up. They can comprehend the child. Adult behavior may also be within their scope of understanding, but this child-adult, this bundle of contradictions who is momentarily one age and momentarily another, is a strain on their powers of adaptation.

Commonly encountered is the child who has grown rapidly, that is, shot up physically almost overnight. Undue demands may be made on him. Literally overnight parents, teachers, and others expect adult judgment from this adult frame and may suddenly become intolerant of momentary relapses into childish behavior, gusts of temper, wide mood swings in which undue optimism or undue pessimism occur. They begin to impose adult demands and to condemn childish impulses, thus increasing insecurity and the need to be childish. Such an adolescent has a difficult time. He has no real place in either world.

Another situation frequently met is that in which parents are gratified by the child's dependence and threatened by his adult behavior. They encourage the childish behavior and combat the child's self-assertion. Reacting with alarm to his growing independence, they sometimes feel it is a rejection of themselves.[7] These parents enhance the safety and comfort of childhood and unconsciously encourage its continuance. Later, these same parents may suddenly find the child objectionable and abruptly reject their self-created infant, thus putting him completely to rout by demanding sudden change. The gist of the situation is that in this period of reorganization and transition, the adolescent is normally a bundle of contradictions. It is as though, before giving up the various stages of childhood, he must relive them or momentarily retreat to them.

Sex identity is in a state of flux

The adolescent is, therefore, all ages in one.[8] For example, in his sex life he is momentarily self-loving, at another moment hero-worshiping individuals of the same sex, again, he is momentarily strongly attracted to persons of the opposite sex. His sex identity is in a state of flux, not yet crystallized in any one form but expressed variously. This self-love is shown in his urge for self-adornment and absorption in "looks." The adolescent will spend hours before the mirror; bodily interest and concern are very great. His impulses toward his own sex are shown in hero-worship and "crushes." He may retreat from spasmodic interest in the opposite sex to his own sex, particularly after any defeat in relationship with the opposite sex, and at such times his hatred of the other sex may become pronounced. His normal attraction to the opposite sex needs no elaboration. The popular terms "girl crazy" and "boy crazy" indicate the intensity and instability of many of these early relationships. Success or failure—that is, gratification or hurt in the first venture—may become a determinant of future experience, and therefore the relationships of a young person at this stage of development are most important. His eventual sex development has been predisposed toward final crystallization in one form or another by the nature of his relationships with his parents. Since, however, his sex identity is not yet formed, these adolescent love relationships may be decisive.[9]

At this age, general social adjustment may show the same two-way pull. The individual may need to be momentarily the lone wolf, going off by himself. A very real purpose may be served by self-imposed isolation, provided it is not prolonged. Or momentarily he may need to gang up with his own sex against the opposite sex. During these phases, there will be great emphasis on likeness to others. He must wear the same clothes, think and act the same way, possess the same gadgets. Hostility toward those who are different may again be pronounced, as during the earlier gang age. The young person's gropings for individuality also may undergo phases of overemphasis. His need to stress his individuality may take bizarre forms in dress, in conspicuous behavior, in unrealistic, independent action wherein he will "die" for some trifling cause or outreach himself in defending those who depart from the group.[10] Normally, as adolescence proceeds, the person seems increasingly gratified with activities in mixed groups, more responsive to the needs of others, more altruistic, more stable in his choices, and more realistic in his strivings.[11]

The adolescent wavers between reverting to childhood and striving for adulthood

What import has this for public assistance workers? Obviously, many of the so-called problems of adolescence can be regarded as normal growing pains. If we see them in this light, rather than as problems, we will focus on providing opportunities for growth rather than on direct correction of the behavior manifestations. *Behavior at this age might be classified into two groups: (1) that which shows the wish to remain a child and (2) that which shows the desire for adulthood and is problematic in that lack of adequacy as an adult may drive the young person to outreach himself in pretending to be more adult that he is.* This striving may take the form of undertaking work beyond his years, seeking sophisticated recreational outlets, and seeking mature sex life of an uncertain nature at an early age. In striving beyond himself, he runs the chance of frustration, defeat, and hurts of many sorts. In general, we help the adolescent most when we grant him the right still to resort to some childish behavior. Condemnation of such behavior should be avoided whenever possible. However, it is well recognized by those who have had wide experience in helping adolescents that frequently they need definite guidance and supportive judgments as to the right way of doing things; preferably this should come from someone they admire and respect. It has been said that fear of insecurity, present in children of all ages, becomes at adolescence an anxiety of the future, in which schooling, career, and marriage are absorbing concerns.

Planning for the future may have a stabilizing effect

We help the adolescent most, then, when we help him make reasonable plans for the future and at the same time help him obtain opportunities in *the present for their eventual realization.* Expert vocational guidance is most important at this age, and workers should make every effort to explain to the family the use of such community resources. Clinics available to child welfare services might well be used more often to determine the abilities of children rather than so predominantly for help with learning disabilities and behavior problems.

Knowledge of the mental capacity and aptitudes of the adolescent is highly important is he is to be educated suitably. Appropriate education is essential to his general social adjustment. In this connection, one study yielded significant findings. The problem chosen was a comparison of the histories and mental make-up of a series of pairs of blood brothers with a maximum age difference of four years, one member of the pair entirely normal in conduct and the other a severe conduct problem or a juvenile delinquent. The findings of particular note were that the problem boys were, on the average, duller in intelligence and inferior in their grasp of school subjects. In mechanical ability, however, the problem boys were superior not only to their brothers but also to 60 percent of the boys in an unselected group of schoolchildren. Thus superior mechanical ability in an unfavorable environment was associated with delinquency. Parents were found to look with greater approval on the nonproblem boys, and the school records seemed to be a factor that won these boys greater status at home. Teachers paid slight attention to the individuality of their pupils, recognizing neither their vocational nor personality needs.

Among other recommendations focused on improving environmental conditions and attitudes of parents and teachers, special emphasis is placed on schools utilizing special abilities of potential and actual delinquents by giving them education through the use of concrete materials, that is, industrial training.[12] In participating with other community groups on the matter of educational opportunities, public assistance agencies should be able to utilize their experiences in observing the need for educational resources better adapted to intellectual ability and vocational aptitudes. It would enable public assistance staffs to interpret to communities the need not only for appropriate educational facilities but also for more liberal policies regarding continued financial assistance to young people in order that they might be trained for a more secure economic future. Lack of proper educational facilities has been a factor operating against the continuance of educational opportunity.

Decisions regarding work and schooling are important issues with which the adolescent frequently needs help. Because of his tendency to outreach himself, his choice will not necessarily be wise. He needs the protection of rigidly imposed child-labor laws and wise counseling on part-time work in relation to his educational goals. *When the future becomes particularly uncertain, the adolescent can be expected to respond with anxiety, expressed in behavior disturbances.* Adolescents in the present wartime are having more adult demands either suddenly imposed on them or opened to them. There is a strong impulse to move in this direction. At the same time, the adult world is more dangerous and the future is much less certain. These factors are believed to be significant causes in the wartime instability of youth.[13]

Adolescents in public assistance families may be subjected to special stresses

Adolescents in families who are living precariously from an economic standpoint are subjected to certain special stresses. Frequently more adult demands are placed on them at an early age. Opportunities to plan for the future are more meager and the future itself has greater uncertainties than in the economically secure family. Frequently also, the parents, anxious, uncertain, defeated because they have found the world a too-competitive arena, convey their insecurity to the child. And so we might expect the children in this age group in many public assistance families to present greater problems in emancipation. They may well cling more tenaciously to the parents or, in the interests of survival, be compelled to escape the uncertainties of their family life through an abrupt and premature "cutting off." They may *needfully* assert their right to keep their own earnings and out of a tragic necessity pursue their own paths unhampered by the burdens of the past.

Supervisors may need to help the worker understand the individual's need for survival apart from the family as something other than a selfishness that is to be condemned and opposed. Young people in economically disadvantaged families may need and seek supportive help in finding and making the most of present opportunities and planning realistically for the future. Today the earnings of young people comprise a perplexing problem for many public assistance workers in connection with assistance planning. Such vital issues as the child leaving home sometimes are at stake. Parents raise difficult questions about their problem in either guiding or coercing their older children to spend their money properly. Because of this, it seems advisable to give rather full consideration to the meaning of money to adolescents. We should probably find that frequently it still has some of the same meanings for adults.

Money has great emotional significance

Money means different things to different people at different ages. For children, money normally takes on meaning in terms of the import it has within the famly. In adolescence one may find either conformity to the family pattern in handling money or a strong reaction against it. Some children learn good money habits within the family and some bad habits, but the handling of money is not as simple as that. *Money is an infinitely complex subject. It has great emotional significance, and the meaning money has for the individual will determine what he will do with it.* Within our society money has been the symbol of adequacy, even of worth. It wins respect for the individual. To be rich sometimes is to be both powerful and wise. To be rich frequently is to be forgiven many sins of omission and commission.

Money may have affectional import

Within the family, money has had great affectional value. When a child is bad, allowances have been withheld; when good, money and things are given. Likewise, when parents are feeling good, they may give freely; when that are out of sorts, they may withhold the pennies. Children early tend to reach out for money as an assurance of love. Beside the very gratifying things it buys to compensate for life's deprivations, it assures one of being loved.

This use of money as an expression of negative or positive feeling may permeate family life. Father comes home and has a tantrum because mother has overspent their funds. Mother, almost unconsciously, may have overspent because she was depressed. She was depressed because tensions have been acute between herself and her husband. Father is anxious and worried because the demands of the family have become oppressive. Mother knows intellectually that he no longer freely gives her either money or love because of harsh realities, but emotionally she needs to be loved and when frustrated her old childish need for money as reassurance is activated. So she spends. Father has a temper tantrum; mother feels all the more unloved and hostile, with perhaps an increased need to spend, and so the pernicious circle is established. Children early sense the affectional values money has in the parental relationship. Father gets a raise; mother loves him for it. Father feels expansive and gives freely to mother and the children, not merely because he has the money to give but because now he has the love to give. And so the child's need for and use of money is strongly interfused with affectional need. In this area he is frequently expressing his gratifications, deprivations, and conflicts and is working through much that is important to him.

Money may be a symbol of power

Money has other import also. *To many it is a symbol of power and strength, a symbol of the adequacy of the adult.* In the social group this value is pronounced. The child early gets the feeling that adults have money—at least they control whatever money there is. So the child begins to feel, "When I get big, I will have money too and I will control it." In some instances, complete control will be expressed in wild spending as an exhibition to others or as an assurance to oneself of one's adult adequacy. For other children, doing s I please" with money—that is, control of it—will mean hanging on to it, ping it all to himself with the illusion that the more money he has, the bigger and more adequate he is. The deeply anxious, unloved child who tends to withdraw into himself may react this way. Or the deeply dependent, insecure child may anxiously and willingly give it all to his mother. Therefore, the little hoarder—the child about whom the parents, teachers, and caseworkers are less anxious in regard to money—may not have more mental health than his spendthrift brother; he may sometimes have even less mental health. What this means is that children frequently are expressing their growth, their impulses toward adulthood, in their combat for money and their use of it. They are working through much in relation to parents and parent persons in their assertion of the right to do with it as they please. When we realize these meanings, we see the importance of understanding what money means to each person. We then may be less anxious about his practices and hopefully more understanding of how he feels when he must meet the (to him) coercive reality of agency policies.

Adult judgment about money cannot be expected from adolescents

As might be expected from all that has been said about normal adolescence, certainly adolescents cannot be expected to use adult judgment about money. We must expect unevenness. The young person may seem to be developing some stability and judgment in this area when, all at once, there may be a relapse into childish attitudes and habits when some compelling need takes possession of him. Take, for example, two young people in families receiving ADC. Jim, aged 16, had been earning money doing chores after school. For two years he had been consistently planful, spending a little on fun, a little for things of substance, and saving some for a technical school course in which his hopes were centered. Suddenly in one weekend he spent two years' savings. His aspiring mother, reduced to tears, berated him. She failed to see the connection between the spending spree and the boy's disappointment at not making the football team and his anxiety over his resultant status with his girl friend. Paul, aged 15, had also earned and saved some money for a technical training course. Intellectually precocious and physically frail, this youngster had led an isolated life with academic achievement his only goal and area of security. Again, an aspiring mother was reduced to tears when a box arrived containing physical training equipment for which all his savings had been expended.

Attitudes toward money are symptomatic of basic individual needs

Money may buy many gratifying material things. It buys new and exciting experiences, one of which may be the longed-for emancipation from the parents. It may even buy friends, and the adolescent cannot be expected to discern that friendship that has been bought is a poor purchase. Beneath these externals money may buy for the child a sense of security, of belonging, of being loved, adequate, even powerful. Again we must remember that the adolescent's attitudes toward the use of money are symptomatic of basic individual needs within the framework of needs peculiar to his age period. His childish impulses in relation to money again are serving a twofold purpose: (1) he is working through many conflicts unresolved in the past, (2) he is reverting to old familiar ways as a needed respite from the harsh reality of the adult world of which he is not yet an integral part. From our adult point of view, what may seem to be random, purposeless spending may be serving an important purpose. Frequently adolescents in some of their seemingly unwise spending actually are, like Paul, putting first things first—always they are revealing their need, that is, telling us much about themselves. Certainly it is through earning and spending, through the management and mismanagement of funds, that the young person may meet certain basic needs and thus realize growth. Only in this way can he learn the value of money and how to manage it. Money management, therefore, is not related solely to intellect, training, and experience. If the child goes into adulthood with many childish needs unmet, then the distorted personality may continue to be manifested in this area of his life as in other areas. What is the import of this to public assistance workers?

Problems arise with wage-earning children in public assistance families

Young people in public assistance families are denied to a greater extent than children in other families the self-determining use of money described above. Although they too may be working through many conflicts unresolved in the past and may also be reverting to childish ways as a needed respite from the harsh reality of the adult world, they are often confronted with the demands of the adult world as imposed by assistance policies. This is not necessarily a destructive experience. While other children may have had less deprivation and with their first earnings may now have more freedom to do as they wish with some of the money, still the helpful parent, while permitting some freedom, has also been stimulating gradual assumption of adult attitudes through encouraging both saving and contributing to others. This has been made gratifying in various ways, notably through helping the child plan for the future and through according him greater recognition in general as an adult. The greater problem in the public assistance family frequently lies in the fact that the whole process has been much less gradual. The youngster has had little money in the past, and when he suddenly gets some, he does not have time to find himself in relation to it but is expected immediately to use it for his ordinary unexciting needs. Furthermore, these children frequently have not had the stabilizing influence on planning for the future.

In public assistance families as elsewhere, the reaction of the young person to earning and spending will reflect the nature of his family life in varied ways. When the individual's affectional needs have been met in childhood and when his family relationships are essentially good, even though certain adolescent dependency and authority conflicts may now be present, his initial protest against restricted use of his money may quickly subside. It is important in these instances that the young person's resentments over denial be understood and that any deprivations be acknowledged. When this is done, he may move toward taking over responsibility, especially if he attains recognition and status by so doing.

Parents may be helped to see the need to give a wage-earning child a greater part in financial planning, more place in the family councils, and more freedom in other areas of his life. In one family where James, a 16-year-old boy, was working and contributing resentfully to the family budget, the worker learned in talking matters over with him that his resentment stemmed primarily from being treated like a child at the same time adult demands were being imposed in regard to money. The mother had unwittingly not recognized the more grown-up status to which his years and earnings entitled him. Furthermore, out of her own economic deprivation and financial worry, she had seized possessively on his earnings and out of her fears of the future had anxiously dictated all the spending. Fortunately, in this instance the mother was able to modify her handling of the situation and the youngster quickly assumed more adult attitudes with considerable gratification in his new status.

In contrast to James, we see a different situation in the case of John P, aged 18, another eldest boy in a family receiving ADC. John's mother anxiously turned to the worker for help in prevailing on John not to leave home. To his mother, James seemed selfish and ungrateful in wanting to keep his total earnings to spend in his own way and threatening to move out and pay board and room elsewhere rather than pay it at home. He was unresponsive to the worker's ill-advised efforts to help him see that he would be losing money by moving, as well as to his appeals to his obligation to his mother and his disabled father. In several discussions it became clear that his attitude was an expression of a strong desire to leave home, where he was entangled in an old attachment to a dominating mother and where he suffered the continual hostile rivalry of his father. Bringing money home had intensified this conflict to such an extent that recently he had solved the problem by staying away from home as much as possible and by squandering his money, behavior that pleased the father, who had done likewise in his wage-earning days. It won the mother's condemnation, however, and her continual comparison of him with his father, which both irritated and gratified him. At least he could reassure himself that he was now a man. A shift had occurred in the family alignments when he became a wage earner. Whereas formerly mother and son had seemingly sided together against the father, now father and son were aligned against the mother.

In view of the limitations of his life situation, the constructive course of action for this youth was clearly his own plan for himself, that of withdrawing from the family and of assuming full support of himself. He was caught in conflict that, if he remained in the home, he could ease only in destructive ways. In the interests of self-survival, he was using his money and the issue with the agency as a means to emancipate himself. The worker could not see the relatively constructive import of this action but considered it bad for him, in the long run, to be permitted to be so selfish. In his opinion it would be better if somehow John could be persuasively coerced into staying at home, where, in doing his part, he might develop more mature attitudes. The worker was powerless to keep him there and so saw him go with a great sense of personal failure.

We can sympathize with the worker's concern over some of the circumstances under which this young person left home. The dependencies and hostilities involved in an unfriendly break may not be a sound basis for real emancipation. They may well go with him to be lived out in other relationships in self-frustrating ways. And yet, in order to survive he may *have* to leave. How much he may grow through the separation cannot be predicted.

The problem of the young person who is earning is widespread, and many examples could be cited to show the difficulties presented. Community attitudes as well as state laws requiring relatives to support create pressure to keep the young person within his own family, obstructing establishment of a family of his own or going forward into any life plan he may make for himself. Unless he is unusually mature, his social adjustment and general personality growth may suffer. On encountering such cases, workers may get caught in the conflict between the individuals' welfare and community attitudes and agency restrictions. They may identify with the young person or the community and agency. When identified with community or agency, they may resort to moral judgments because they see the youth as irresponsible or ungrateful. They may fail to see that he is struggling to take responsibility for himself, commonly a prerequisite to assuming it for others. In either instance, they may fail to understand the youth's own conflict, for he may be torn between wishing to go forth to a life of his own and feeling his obligation to remain. When caught in the conflict, one way or another, the worker may fail to be helpful as in the case of John. The worker, even though understanding all the factors involved and the welfare values for the individual, may be blocked in meeting the applicant's needs because of statutory provisions or policies that do not permit individualized measures.

Young people's attitudes toward money reflect social problems

Repeatedly, social workers have been expressing concern over self-aggrandizing attitudes evidenced by young people who prematurely are earning "big money." This manifestation may well be a commentary on the lacks in many lives. It must be remembered that *we can expect mature attitudes toward money and enlightened use of it only in the adolescent who does not have too much at stake emotionally in earning and spending.* When he has many deprivations for which to compensate, deep conflicts to appease, and great frustration to ease, he may be driven to meet his own compelling needs without reference to others. He may have small capacity to endure denial and, therefore, may be unable to postpone until tomorrow the gratifications money will buy for him today. In these cases there is not so much a money problem as the reflection of many profound social problems, which, belatedly, we may be unable to help the individual to solve. The children of tomorrow are another matter. These young people today point the need for broad social and economic measures to safeguard family life in order that more mature personalities gradually may emerge.

When assistance policies bearing on these questions are formulated, when the assistance plan is discussed with the family, or when we are called on to advise in such problems as those cited above, it is important that we understand the meaning of money to the specific individual. How many workers gain this understanding? The young person frequently will not be able to put into words precisely what money means to him. We therefore must derive the meaning from an array of factors such as the character of his relationships with his parents and their attitudes toward money in general as well as toward his money, the character of his relationships with his brothers and sisters, rivalries in which the individual feels outdone, and his status in school and social life. Is he doing well in school or failing? Is he physically adequate in competitive games? Is he accepted or rejected by his social group? How does he spend his money? For what? And on whom? These are all important questions in determining what he is striving to get other than the actual material goods or pleasures in and of themselves.

Money has import for total personality

When we consider the value of money for the individual, adult, or child, when we realize that is has import in terms of the total personality in relation to the life situation at any given time, then perhaps we will bring more understanding to the administration of public assistance. In the light of this understanding perhaps we will appreciate, even more than previously, the wisdom in general of the unrestricted money-payment policy that safeguards for the individual his customary freedom and responsibility in the use of money.[14] Perhaps we will see more meaning also in the varying response of individuals to our statutory regulations for support by relatives. As our appreciation of individual difference grows, we will increasingly anticipate wide variation in response to all our policies and legal provisions, of which only a few examples can be presented.

For most people, the lack of restriction on expenditures will afford genuine security in that they have a continued opportunity to plan and manage their own lives within the limits set by meager grants. There will be some individuals who, unable to plan or manage resourcefully, will build up resentment unless they receive more help through additional services. They may want and need additional help in budgeting and planning so that they may experience a feeling of adequacy rather than failure with resultant insecurity. Insofar as payments are inadequate, this situation can be expected to occur with greater frequency. The problem then arises of giving such help without conveying the impression that we are dictating the use of the money. This may involve clarifying repeatedly with the recipient the fact that he has a right to this help and that it is proffered for him to use as he wishes.

We place a great deal of emphasis on the individual's *right* to assistance in the belief that it dignifies, that it frees him from humiliation, and that it leaves him unshackled by feelings of personal obligation to the agency, all elements that should operate against the production of dependency. In the light of our understanding of the emotional import money has for people, we will realize that the values of such a right may be greatly undermined for many persons when payments are inadequate. *Many individuals who have repeatedly met eligibility requirements are more impressed with the deprivation than with the right, if they are continuously granted less than they need.* For many people, to be deprived is to be humiliated. Humiliation evokes resentment, and feelings of resentment in turn engender feelings of heavy obligation when these feelings occur in a relationship in which the individual is being accorded his right to survive. It may seem strange to many of us that feelings of resentment can evoke excessive feelings of obligation. Perhaps it may seem less strange if we can recall a time when we ourselves had to take something from someone we did not like or from someone who gave, begrudgingly, less than we needed. Perhaps we may recall that we felt more obligated in these instances than to persons who helped us generously, freely, and unquestioningly.

What happens between individuals may happen between an individual and an agency. We have ample evidence that clients do personalize agencies, the agency's wishes to the contrary. In spite of the concept that the public agency is not a person who gives or withholds but instead an agency that respects the right to which every citizen is impartially entitled, the agency may well represent to the client "the worker up there who gives too little and asks questions with tiresome regularity." He may come to feel that he is given to

begrudgingly and with great question. The resultant sense of undue obligation places him in the defensive position of an individual with a debt he cannot pay, thus leaving him humiliated and helpless. When we realize this, we
see how important it is that workers apply this understanding of individuals
as eligibility is established and re-established. This does not mean that eligibility
requirements will be relaxed or that grants will be individualized beyond the
limits of the law. It merely means that the individual's feelings about his stress
will be understood. We also see the importance of bending every effort toward
the attainment of adequate payments if public assistance programs are to
achieve their constructive purpose.

Notes

1. Franz Alexander, MD, *Our Age of Unreason; A Study of the Irrational Forces
in Social Life* (1st ed.; Philadelphia: J.B. Lippincott Co., 1942), pp. 141 and 142.

2. For full discussion of the relationship between physiological growth impulses and
the emotional development of the child *see* C. A. Aldrich and M. M. Aldrich, *Babies
are Human Beings; An Interpretation of Growth* (New York: Macmillan Co., 1938);
or Margaret A. Ribble, MD, *The Rights of Infants* (New York: Columbia University
Press, 1943).

3. For further study of the relationship between maternal overprotection, the needs
of the parent, and personality development of the child, *see* David M. Levy, *Maternal
Overprotection* (New York: Columbia University Press, 1943).

4. For a full discussion of the needs and care of the infant, *see* Agatha H. Bowley,
Guiding the Normal Child (New York: Philosophical Library, 1943), chaps. 1–3;
Margaret E. Fries, MD, "Mental Hygiene in Pregnancy, Delivery, and the Puerperium,"
Mental Hygiene, Vol. 25, No. 2 (April 1941), pp. 221–236; Arnold Gesell *et al.*, *Infant
and Child in the Culture of Today; Guidance of Development in Home and Nursery
School* (New York: Harper & Brothers, 1943); Ribble, *op. cit.*, p. 5; and Susan Isaacs,
The Nursery Years (New York: Vanguard Press, 1937).

5. For further study of the needs of the school-age child, *see* Bowley, *op. cit.*, chaps.
4 and 5; Ruth M. Bakwin and Harry Bakwin, *Psychologic Care During Infancy and
Childhood* (New York: D. Appleton-Century Co., 1942); Margaret W. Gerard, "Learning
to Know the Child Through the Everyday Contacts of the Case Worker," *Proceedings
of the National Conference of Social Work, 1939* (New York: Columbia University
Press, 1939), pp. 360–369; Anna Freud and Dorothy T. Burlingham, *War and Children*
(New York: International Universities Press, 1943); and Douglas A. Thom, MD, *Everyday Problems of the Everyday Child* (New York: D. Appleton-Century Co., 1938).

6. *See* Peter Blos, *The Adolescent Personality* (New York: D. Appleton-Century Co.,
1941); Irene Josselyn, MD, *The Happy Child*, "Stages of Maturation, Infancy Through
Adolescence" (New York: Random House, 1955); M. O. Sklansky, MD, and S. A.
Lichter, "Some Observations on the Character of the Adolescent Ego," *Social Service
Review*, Vol. 31, No. 3 (September 1957), pp. 271–276; and Josselyn, *Psychosocial
Development of Children* (New York: Family Service Association of America, 1948).

7. As an example of a parental response of this sort, *see* Charlotte Towle, *Social Case Records From Psychiatric Clinics; With Discussion Notes* (Chicago: University of Chicago Press, 1941), case of John Stanley, pp. 41–82.

8. For further study of adolescence, *see* Blos, *op. cit.*; Katherine Whiteside Taylor, *Do Adolescents Need Parents?* (New York: D. Appleton-Century Co., 1938); Caroline B. Zachry and Margaret Lighty, *Emotion and Conduct in Adolescence* (New York: D. Appleton-Century Co., 1940); James S. Plant, "The Problems of Older Children in Personality Adjustment," *Proceedings of the National Conference of Social Work, 1941* (New York: Columbia University Press, 1941); and Frankwood Williams, *Adolescence; Studies in Mental Hygiene* (New York: Farrar & Rinehart, 1930).

9. For the importance of early family relationships and sexual development, *see* Peter Blos, *op. cit.*; Irene Josselyn, *The Happy Child; George Mohr, MD, and Marian Depres, *The Stormy Decade* (New York: Random House, 1958); and Sklansky and Lichter, *op. cit.*

10. *See* Sklansky and Lichter, *op. cit.*

11. For a vivid and penetrating description of normal adolescence, *see* Booth Tarkington, *Seventeen* (New York: Grosset & Dunlap, 1937).

12. State of New York, *Report of the Crime Commission* (Albany: J.B. Lyon & Co., 1929), pp. 205–209, 231–249. *See also* Solomon A. Lichter, Elise B. Rapien, Frances M. Seibert, and Morris O. Sklansky, MD, *The Drop-Outs: A Treatment Study of Intellectually Capable Students Who Drop Out of School* (New York: Free Press of Glencoe, 1962).

13. Charlotte Towle, "The Effect of War Upon Children," *Social Service Review*, Vol. 17, No. 2 (June 1943), pp. 144–158.

14. Social Security Board, *Money Payments to Recipients of Old-Age Assistance, Aid to Dependent Children, and Aid to the Blind*, Circular No. 17 (Washington, D.C.: Bureau of Public Assistance, March 1944).

4

Adulthood and old age

I t has been said:
>   After reaching maturity the organism is biologically independent and can per-
>   form its vital functions without external help. This independence is never com-
>   plete in the case of organisms living in society; man remains to a certain degree
>   dependent upon his fellow men. However, if necessary, he can survive like
>   Robinson Crusoe, alone.[1]

Among other factors, this physical self-dependence is important in giving the adult greater security than the child. A significant factor in the social
structure within which social workers help people, however, is the fact that
man does not have full use of this biological capacity for survival. To be sure,
he may be able to survive alone on an island abounding in natural resources.
However, he has much less chance for survival alone in modern society, for
the goods that surround him are not his for the taking. *Therefore, unless broad
social security provisions are made available to man as his inalienable right
to survival, he is doomed to continue in the psychological state of childhood,
anxiously dependent on others, insecure, and unfree to move courageously
into full assumption of adult responsibilities. There is no better base than this
for the continuance of self-aggrandizing strivings and for the persistence of
irrational behavior.* Social security and public assistance programs are a basic
requirement for the development of the mature personality, a state of being
essential if democracy as a way of life is to be realized in full measure.*

If the adult's basic needs have been met fairly adequately throughout infancy, childhood, and adolescence so that growth toward maturity has been
realized normally, then he will inevitably have needs and wants beyond the
mere privilege of survival. He will bring ambition, an urge for accomplish-
ment, a desire for participation in group life, an impulse to give and live beyond

---

*In the 1945 edition, Towle stated: "Social security and public assistance programs are a basic
*essential for attainment of the socialized state envisaged in democratic ideology, a way of life
which so far has been realized only in slight measure."* —Ed.

61

himself in many ways. If circumstances deny him the opportunity to work and to realize some of these aspirations, if they limit his relationships in the family and the community, he may be deeply frustrated and experience a hunger equivalent to actual physical hunger. ("Man cannot live by bread alone.")

Social workers have come to know the emotionally starved adult and to recognize some of the ways in which he commonly appeases that hunger. Frequently they are not constructive ways. To the inexperienced social worker they may seem quite irrational. To the social worker whose knowledge and experience enable him to see the *meaning of behavior*, these "unwise" solutions take on a wisdom of their own. The parent who buys his toddler a pink elephant instead of the shoes the child needs; the harassed and overburdened mother who periodically falls ill and obviously takes pleasure in clinic visits and hospital care (in one such instance, the woman commented enthusiastically to her worker as she was being returned to the hospital, "The doctors and nurses there are the nicest people I've ever known"); the parent who, living vicariously in the accomplishments of his children, makes demands on them beyond their years; the unemployed man who takes to the tavern—all these reactions have been known in individual instances to bespeak potentials for a healthier life that have been frustrated.

The emotionally mature adult

In general, there are two major concerns with respect to the needs of the adult—preparation for work that will assure survival and the attainment of some degree of social productivity. On reaching maturity, the individual's energies will be concerned largely with the struggle for existence, but he will be concerned also with the establishment and maintenance of family life and with other creative activity or socially productive work that contributes to the life of the group. Effective fulfillment of these needs will depend largely on the nature of relationships the individual is able to establish and maintain and on the meaning of these relationships to him and others. It will depend also on opportunities to continue to learn. Since the course of life can be described as a continuous process of learning, that is, of adaptation to ever changing external and internal conditions, the need for opportunity to understand and learn to meet the changing factors and forces of life is ever present. The need to be loved and cared for, the central issue of the young child's life, continues but becomes less self-centered. Insofar as the individual builds up a surplus through having been loved adequately, an impulse and capacity to love others develop.

That largely hypothetical person, an emotionally mature adult, defies a precise descriptive definition. Perhaps certain characteristics of what we mean by "maturity" might be stated roughly as those of *a person in whom enjoy-ment of dependence or inordinate pride in independence are replaced by gratification in interdependence. He still has considerable need to depend on others, a need to be loved, and a need to be cared for at such times and in those areas of his life in which he is unable to care for himself. He has a need also to have an opportunity to care for himself and to contribute to the welfare of others.* Growth from infancy to adulthood may be described as a process of change in which the individual moves from loving the world as part of himself to loving, that is, respecting, himself as part of the world.[2] Insofar as the individual is basically secure through having experienced relationships in which he has been adequately loved and through having experienced op-portunities for maximum development of his mental and physical capacities, his emancipation from his parents will have occurred naturally, gradually, and completely. He will, therefore, have little anxiety about either his need to depend on others or his need to compete with others, that is, his wish to excel others.

Mature people can be distinguished through the way they use their right to assistance

Social workers have learned, through experience, what at first seemed a strange contradiction to the traditional ideas in which we had been reared, namely, that *it is the relatively secure adult with considerable strength and capacity for independence who becomes least anxious, least resentful, and least humiliated when through force of circumstance he turns to others for help.* This is not to say that he has no discomfort in asking for help even when it is clear to him that this help is a right to which he is entitled. In our society, in which the adult of today has been reared in the ideology that self-support and self-respect are synonymous, even the most secure adult may experience some feelings of inadequacy in relation to this ideal. Even he may feel some strangeness and uncertainty and loss of adequacy in that for the first time in his life he has been unable to cope with circumstance. His anxiety, however, will be more readily allayed through our interpretations. He will more readi-ly than others take hold of the idea of "right" and use it to ease his own hurt feelings. He will be less prone to slump into prolonged dependency and, therefore, less fearful and protesting or less resentful and critical of what we do for him. He will be more likely to participate actively in establishing eligibili-ty and in general will continue to be active in handling his affairs. He will be less prone to carry over the disturbed feelings in this experience into other life relationships, like the man who responds to loss of status as a wage earner in the home by becoming hostile and competing with his children for the at-tention of his wife. During the Depression years, social workers had an op-portunity to distinguish mature and resourceful people through the way in which they used their right to assistance. They learned that *these individuals could use or freely could refuse the right to other casework services without becoming anxious or threatened as to their right to financial assistance.*

How the worker feels about dependency is important

The worker who has little respect for the person who is in economic straits, who does not have a conviction of the needy person's right to agency provisions, and who therefore mistrusts the applicant and is more intent on proving his ineligibility than determining his eligibility, will question provocatively rather than respectfully. This intensifies the applicant's discomfort and tends to lower his morale. Unless the applicant has unusual inner strength, he may experience a threat to his adequacy, resulting sometimes in a regressive response in his relationship with the agency. When a worker brings such attitudes to the task of helping the individual establish his right to assistance, they operate against the recipient's constructive use of all the agency's services, which in the long run will mean the strengthening of self-dependence and a diminishing need for the agency's support.

Most individuals feel some discomfort in applying for and receiving assistance

Social workers deal with relatively few so-called "mature adults." Many people only approximate this state. Out of frustrations experienced in childhood relationships and out of the obstacles to full realization of mental and physical capacities, many people bring to adulthood vestiges of their childhood selves. Most, however, manage to get along in fairly adequate fashion. The people served by public assistance programs frequently are those whose adverse life circumstances have been exceptionally frustrating and whose relationships have suffered the strain of limiting life conditions. More often than not, therefore, workers encounter disturbed feelings symptomatic of profound discomfort when major catastrophes of life drive these people to others for help. They too, however, often have had considerable capacity to get along in adequate fashion, and that capacity may be restored as present strains are eased if early frustrations have not been profoundly damaging.

Even though our conception is that we proffer public assistance as both a right and a helping service, many people will be inclined to feel dependent and to assign to the agency the identity of helper. Lifelong insecurities will render them anxious. Lifelong feelings of inadequacy may be the base for feelings of humiliation. Lifelong feelings of resentment stemming from deprivation, frustration, and humiliation will be intensified and may well be directed toward those on whom they are now forced by circumstance to depend. Furthermore, many problems other than the need for financial assistance frequently will be exerting pressure in this relationship with the agency that proffers help in at least one area.

The anxiety of these people, therefore, may not readily be allayed through our interpretations. They may not take hold readily of the idea of *right* to ease their own discomfort. Instead, that very discomfort may find expression in varied ways, depending on the meaning of the present need in relation to old failures, former conflicts, frustrations in relationships, and previous sources of security or insecurity. They may be more inclined to relapse into dependency, less free to participate in establishing eligibility, with many anxieties about and resistance to agency demands. Fearful of their own impulses toward dependency, they may be full of protests about the service, resentful and critical of what is done or not done for them. Conversely, they may react with abject gratitude and feelings of obligation that reinforce the original feelings of helplessness and operate against resumption of activity in their affairs. As previously indicated, they may tend to carry over the disturbed feelings in this experience into other life relationships. How services are rendered becomes important. Decisive here is the extent to which we can offer them a helping experience that restores self-respect through giving them as much command of the situation as they can assume.

Offer services as a right with no obligation to accept them

All services must be proffered as a right to which recipients are entitled but which they are not obligated to use by reason of the fact that they have utilized their right to financial assistance. This distinction implies careful and sometimes repeated clarification of the fact that they may have both kinds of help without endangering the right to "relief." Because humans tend to react to any one phase of an agency experience in terms of the total self and in terms of a totality of need, it may not be a simple matter to render services clearly distinguished one from another. An agency may conveniently divide itself into two sets of services and proffer them like two different commodities. But a man has not two separate sides to his head or his heart. Therefore, regardless of an agency's particular conception of its service, the administration of an individual's right to financial assistance at time of dire need in some instances may be identified in his feelings as an understanding readiness to see and meet his various needs. *Therefore, services related to financial assistance imply a more complete acceptance of him as a person, reassuring him of his right of financial assistance instead of threatening that right.*

In other instances, the person's resentment over taking help in any form may be intensified by the offer of additional help. He may want the help in the objective interests of himself and his family. At the same time, he may not want the help in the subjective interests of his self-esteem. Or the desire for help may be the dominant impulse, so he does not refuse it. This is a decisive differentiation that should serve as a guide to use in our subsequent efforts. If he accepts the help, his discomfort may not be allayed readily by our interpretations of right and freedom of choice, and he may need to use his feelings of obligation resentfully against us. We then encounter responses that say in word or act, "because you got me 'relief' I have to depend on you in general." *In such instances we should focus on understanding his resentment and easing it through an interpretation of his dual rights with the hope of reconciling the two facets of his need—i.e., taking help and maintaining self-esteem.*

Work is important to the adult

The importance of work in the life of the adult is well recognized. It is commonly agreed that work is "good for people" and that in idleness man deteriorates in one way or another. The conflicting impulses toward regression and progression persistent in some measure throughout life may have led to the puritanical assumption that because work is good for man he has a disinclination for it and, conversely, because idleness is bad for him it is highly desirable to him. If this is so, it is indeed a sad commentary on the mental health of great masses of people. This conception has influenced relief practices throughout generations. It is at the roots of our fear of pauperization and of the conviction of some that relief should be inadequate, because if it were adequate man would prefer to luxuriate in idleness rather than work for an equal amount of money. During the Great Depression, when a cross section of the population lived in enforced idleness, social workers observed much that led them to qualify, if not wholly to refute, this assumption, notably the following: (1) The experience of the Works Progress Administration in which administrators grew increasingly impressed with man's eagerness to learn and to participate in socially productive activity. (2) The observations of the Tolan Committee, seeing people make extreme efforts to get work, to the extent of risking the loss of security of receiving relief through crossing state lines to find jobs. (3) After prolonged periods of idleness the eagerness with which men returned to work when it was again available, indicating that these impulses were strong and that individuals were not as readily infantilized through enforced dependency as had been feared. The substantial decline in assistance rolls during the war period gave further evidence of man's eagerness for productive contribution to the world's work.

> Between December 1941, when Pearl Harbor was attacked, and July 1944, the number of cases on the general assistance rolls declined 68 percent and the number of families receiving aid to dependent children, 34 percent. Recipients of old-age assistance declined 7 percent in number, and there was even a decrease of 6 percent in the number of persons getting aid to the blind.[3]

The countless pleas for work, the complaints of boredom, the intense dissatisfaction expressed in terms of not having anything to do as often as in terms of not having enough money to spend numbed the ears of caseworkers and left a deep conviction that *men live by their work and it has in countless instances more than mere survival value for them.* Furthermore, this conviction is supported by modern insights into human personality that have been gained through scientific study.[4] Based on observations made in the study and treatment of humans, the student of human behavior has a strong conviction that *normally* the adult wants to work, that he has an imperative need to work, and that he is deeply frustrated in his growth impulses when denied that opportunity. Furthermore, it [is] his conviction that *it is not idleness itself but the frustration in idleness that sets in operation the regressive process through which men break down or become what is commonly termed "pauperized."* As social workers increasingly comprehend this fact they will have more faith in the client's willingness to work. This, then, may affect their attitudes as they help him determine need and establish his eligibility.

Today, with a labor market in which work is available to people of all ages and nearly all conditions, the general relief loads include a relatively large proportion of persons who are physically, mentally, and emotionally disabled and hence unemployable. Among these may be encountered some legendary instances of pauperization. A careful study of the background of these people may give a better understanding of this condition. Employability from the standpoint of physical fitness is sometimes carefully determined by medical examinations. When physical unfitness has been ruled out, an individual's disinclination for work, continued complaints of physical symptoms, ineffectual attempts to get or hold jobs, any or all of these manifestations commonly are diagnosed by lay staff under some such nomenclature as "work-shy," "malingering," and so on. Until it is recognized that man normally wants to work and that disinclination for work may well be a symptom of mental or emotional illness, available psychiatric services will not be utilized for the study and treatment of this condition. Until this is done, we may fail to be helpful to persons who might be helped and we may treat unjustly those who are incurably ill.

In this connection, it is recognized that the general unavailability of psychiatric services will long be an obstacle to the determination of employability on a mental-emotional basis. Use of these resources when available might throw valuable light on the problem of the "work-shy" individual. In the meantime, one can only speculate that long-standing economic deprivation might be observed in many instances, and one might wonder whether emotional deprivation in early life relationships, infantilizing parent-child relationships, repeated hurts through failure in relationships, repeated frustration in aspirations beyond the survival level, may not have been common. It is doubtful whether *adequate* assistance would loom large as a factor in the demoralization of the individual. It has long been a conviction of caseworkers in many agency settings that adequate support would be a positive factor in the rehabilitation of individuals who through force of circumstance must use their right to public assistance.

Establishment of a family is crucial

As the adult establishes and endeavors to maintain a family, the success of the venture will depend in large measure on the extent to which he is no longer immersed in a self-centered struggle to meet his own needs but has instead some "surplus" to spend outside himself. The stability of his family life will also depend on chance factors and on the extent to which limitations in his capacity for relationship are balanced by his partner's capacity to give. Out of affectional and economic deprivation in her earlier years, a woman may bring to marriage a childlike need to be loved and cared for. Her husband may be able to meet her execessive need as long as he is feeling adequate through having satisfactory work, so that he has status as head of the family and status in the community as a wage earner. Some of the gaps in the relationship may have been filled and the marriage sustained through his ability to provide for his wife. Loss of satisfying work and the loss of status entailed in unemployment may, however, create feelings of inadequacy in the husband that make him temporarily dependent on his wife for assurance of love. Unable to meet his affectional need, she may be irritated, particularly when he is showing less affection and providing so little financially. She is even less able than usual to meet his need. And so mutual frustration may lead to a breakdown in a relationship that might have continued had not changing circumstances brought a shift in the balance of needs.[5]

The arrival of children is a crucial test of the maturity of the parents and the stability of the marriage relationship. Social workers have long been familiar with the father who deserts, turns to drink, or in other ways becomes irresponsible and hostile at the birth of a child. They also are familiar with the mother who is irritated beyond endurance and whose resentment and anxiety over having to meet demands beyond her capacity are expressed in various ways, such as discouragement, self-pity, depression, overt display of temper, nagging, erratic discipline, poor management, neglect, or excessive efforts to outreach her scope. Even under advantageous circumstances, the complete dependency of infants and the prolonged demands of children make parenthood a responsibility that generally is carried with ease and enjoyment only by those whose life relationships have given them capacity to meet the needs of others freely and flexibly. When an individual has this capacity, he is not only able to meet the dependency needs of the children but also—because he does not need to realize his own frustrated self in them—is able to grant them self-identity and release them for growth toward independence. Since most indivduals bring vestiges of childish need into marriage and parenthood, some problems are normally found in parent-child relationships.[6]

Economic insecurity heightens the stress of parenthood

It is generally agreed that lack of basic economic security heightens the stress of parenthood and intensifies relationship problems. One may expect more regressive responses on the part of parents in families where there is economic strain. When regression occurs in the adult, it is not as normal an aspect of the growth process as it is in the adolescent. Because the demands of adult life are likely to be more consistently inescapable than those in adolescence and because the personality is more rigidly formed, retreats to more satisfying life periods of the past may bring a more lasting fixation. Affirming the adult's strengths, helping him look and plan beyond the overwhelming present, relieving sources of insecurity, pressure, and strain so that his burden is more nearly commensurate with his capacity—all these are measures public assistance workers have used in order to help the adult in an economic crisis to carry his important task of parenthood more competently. Helping him look beyond the present to the future is not always a simple task when the present is exerting great pressure. Yet innumerable examples of help of this nature that has been deeply influential in the lives of people could be cited.

For example, Mrs. J, the widowed mother of four children who were receiving ADC, had grown deeply discouraged and apathetic in the struggle to maintain her family. Her physical complaints (without organic basis), lax housekeeping, impatience, and a general state of unhappiness were affecting the lives of the entire family. Mrs. J expressed a feeling of hopelessness; not only did her own life stretch out ahead as an endless path of meager living and unfulfilled aspirations, but also she keenly felt the poor prospect for her children. What chance had they to do any better? The worker's resourceful suggestion of a scholarship association to enable the intellectually able eldest son to continue his education beyond high school and his help in putting the mother in touch with settlement music and art classes for two other children brought a marked change in this woman's morale. Through her children she could now envisage a better future and with them work for its realization.

Sometimes social workers grow discouraged—so many families need so much that the little that can be done hardly seems to matter. Sometimes this is true, yet once again we encounter a surprising element in human nature. With persons in great need a little help may go a long way and prove to be the toehold in a seemingly insurmountable wall.

Some workers tend to be intolerant of parental failure

Among all human limitations, parental shortcomings often are the most difficult for a social worker to accept. To the neglectful, punitive, complaining, begrudging parent who has meager capacity to meet his children's needs, the social worker may respond with deep feelings of condemnation. While he may not let these feelings interfere with helping the parent establish his right to assistance, still he may render the agency's service in such a way as to convey his feelings. Also, in rendering casework services in accordance with the need and request of such parents, he may fail to accord them understanding help and unconsciously may become authoritative or depriving. Out of his identification with the children as opposed to the parents, he may exert demands in their behalf that are beyond the parents' scope. In so doing, he increases the pressure of parental responsibilities and may stimulate in the parent greater neglect or hostility toward the children. This behavior adaptation, formerly described as regression, occurs when the demands of the external world exceed the individual's capacity to meet those demands. Idealization of their own parents, adherence to the traditional concept of parents as all-giving and all-enduring, together with elements of frustration in their own relationships with their parents, may combine to make workers singularly intolerant of parental failure.

As public assistance workers gradually learn that the parent who fails frequently has been failed, as they comprehend the principle that we give as we are given to and that none of us can give from a vacuum, then they may become more sympathetic with an understanding of the deprived person who deprives, the punished one who punishes. Gradually, then, they may perceive the futility of their own unwittingly retaliative treatment of these parents. It becomes obvious that sympathy, understanding, and supportive help may enable these parents to carry their responsibilities more competently, provided their need is not insatiable, as in the case of many people who should be considered emotionally ill. It becomes equally obvious that dislike, condemnation, and denial will only undermine further their adequacy as parents.

Focus should not be wholly on the children

In our attempts to help ADC parents with problems of child rearing, we frequently defeat our purpose through focusing wholly on the children and their welfare. In such instances, we may give the parent a feeling that we have little faith in his competence. He may infer that, because he is receiving financial assistance of the grounds of parenthood, we now are demanding that he meet our requirements and are tending to direct the management of his parental responsibilities. Repeatedly, in response to this approach, we see parents become defensive and antagonistic. This might be avoided if the parent had an opportunity to reveal his problems spontaneously in response to our interest in him and to an expressed concern as to how things are going. Our understanding of his experience as a parent frequently will free him to bring out the negative elements in this experience and enable him to reach out for help if he needs it. Instead, we more often make him defensive about his need for help through immediate routine and meticulous inquiries about the children, their health, their school records, their behavior, and the like. It is commonplace knowledge that in order to help children, frequently we must first help the parents. Often, however, our well-intentioned help has taken the form of coercive measures or persuasive efforts based on our understanding of the child's needs rather than the parent's equally imperative need. When we learn to give to parents in order that they may give to their children, we work more effectively. This principle is particularly significant in our work with families receiving ADC, in which the purpose of the program emphasizes meeting the needs of the child in his own home under the care of his parents or other relatives.

Old age can be a satisfying period

Old age is the last of a series of adaptive changes in the life of the individual. Like other life periods, the person's adaptation to it depends on the general life situation, the extent and suddenness of circumstantial change, the nature of previous relationships, and the way in which earlier life crises such as puberty, separation from parents, marriage, parenthood, and menopause have been met. Normally, it is a period of diminishing powers in which the individual's inner resources decline, while at the same time his external world narrows, in some instances markedly. *In favorable circumstances of economic security, a gradual decline in physical and mental powers, the continuance of sustaining relationships, the continuance of some satisfying activity, and an inherent capacity on the part of the individual to accept change without undue anxiety and resistance, one may encounter no marked problems of adjustment.* This life period may be one of continued fulfillment, a beneficent twilight period, a reflective and peaceful respite, as glorified by Cicero in "DeSenectute."[7]

A competitive society tends to make old age difficult

The modern social and economic order operates against this idyllic state in the closing years of life even when physical health factors are relatively favorable. A competitive society in which the individual's sense of worth has been maintained through achievement and in which people in general have been improvident in the arts of leisure implies a profound loss of security and of satisfying activity in old age even for many advantaged people. Competitive society has made it impossible for the majority to enjoy economic security and to remain highly valued in the group as they become economically useless and a threat to those who are struggling for a precarious survival. *The aged have tended to become a burden rather than an asset in a society in which change has been so rapid that the knowledge and experience of the past have*

been quickly outmoded and in which productivity oriented to the present and
the future is valued more highly than historical perspective or the wisdom
of the ages or the affectional contribution in relationship the aged can give.

More often than not, the individual also undergoes marked physical
change, a general lessening of capacity for sustained work, increased fatigabili-
ty, a general slowing up, often accompanied by chronic and progressive illness of a disabling nature. Loss of physical adequacy, lessened mental adequacy, accompanied by affectional deprivations occasioned through the death
of contemporaries and loss of children to the other relationships that now
become primary for them, loss of gratification in work and in an active social
life in the group—all these deprivations and frustrations may combine to give
the aged person a deep sense of helplessness. All this may cause a heightened
need to depend on others in a life situation in which relationships are less sustaining than before. Frequently old people have a wish to feel adequate and
a longing to be needed at a time when reality makes their wishes unrealistic.
These are some of the outstanding conflicts of the aged; any one of them could
well provide anxiety, and a combination of them frequently results in profound anxiety and acute fears. How may old people handle this anxiety?

The aged person deals variously with his anxiety

Denial and compensatory activity are common ways of dealing with anxiety. We are all familiar with the aged person who denies his failing vision,
insisting that he can see just as well as ever, or who denies his loss of physical
strength, refusing to be waited on and repudiating the small considerations
and social amenities extended to the aged. We are familiar with the compensatory features that may accompany such denials, in which the individual attempts by force to preserve his earlier status. A denial of displacement as head
of the family may be accompanied by despotic authority over children and
grandchildren. If the authority is not unquestioningly accepted as of old,
recourse may be taken to hysterical episodes or to illness. When change is
denied, the individual may show deep resentment when any help is offered
and may construe it as an attempt at authoritative management. Sometimes
there is a two-way feeling, for the person, sensing his growing helplessness,
wants on the one hand to give up and become more dependent, while on the
other hand he resents his loss of adequacy and wants to maintain it. His protests against management are sometimes a bid for it, and he may quickly and
with gratification succumb when circumstances force the issue.

Miss S, a recipient of old age assistance, was growing so infirm as to be
unable to care for herself adequately. The public assistance worker tried to
help her face her need for institutional care, only to have the suggestion
staunchly repudiated. Finally, eviction by three successive landlords because
of neighbors' complaints about the state of her rooms and inability to obtain

a fourth lodging led to her placement in a home for the aged where she subsequently led a more comfortable and satisfying life. On the day of removal, she angrily reproached the worker for not having "made her" do this earlier, and at this time she recounted the discomforts and loneliness of the past months.

It is possible that this woman had to live through this last defense against becoming dependent, that she had to experience this final unrealistic assertion of her ability to manage her own life, and that impersonal circumstance alone could serve as an acceptable coercive agent. One wonders, however, whether the public assistance worker who tried to help her face her need for institutional care might not, without using either coercion or persuasion, have been more helpful than he was. The record shows that the worker focused narrowly and directly on the woman's limitations, pointing out her helplessness, the dangers to her welfare in remaining alone, and stressing the benefits of an institution. Had he helped the woman express her fear of change, her preconceived notions of institutional life, what it meant to part with her own things and to give up the management or her own affairs, the woman might have made this choice for herself. We cannot talk people out of their resistance to change, but frequently that resistance may dissipate itself when the individual has an opportunity to give expression to it, especially to a person who understands but does not necessarily feel the same way about it.[8] In this instance, the woman might have been spared months of uncomfortable living and much anxiety.

Adaptations are the same as at earlier life periods

In old age the future is uncertain, even frightening, while the present has many frustrations. It is, therefore, inevitable that there is considerable regression to the past. Regressions at this period are normal and abscence of them is unusual. Regressions are manifested in many forms varying from individual to individual. Aged people frequently attach themselves to old things; they fall back on fixed routines, becoming irritated when forced into unfamiliar regimes. They tend to reminisce about old friends and to idealize the past. They may become untidy or sometimes more meticulous, demanding excessive personal care. They may become blissfully oblivious to present threatening realities, showing an exaggerated optimism and a complete disinclination to plan realistically. Or they may exaggerate present problems, showing marked anxiety about trifling incidents and taking excessive measures to safeguard their health, their finances, and the like. As they experience the reversal of roles in which they feel themselves to be dependent on their children, rather than the children dependent on them, they may ally themselves with young grandchildren and, combating parental authority, may seek indulgence for them. Or they may be rivalrous with the grandchildren. Personality changes may have an organic basis in cerebral damage in the aging process or may be owing primarily to factors previously enumerated—that is, to the individual's emotional response, to the many marked changes time brings, sometimes gradually or often quite suddenly. In work with the aged, therefore, it is often important to determine the basis of personality change through medical examination. This differentiation may guide us in deciding how much to rely on any possible modifications in environment to bring change in the individual's response.[9]

Implications for public assistance

The decisive point in this life period is that the same behavior adaptations are being used as at earlier life periods and that the denials of reality, the compensatory efforts, the regressions are serving the same purpose. Now, as formerly, the individual is striving for a feeling of safety and of security. We may do rather different things for the aged, our work with them will have a different focus and emphasis, but notably the same principles will be utilized.

1. We are interested first in gauging what strengths the person still has to manage his own affairs and helping him to find satisfying activity within the limits of his physical and mental condition and his environmental situation. We try to afford every opportunity for him to utilize these strengths in planning for himself. We give him as much help as we can in relation to what he needs in securing a life situation that makes continued activity possible. Our help may involve utilization of community resources and resources in family relationship.[10]

2. After making sure that the individual has every opportunity to utilize the present to the utmost, so that he is not needlessly driven to the past, we accept some regression to the past as natural, inevitable, and essential to his comfort. When we accept this, we may then expect to meet dependency through giving supportive help in many ways, with recognition of the difference between the import of these measures at this life period and at earlier ages.

Legal provisions cause hardship

When we understand the needs of the aged and their behavior tendencies, which are not peculiar to aged but common to all humans, we see the destructive import for them of present rulings in many states on the responsibility of relatives for financial support. *We know that this is a time of life when the individual needs more than ever before the security of harmonious relationships with members of his family. Enforced support may make him a burden and an irritant to his frequently already disadvantaged family.* Thus, insofar as his family relationships become strained rather than strengthened, as they frequently do, he experiences deprivation and frustration in the present that drive him to the past, thereby stimulating and reinforcing regressive impulses. Furthermore, one of the conditions of old age that has induced more regression than would otherwise be necessary has been the humiliating reversal of roles that occurs when the person is forced from the position of parent to that of dependent child.

It would seem that in America, where the dignity of man is presumably the keystone of its democratic structure, every individual should be entitled to conditions that enable him to maintain what strength and dignity of his adult years remain to him in spite of or apart from the inroads that time may have made on his mental and physical capacities.[11] In this area, public assistance administrators and staffs, with knowledge of common human needs and principles of human behavior, will have deep convictions. The destructive effects of many of our present legal provisions indicate the need for every effort to change the laws. An unnecessary burden is being placed on the worker's shoulders, not only in investigation and persuasive and coercive efforts to induce relatives to support but also in dealing with the resultant difficulties in relationships. There are hurts here, with resultant problems, and these are better avoided through legal change than than through casework ministrations to the aged that, however discriminative and tender, cannot compensate for damages wrought by humiliating wrongs.[12]

Notes

1. Franz Alexander, MD, *Our Age of Unreason; A Study of the Irrational Forces in Social Life* (1st ed.; Philadelphia: J.B. Lippincott Co., 1942), p. 142.

2. For a more comprehensive coverage of maturity, *see* Therese Benedik, MD, "Personality Development," in Franz Alexander, MD, and Helen Ross, eds., *Dynamic Psychiatry* (Chicago: University of Chicago Press, 1952), pp. 63–111; Bruno Bettelheim, *The Informed Heart: Autonomy in a Mass Age* (Glencoe, Ill.: Free Press, 1960), p. 309; Robert J. Havighurst, *Middle Age: The New Prime of Life* (Ann Arbor: University of Michigan Press, 1956); Ives Hendricks, "Work and the Pleasure Principle," *Psychoanalytic Quarterly*, Vol. 12, No. 3 (1943), pp. 311–329; Leon J. Saul, MD, *Emotional Maturity* (Philadelphia: J. B. Lippincott Co., 1947); Robert W. White, *Lives in Progress. A Study of the Natural Growth of Personality* (New York: Dryden Press, 1952); Franz Alexander, MD, "Development of the Fundamental Concepts of Psychoanalysis," in Alexander and Ross, eds., *op. cit.*, pp. 3–34; Erik H. Erikson, *Childhood and Society* (New York: W. W. Norton & Co., 1950); and Marie Jahoda, "The Meaning of Psychological Health," *The Social Welfare Forum, 1953* (New York: Columbia University Press, 1953).

3. "Public Assistance Goals: Recommendations of the Social Security Board," *Social Security Bulletin*, Vol. 7, No. 11 (November 1944), p. 2.

4. For further study of this long-controversial question, *see* Abram Kardiner, *The Individual and His Society* (New York: Columbia University Press, 1939); *Men Without*

Work; A Report Made to the Pilgrim Trust (Cambridge, England: Cambridge University Press, 1938); E. Wight Bakke, *Citizens Without Work* (New Haven: Yale University Press, 1940); U.S. Congress, *Report of the House Select Committee to Investigate the Interstate Migration of Destitute Citizens* (Tolan Committee), H. Rept. 369, 77th Cong., 1st sess., 1941. For comments on findings of the Tolan Committee, *see* Edith Abbott, "Social Work After the War," in Helen R. Wright, ed., *Social Service in Wartime* (Chicago: University of Chicago Press, June 1944), pp. 180–181; Abbott, "People Prefer to Work," *Social Service Review*, Vol. 18, No. 1 (March 1944), p. 92; Bettelheim, *op. cit.*; Henry H. Hart, "Work as Integration," *Medical Record*, Vol. 150, No. 12 (1947), pp. 735–739; Norman W. Bell and Ezra F. Vogel, eds., *A Modern Introduction to the Family* (Glencoe, Ill.: Free Press, 1960); Reuben Hill, *Families Under Stress* (New York: Harper & Bros., 1949); and Hill, "Generic Features of Families Under Stress," *Social Casework*, Vol. 39, Nos. 2 and 3 (February–March 1958), pp. 139–150.

5. Jeanette Hanford, "Family Case Work With Marital Difficulties," *Proceedings of the National Conference of Social Work, 1937* (Chicago: University of Chicago Press, 1937), pp. 226–242; Charlotte Towle, "The Social Worker and the Treatment of Marital Discord Problems," *Social Service Review*, Vol. 14, No. 2 (June 1940), pp. 211–223; Gerald H. Caplan, MD, "Mother Child Relationships: Origin and Development of," and "During the First Year of Life," *Concepts of Mental Health and Consultation*, Children's Bureau Publication No. 373 (Washington, D.C.: U.S. Department of Health, Education, and Welfare, 1959), pp. 57–78 and 79–109; O. Spurgeon English, MD, "The Psychological Role of the Father in the Family," *Social Casework*, Vol. 35, No. 8 (October 1954), pp. 323–329; and David M. Levy, *Maternal Overprotection* (New York: Columbia University Press, 1943).

6. Percival M. Symonds, *Psychology of Parent Child Relationships* (New York: D. Appleton-Century Co., 1939); and Morris D. Riemer, MD, "Loving Versus Spoiling Children," *Mental Hygiene*, Vol. 24, No. 1 (January 1940), pp. 79–81.

7. *See Mental Hygiene in Old Age* (New York: Family Welfare Association of America, 1937).

8. For discussion of this concept, *see* Chapter 1, pp. 9–11.

9. *See* "Old Age and Aging," *American Journal of Orthopsychiatry*, Vol. 10, No. 1 (January 1940), pp. 27–87; Ruth S. Cavan, E. W. Burgess, Robert J. Havighurst, and Herbert Goldhamer, *Personal Adjustment in Old Age* (Chicago: Social Science Research Association, 1949); E. H. Friedman and Robert J. Havighurst, *The Meaning of Work and Retirement* (Chicago: University of Chicago Press, 1954); Lawrence Greenleigh, "Some Psychological Aspects of Aging," *Social Casework*, Vol. 36, No. 3 (March 1955), pp. 99–106; George Lawton, *New Goals in Old Age* (New York: Columbia University Press, 1943); Charlotte Towle, "Factors in Treatment," *Proceedings of the National Conference of Social Work, 1936* (Chicago: University of Chicago Press, 1936); "Casework with the Aging," *Social Casework*, Vol. 42, Nos. 5–6 (May–June 1961), pp. 219–290; Helen Lokshin, "Critical Issues in Serving an Aging Population," *Social Casework*, Vol. 45, No. 3 (March 1964), pp. 21–27; and Edna Wasser, "Responsibility, Self-Determination and Authority in Casework Protection of Older Persons," *Social Casework*, Vol. 42, Nos. 5–6 (May–June 1961), pp. 258–266.

10. Elizabeth Dexter, "New Concepts and Old People," *Proceedings of the National Conference of Social Work, 1939* (New York: Columbia University Press, 1939), pp. 381–389.

11. George Lawton, ed., *New Goals for Old Age* (New York: Columbia University Press, 1943).

12. Edith Abbott, "Abolish the Means Test for Old Age Assistance," *Social Service Review*, Vol. 17, No. 2 (June 1943), pp. 213–215; and Abbott, "Public Homes for the Aged and the Social Security Act," *Social Service Review*, Vol. 17, No. 4 (December 1943), pp. 501–502.

5

The handicapped

A ll public assistance workers encounter many individuals who are chronically ill or have a physical handicap. These people present special problems, and therefore workers frequently set them apart as persons who must be treated differently. It is important to bear in mind that, in spite of special problems that demand special services, work with the ill and the handicapped is governed by the same basic principles as work with any other group of individuals.

Meaning of disability to the individual is important

It is important, first, to understand the meaning of the illness or handicap to the individual. His life will be affected circumstantially and psychologically in varied ways and varying degrees. Insofar as they bring change, the factors determining the nature and degree of the individual's response are age, sex, prior life experience, prior personality development, and the timing of the onset of disability in relation to other events in his life.[1] This factor of timing is sometimes decisive. For example, a man immersed in humiliation and defeat at being unemployed may sustain an injury or fall ill. At such a time the disability may be seized on and used to the utmost as a more acceptable basis for being unemployed than not being wanted in the labor market. The same mishap in time of employment might not have brought the same gratifications and therefore, not being useful, would not be clung to in the same way.

Or in old age, when the future is uncertain and life in general has become frustrating, illness or handicap may be used as a means to return to earlier infantile gratifications. The person may derive attention and a feeling of safety and comfort through the care his disability earns him. This is not necessarily the case, however, for if the person has well-entrenched patterns of self-dependence he may resist his disability or deny its existence through refusing medical care and attempting to carry on as of old. An important factor determining his choice of a solution may be the response of family members to his disability. Their anxious overprotection may drive him to further lengths in denying his limitations or it may encourage regression. Their indifference and neglect may provoke regression in order to command attention or it may block him in getting the help he genuinely needs.

Likewise in adolescence when the young person has not a secure place in the adult world and when he has considerable anxiety about his status among his peers, a physical handicap or chronic illness that limits his activity may be deeply disturbing. He may solve the problem by a regression to childhood or may resist the limiting reality of his handicap through overreaching himself in activity and refusing to use measures proffered to safeguard his welfare. Again, decisive factors determining the nature of his response are his prior personality development and the response of others, notably his family and friends, to his disability.[2] Above all, he may need help in planning realistically for the future.

Illness or disability may serve a useful purpose

If we understand the meaning of illness or disability to the individual, we may see the purpose it serves for him. Within the framework of his present situation and the interplay of his family relationships, we need to try to understand what *use* his disability has for him—what unmet need it fulfills— now, in his present life situation. Accordingly we ask ourselves such questions as: Why does he not want to give up his handicap? Why does he need to deny it? Is it enabling him to escape overwhelming pressures, to compensate for certain lacks, or to gain satisfaction in one way or another? We seek the answer through knowing the individual, focusing on more than his handicap; frequently we fail to understand the disabled person because we do not see beyond his disability. Perhaps our own limitations, physical or otherwise, brought us the experience of feeling different, so that as we encounter "the disabled" it may be difficult not to emphasize his difference and to stress the handicap as though it were the total person rather than merely an aspect of him or as one problem he presents.

The worker in the case of Miss S tended to do this.[3] In attempting to help her see that an institution would afford her a more comfortable life, he focused on the woman's physical ineptitude, her inability to get along, and thus, perhaps, aroused a strong defense in which Miss S may have been driven to prove that she could and would get along on her own. Had the worker focused on understanding Miss S as a person, he would have helped her express something of what her infirmity meant to her, something of the loneliness and dissatisfactions of her present life as well as her fear of institutions. Thus he might have enabled her to make this choice and thereby to realize constructively her desire to manage her own affairs. Likewise, in the D case, the worker saw Mr. D as a turberculous patient rather than as a man who had been the head of his family and who still had both the inclination and the capacity for participation in the management of family affairs.[4]

Congenital handicaps may shape the personality

When physical handicap has been congenital or has had its onset in infancy or early childhood, it does not have the same threat of change as when it occurs later in life. It may have been deeply influential, however, in forming the personality of the individual. The effect it has had in these instances will depend largely on the meaning the handicap has had for parents and other family members responsible for the care of the individual during childhood.[5] Frequently, a parent brings to the experience of having a child certain predetermined needs that may lead him to seek self-realization, or sometimes even to strive for adjustment, through the child. When the child is born handicapped or early suffers injury or chonic illness, the parent may experience great personal frustration. It may also be a threat to his pride, thus making him feel inferior. The resultant feelings of irritation, especially if he feels at all to blame for the child's condition, may lead to feelings of rejection. This rejection may be expressed openly or, if the parent feels guilty over his hostile feelings, may be disguised through overprotective handling that eases the guilt.

If the parent has had deep feelings of inadequacy or great frustrations, he may identify himself closely with a handicapped child, and in such an instance protective handling or unrealistic, wishful strivings may characterize his relationship with the child. In a family receiving ADC, Mr. V, unemployed because of a serious cardiac condition, had cut short an able career in the engineering field. He responded to his son's post-infantile-paralysis handicap and mental retardation with refusal to accept a clinic's advice regarding medical care and vocational training. He needed to deny that there was anything much wrong with the boy. He blamed the school for the boy's failure and resisted placing him in a school for crippled children where it was thought the youngster would have a better chance for some success. In ADC and other programs, as workers confer with parents on problems presented by their handicapped children it is important that they understand what the child and his disability mean to the parent.[6] This understanding can serve as a guide in our efforts to help parents who turn to us not only in relation to management of their children but also in such vital decisions as to whether to place children, allow them to have special educational opportunities, or co-operate in medical care.

Understanding an adult's response may enable the worker to be more helpful

When we work with the adult whose handicap has been lifelong, it may be too late to bring about basic personality change. Understanding his response may, however, enable us to be more helpful in many ways. For example, in the case of Mr. and Mrs. N, the worker encountered a young couple who were both blind. They were living in basement rooms in a dilapidated building, quarters provided by the town authorities or families receiving assistance. Mr. and Mrs. N had met in the state institution for the blind and had been married shortly after leaving there while both were employed at broommaking in a blind and disabled workers' shop. Mrs. N, aged 20, applied for and received Aid to the Blind when she became pregnant and could no longer work. Because of his age—19 years—the husband was not eligible for Aid to the Blind. When his wife was unable to accompany him back and forth from the shop and in their rounds in broom selling, he gave up his work. maintaining that he could not get along without her. During the subsequent months he became increasingly dependent on her. After the birth of a child with normal sight he became irritable and difficult, since the mother became quite absorbed in this fulfillment of her fondest hopes.

It was at this point that Mrs. N unburdened to the worker her great discouragement over Mr. N's inability to assume the responsibilities of a husband and father. She described him as always having been childish, which she attributed to the fact that he lost his parents during infancy and was left to the care of a grandmother who gave him excessive care because of his disability. Upon marriage he immediately looked to her to plan for both of them. She contrasted her own situation with his in that she had come from a family in which there was hereditary blindness, five of eight members having been sightless or having markedly impaired vision. She said that her disability had been taken for granted. Her family was sociable and of great solidarity. The children accepted responsibility and participated almost normally in the life of the community. Mrs. N impressed the worker as being an outgoing, sociable woman with the unusual self-dependence in managing her affairs and in caring for her child.

As Mrs. N spoke of her concern over her husband the worker directed her to consider what the child meant to him, and she was able to identify his difficulty as one of rivalry, although at the time this did not help her to feel any more tolerant of his limitations. The worker's suggestion that she place more responsibility on him did not bring results. Later the worker tried to get acquainted with Mr. N, who had until this time remained almost unknown because all financial planning had been done with Mrs. N. The worker found him very unhappy because he was not working and earning, and also because his wife had money and he did not. He disliked broommaking. He claimed to be mechanically inclined and said that he enjoyed working on old radios. He recalled his life in the institution with some pleasure, especially as he talked of having studied the violin, played in the institution's orchestra, and participated in musical activities at church. In this community he had missed his religious and musical activities and had wanted work of a different sort but had felt that he would not be considered for anything. He was discouraged and depressed about their physical surroundings, and the worker got the impression that their living arrangements had operated against community contacts. The worker agreed that there might be difficulty in finding a job but, in view of the labor shortage and the fact that some industries were now employing blind workers, held out hope that he might get work. He made suggestions as to where Mr. N might apply. He showed interest in his musical ability also, and interest in the possibility that he and his wife might find community activities and church connections similar to those they had enjoyed in the past. Later Mr. N obtained work, and shortly thereafter the worker helped him apply for residence in a housing project.

Some months after the worker learned from Mrs. N that Mr. N had continued to be fairly regularly employed, that they were planning to have the child admitted to a nursery school group, and that they had become affiliated with a group of young married couples who lived in the housing project and gave parties. Both Mr. and Mrs. N were playing in the orchestra for the group's dances. In their last conversation Mrs. N stated that her husband had become tolerant of the baby; that he had bought him an electric train for Christmas and, since the baby was too young to enjoy this toy, Mr. N was playing with it a great deal. She complained that he had spent a considerable sum of money on a watch, which was foolish in that he could not use it. The worker directed her to consider the importance of this possession to him in terms of "being like other men." Mrs. N reported general improvement in their relationship, their only present difficulty being over the spending of money. She recounted that their worst quarrel had occurred over some curtains—Mrs. N wanted pink ones, while Mr. N wanted blue!

Influence on use of public assistance

This case affords discussion of a number of important points in work with the handicapped:

1. Basic personality differences in Mr. and Mrs. N result in part from their differing life experience with the same handicap. It is clear that each brings different needs to adulthood. There can be no great change in the personality of Mr. N, but, insofar as his needs are met, he functions more adequately within the limits of his personality.

2. Because Mr. N was not the recipient of aid, he apparently was ignored. That aid had meaning for him, however, in that it became a disturbing factor in his relationship with his wife. The worker's eventual recognition of him as a person important in the family scheme apparently brought a ready response. Perhaps because of his handicap and also because of his dependency he needed this recognition all the more.

3. We note also that marked change had come into the lives of Mr. and Mrs. N through transferring from the protected regime of an institution, where

they lived among the handicapped, to a competitive community in which they must find their place among those who are not handicapped. This adjustment was probably more difficult for Mr. N because he was basically a more dependent person than his wife. He had clung to her to support him within the community, so that when she withdrew from work he had to accompany her. He needed encouragement and supportive help from someone who represented the community. It might be expected that in work with blind individuals who have lived in an institution there would frequently be a need for help in using community resources and in finding some of the interests of their past life in the strange situation. In this connection the difficult problem introduced by living in wretched housing, stigmatized as town property for the use of the indigent, deserves careful consideration. The value for these people of the community life existing in many housing projects is worth noting.

4. This case also emphasizes the deeply significant fact that "the blind" are not necessarily helpless, and that in spite of, or perhaps all the more because of, their difference from others, they long for identification and association with those who have normal vision. They try to see the world through our eyes to a greater extent perhaps than we try to see it through theirs. Watches and colors and respectable surroundings still matter. All Mr. N's needs were needs frequently encountered in work with sighted fathers and husbands. The blind individual is a *person* who happens to be blind. We need to know the person in order to help with the problem of blindness.[7] This same principle would apply with handicaps other than blindness.

5. This case presented the need for more adequate rehabilitation measures in state schools and for use of state rehabilitation resources. Correspondence with the state school in the case of Mr. N revealed that there had been no attempt to determine his intellectual capacity, vocational aptitudes, or aspirations and interests. It is obvious that persons with a major handicap need special help and special opportunities that may enable them to overcome their limitations as much as possible. Dependence, actual and psychological, is an inevitable result of a lack of preparation for the life of the community. When the person's prior life experience has been such as to induce dependency, he may have all the more need for this help.[8] We note the importance also of using all available community resources both for preventive and remedial medical care.

Worker's feeling about handicaps is important

In our work with disabled people, traditional attitudes—certain time-honored emphases—frequently obstruct us, perhaps because we feel deeply about them. We encounter our own mixed feelings about persons who are different. In many of us there probably are vestiges of our early childhood anxiety about difference. In any group of children we can note anxiety about the child who is a stranger until the group has felt him out and been assured of his likeness to them. We have all observed their reactions to the child who is markedly different—in dress, in ways, or in language. A disabled child frequently becomes the target of much hostility. They cannot permit themselves to identify with him. Perhaps this is because of an unconscious fear that whatever happened to him might happen to them. Therefore, they ostracize him in one way or another as a protection against entering into a relationship that is somehow threatening. As they grow older parental disapproval checks their savagery. Also, as they mature they become more altruistic, and guilt over past feelings toward or treatment of those who are less fortunate may bring a reversal of attitudes and behavior. They may become as overprotective of the handicapped person as they were rejecting of him in earlier years.

Adult attitudes toward disabled persons are characterized by an inability to take handicaps for granted, by overprotective tendencies, and by a degree and kind of emotional involvement that tends to set the disabled person apart. These feelings are reflected in disability-conscious efforts to help them. Perhaps these feelings explain our studied attitudes, our concentration on just *how to treat* the handicapped—as though they were a separate species. Perhaps they determine our tendency to view these individuals in terms of their disabilities and to plan for them primarily with reference to their difference, thereby frequently enhancing their discomfort and feeling of isolation.

Feelings as a person must be understood

Much work with the handicapped has been done with the self-conscious conviction that certain attitudes should be maintained by individuals who work with them. We have long been aware that some handicapped persons have tended to become dependent. The prominence of regressive impulses in response to the obstacles or the change incurred in the individual's life led to a creed against infantilizing the disabled. Workers have been cautioned to avoid sympathizing with them and to encourage a certain bravado through reassuring them and "bucking them up." In accordance with this, some workers have avoided discussing the handicap lest the individual become too centered in his disability. A number of such attitudes could be cited that bespeak our studied efforts to help those *we feel* are different. Our helping efforts have swung from the extreme of coddling and sympathy that weaken to the discipline and denial that also may not strengthen. The decisive point is that these stock attitudes are not valid for general use. They meet the needs of some individuals but to the same degree frustrate others. We will help the handicapped individual only as we understand his *needs as a person*, not only the needs created by his handicap but also those he has in common with other human beings. This focus implies readiness to acknowledge his difficulties, help him express his feelings about them, offer protective measures and supportive help in accordance with his need, and let him use his strengths and resourcefulness in managing his own affairs. The same principles we use in helping people with other problems are appropriate in work with those who are chronically ill or physically handicapped.

Notes

1. For consideration of the social and emotional implications of physical handicaps, *see* Charlotte G. Babcock, "Inner Stress in Illness and Disability," in Howard J. Parad and Roger R. Miller, eds., *Ego-Oriented Casework: Problems and Perspectives* (New York: Family Service Association of America, 1963), pp. 45–64; James F. Garrett, ed., *Psychological Aspects of Physical Disability*, Rehabilitation Service Series No. 210 (Washington, D.C.: U.S. Office of Vocational Rehabilitation, 1952); Michael Smith, ed., *Management of the Handicapped Child* (New York: Grune and Stratton, 1957); *Emotional Problems Associated with Handicapping Conditions in Children*, Children's Bureau Publication No. 336 (Washington, D.C.: U.S. Children's Bureau, 1952); *Interview Guide for Specific Disabilities* (7 vols.; Washington, D.C.: U.S.Employment Security Bureau, 1954–57); and William A. White, *The Meaning of Disease: An Inquiry in the Field of Medical Psychology* (Baltimore: Williams and Wilkins, 1926).

2. Henry B. Richardson, MD, *Patients Have Families* (New York: Commonwealth Fund, 1945).

3. *See* Chapter 4, p. 73.

4. *See* Chapter 2, p. 14.

5. For a picture of how family reactions determine in considerable measure the child's response to physical disability, *see* Katherine Butler Hathaway, *The Little Locksmith* (Toronto: Longmans, Green & Co., 1943); and Somerset Maugham, *Of Human Bondage* (New York: Doubleday, Doran & Co., 1936).

6. For examples, *see* Charlotte Towle, "The Social Content of Work for Crippled Children From the Standpoint of the Psychiatric Social Worker," *Crippled Child*, Vol. 15, No. 1 (June 1937), pp. 9–12.

7. *See* Ruth Emerson, "In the Interest of Preventing Blindness: Psychological Attitudes of the Visually Handicapped Toward Treatment," *Social Service Review*, Vol. 16, No. 3 (September 1942), pp. 477–496.

8. For further discussion of vocational guidance, *see* Bertram J. Black, "Vocational Rehabilitation," in Harry L. Lurie, ed., *Encyclopedia of Social Work* (New York: National Association of Social Workers, 1965), pp. 816–823; Black, "Principles and Trends in Rehabilitation," *Journal of Jewish Communal Service*, Vol. 32, No. 4 (Summer 1956), pp. 351–355; Caroline H. Elledge, *The Rehabilitation of the Patient. Social Casework in Medicine* (Philadelphia: J.B. Lippincott Co., 1948); Minna Field, *Patients Are People* (New York: Columbia University Press, 1953); Babcock, *op. cit.*; Garrett, *op. cit.*; Smith, *op. cit.*; *Emotional Problems Associated with Handicapping Conditions in Children*; and *Interview Guide for Specific Disabilities*.

6

The family

W̲e have considered some of the common needs of people as individuals at different stages of life and as individuals participating in the group, family, and community. The importance of family life to the child as preparation for life in the world and for the part he will play in the establishment and maintenance of another family has been suggested although not depicted comprehensively. The interplay of relationships within a family normally is complex and to discuss the various anomalies in human adjustment that related to the organization of the family and to the varying nature of its interrelationships is beyond the limits of this presentation.[1]

What occurs in the individual's struggle for survival as he participates in family life has been depicted clearly by many novelists and storytellers, among them Katherine Mansfield, of whose ability to portray family life Willa Cather writes:

> I doubt whether any contemporary writer has made me feel more keenly the many kinds of personal relations which exist in an everyday "happy family" who are merely going on living their daily lives with no crises or shocks or bewildering complications to try them. Yet every individual in the household...is clinging passionately to his individual soul, is in terror of losing it in the general family flavor. As in most families, the mere struggle to have anything of one's own, to be oneself at all, creates an element of strain which keeps everybody almost at the breaking point. One realizes that even in harmonious families there is this double life: the group life which is the one we can observe in our neighbor's household, and underneath another—secret and passionate and intense which is the real life that stamps the faces and gives character to the voices of our friends. Always in his mind each member of these social units is escaping, running away, trying to break the net which circumstance and his own affections have woven about him. One realizes that human relationships are the tragic necessity of human life; that they can never be wholly satisfactory, that every ego is half the time greedily seeking them and half the time pulling away from them. In those simple relationships of loving husband and wife, affectionate sisters, children and grandmother, there

are innumerable shades of sweetness and anguish which make up the patterns of our lives day by day.[2]

Conflicts may be heightened in public assistance families

Since public assistance workers deal with families at times when bewildering complications try them, families who frequently have known repeated crises or shocks, this normal struggle of each family member for closeness to the family and for apartness from it can well be heightened. *The conflicts are essentially the same, only perhaps more intense, with a greater emotional stake in decisions that involve dependency or separation.*[3]

Mr. J, who grew up in a family where he was the mother's dependent son, has had a difficult time maintaining his place in the world apart from his parents by supporting his wife and children. Now, in establishing his eligibility for assistance, he must draw the parents into the investigation. While he knows that with some sacrifice they not only could help him but would willingly do so, his very survival as an adequate adult male is at stake in his protest against turning to them or having them know of his predicament. Even his illness does not justify or ease the situation. His marriage is threatened, for again, as in its early days, his mother will hold the ascendant position and the struggle to place his wife first, which he had practically won, could well be lost in the return to dependence on his parents.

Miss C had long clung to her family in spite of early impulses to break away. Throughout her childhood and adolescence she had been outdone by a sister whom she felt her parents greatly preferred. Her resentment bade her break off and find a life of her own, but guilt over this same resentment, together with a persistent need to be needed, forbade the going. This seemingly curious reaction of staying because one wants to go is not uncommon. A normal separation would have been an enactment of her rejection, so she stayed, contributing to the support of the family group for many years. Finally, the "life of her own" came about through the death of the mother, when the father went to live with the "preferred" sister. Later, financial reverses in this family and the father's application for old age assistance brought an inquiry as to Miss C's ability to support him. The worker found a woman who unquestionably was earning enough to contribute but who offered many reasons for being unable to do so and who finally, under pressure, strongly asserted her right to her own earnings—in her words, a right to a life of her own. Perhaps she had an unconscious need to withhold love as she felt the father had withheld love from her, expressed in her words to the effect that her sister could take care of him, he always liked her, he chose to go live with her, and so on.

Mr. O, a successful engineer, was earning $400 a month in wartime. His wife also was earning and yet, when approached regarding the support of his aged father, he gave Depression debts, educational plans for his children, medical expenses, and the like as his reasons for being absolutely unable to give his father a home or to contribute to his support elsewhere. The real reason lay in this man's long-standing resentment toward his father who, in his opinion, "let me and my sister down" following their mother's death, when he married another woman. "Let *her* children support him" was his attitude, since it was their mother who enjoyed the most productive years of the father's life and spent his money. Rigid enforcement of the laws on responsibility of relatives brought compliance in this case, but with no feeling on the part of the son that social justice had been administered to him.

Understanding family life gives new meaning to legal provisions as to responsibility of relatives

As the carry-over of the family conflicts in the area of dependence versus separation in later life is viewed in relation to attitudes toward financial support of family members, one might, at the risk of oversimplification, make the following tentative statement:

1. In general, when an individual has had satisfying and constructive love relationships within the family, he attains the capacity to meet the dependence of family members. Unless there is lack of means there is no problem of non-support. In such relationships, the impulse is to share and to contribute if it is humanly possible to do so. If it is not possible, the individuals concerned may state their inability to support without undue self-justification or anxiety over this inability.

2. Frequently, when the individual is still tied to the family but has much resentment over those ties plus a fear of loss of love and anxiety over guilt if he should not fulfill his obligation, the support problem is that of the relative himself who is unrealistic about his ability to contribute. He may share his last crust and mortgage his own future because he is not emotionally free to say, "I am not able to contribute." To refuse would be to enact his feelings of rejection and also to risk loss of relationships in which he still has a certain childish dependence. Or sometimes his two-way feelings find expression as follows. When he could contribute, he may enact his resentment through refusal to contribute, accompanied by many rationalizations. Or he may, through placing on others the responsibility of enforcement, make society through court action force him to carry his unwelcome burden.

3. In general, when the individual's separation from the family has not been a normal process of emancipation but a cutting off or breaking away in order to survive, involvement in the family through a renewal of dependency or through contributing to its support constitutes a painful reopening of old wounds or a threatening entanglement in an old frustrating net. In such an instance the person may unrealistically refuse help or maintain his inability to

help, building up a strong case for himself. Sometimes, in order to survive as a relatively free person with some chance for growth, he cannot permit himself to become entangled in his past.

In summary, then, we might say that when relationships are sufficiently good to make acceptance of support or contribution to the support of others a constructive experience, the individual will be inclined to assume this responsibility if he is financially able to do so. Statutory provisions and administrative policies that express a respect for the right of the individual who is not applying for assistance as well as for the one who is would permit some individualization to afford consideration of the factors that affect a person's readiness to give or take help from members of his family.

Adversity need not undermine family life

While recognizing that conflicts in economically disadvantaged families may be heightened through the anxieties and uncertainties implicit in their circumstances, we must *not* assume that this is always true or that these families inevitably abound in problematic relationships that obstruct normal development of the children. Sometimes these very stresses seem to have made relationships more meaningful in constructive ways. Social workers have long known that in the families of the poor one may find solidarity, a willingness to share, to live beyond narrow absorption in self for others, on the part of both parents and children. It has sometimes seemed that because they have so little else, family ties have been enhanced and used to the utmost in this realization of growth. The fortitude, the resilience, the capacity for resourceful planning—in short, all the many strengths that long have aroused our wonder and our respect—bespeak good basic relationships. Whether these have endured in spite of adversity or whether they are in part its product is difficult to say. A long tradition exalts the benefits of poverty. It has always been an easy way out as well as a comfortable philosophy for the "haves" in relation to the "have-nots."

Traditional attitudes, however, frequently stem from wishful thinking as an escape from the solution of difficult problems or to ease our social conscience.[4] On the basis of his findings, the modern student of human behavior and social conditions departs from traditional casual attitudes toward adverse circumstance. He concludes that, while poverty may not necessarily undermine family life, it greatly endangers it and makes the individual's survival as a socialized person a more precarious struggle and one with a more dubious outcome. He has a conviction that in more advantageous circumstances the strengths frequently manifested among the disadvantaged might be reinforced and utilized beyond the end of self-survival. In his own eyes, man's fortitude and resilience under adversity constitute a strong argument for greater opportunity.

Public assistance services should strengthen family life

Public assistance programs should be administered so as to strengthen family life in the interests of the individual and society. That our legal provisions, our agency policies, our ways of working may or may not fulfill this purpose in individual instances is becoming increasingly clear. What the service is doing to the life of the family is a question that should be uppermost in the minds of each staff member. Obviously, our services will have varying values in individual instances. The meaning our ways of helping to establish eligibility may have for the applicant has been discussed, as has the import of decisions dictated by relative-support laws that permit no discretion. Likewise, adherence to residence laws, the undeniable obligation of public assistance staffs, as well as all our procedures, will have significance in family life not only in and of themselves but also in the way in which they are interpreted and executed.

Interplay of family relationships

Understanding what is happening to family life implies some knowledge of what it has been, some perception of its strengths and weaknesses. This involves learning something of how the family functioned as a group prior to the present difficulty. Just as the individual commonly has varying needs at different age levels and common ways of responding insofar as these needs are met or not met, just as these needs and ways of reacting must be respected if the individual is to be helped, so the family group presents a varied interplay of relationship needs that must be considered if its strengths are to be conserved and disintegration guarded against. Furthermore, often we encounter the family at times of marked change. The difficulties that bring a family to public assistance agencies may have set in operation a realignment of the roles played by individuals within the group.

Workers enter the scene at a time of instability

Public assistance workers therefore enter the family scene at a time of instability when the life of the group is reshaping itself or is being refashioned by circumstance. Our service and the way it is rendered, as a new and foreign element in a changing scene, may play a decisive part in the family's future. It is well for workers to have some awareness of the part they play in order (1) not to unwittingly interfere either with the formation of new interfamily patterns or with the old interrelationships, which still serve a purpose, and (2) to lend themselves to constructive rather than destructive use in the interplay of the group.

In the D family we encounter a group in which the father, the head of the household in more than a nominal sence, seemingly had been withdrawn from participation in family life through illness.[5] Understanding of his old position in the home and of the mother's unreadiness to assume his role, together with information on his present health condition and attitudes toward his family responsibilities might have enabled the worker to be more helpful with the medical plan suggested by the physician for the welfare of the group. This would have implied recognition and utilization of the father's established patterns as head of the household in planning for himself. In the case of John P, the family was first seen at a time of change when the boy's new adult status as wage earner brought him into a new relationship with his parents, one so problematic that he had to solve it through withdrawal from the group.[6] Some understanding of the significance of the family interplay might have saved the worker futile efforts and enabled him to be more helpful to the mother in her search for assistance in coping with a recalcitrant son.

Workers must understand family patterns and their implications

It is important that workers be encouraged to observe and try to understand the interplay of relationships within the family. This implies some knowledge of common family patterns and awareness of the significant indicators of the nature of the relationships and their meaning to the individuals concerned. Roughly speaking, these family patterns might be grouped as: (1) family responsibilities shared by both parents, (2) father the head of the household and the dominant member, (3) mother the head of the household and the dominant member, (4) family responsibilities evaded by both parents. With great oversimplification, some of the implications of these types of family organization for children might be described as follows:

1. The family in which parental responsibilities have been or are carried jointly and in which there seems to have been mutual sharing in many aspects of life, such as financial management, companionship with children, discipline of children, recreation opportunities, religious activity, and the like, theoretically shows the pattern most favorable to the child's development. Such a sharing is generally conducive to a harmonious home atmosphere, security in relationship with both parents, a minimum of hostile rivalry between brothers and sisters, and a minimum of conflict in growing up. In most families, certain individuals will be found in close identification with one another; these identifications will normally shift from time to time, frequently in accordance with the age of the child and with his growth needs at a particular period. For example, Johnny may be clearly seen as a "father's boy." It is not merely that he looks and acts like him; there is a bond of feeling between the two that defies analysis

but which is a discernible "feeling together" about all things and toward all the others in the group. Johnny, of several sons, is "the apple of his father's eye" and the father is the pivot of Johnny's world. These alignments, which occur normally in all families, may be less well defined and less fixed in the family in which both parents have a real place through joint sharing of family life. Certainly, although they are present they may escape becoming the focal points of controversy, of rivalry, and of antagonism as in other families.[7]

In public assistance services, we often encounter these families when the joint relationship of the parents is thrown out of balance temporarily or permanently. The inability of one parent or the other to function normally—because of unemployment, illness, or handicap, or the loss of one parent from the group—will bring some change throughout all the relationships in the group. In many instances, a relationship of mutual sharing between parents may have been dislocated through the addition to the family of an aged grandparent. The significant factor to observe is how the remaining parent, or the parent with a changed status, is adapting to his or her new part and how others are responding to the change. Is a widowed mother taking over formerly shared responsibilities readily, with great uncertainty, or with a marked protest against her fate? Is the wife of a now handicapped man assuming her heavier load with irritation, with some gratification, with hostility toward or understanding of her husband's predicament, with some acceptance or with complete rejection of the adverse circumstance in her life? Is the place of a woman whose aged mother-in-law now lives in the home being usurped? And if so, how is she responding to the situation and what reverberations are being registered throughout the group? Because a relationship that has been one of joint sharing often has been based on the relatively mature development of each individual, one frequently finds resourceful adaptation to the imposed change with a minimum of threat to the solidarity of the family group. Change may be causing discomfort or stress, but the essential strengths of the relationship still make possible a constructive adaptation of one sort or another. These families present fewer problems in their use of assistance than some other families, but even so there are advantages in the worker's recognition of the needs they present and the strengths that are here to be maintained and utilized. The G family seemingly typifies such a situation.[8]

2. A second pattern appears in the family in which the father carries the major responsibility and occupies first place in the affairs of the family. He not only brings in the money but decides how it shall be spent. He dictates the management of the children, assumes the major disciplinary role, and fashions the family's recreational life, educational plans, and religious practice primarily in accordance with his own taste and inclination. Whether or not the family life is essentially harmonious will depend on many variable factors, such as how hostile or beneficent a head the father is, how rigid his need is to play the dominating part or the extent to which he can modify it in accordance

with the needs of others, and what his dominating ways mean to the mother.[9] If her dependency needs are met in ways that are gratifying, there may be little parental conflict and the children at least have the security afforded through a vested authority in the home. If the mother is deeply frustrated and only outwardly submissive, her irritations may be expressed in devious ways and the children may live in a tense atmosphere and be surrounded by a parental conflict in which they become pawns.[10]

This family pattern is more usual in some cultures than in others, but from the standpoint of modern psychology—regardless of the culture factor— this family structure theoretically is not altogether favorable for preparing the child for life in the American scene. Whether or not the home is harmonious, there will be less security in relationships with both parents and greater variation in values for the several children within the family. Those children, especially the boys who happen to identify themselves with the father, may have secure status, but more often than not in the process of growing up they may come into acute conflict with his authority. There is a great chance for the development of deep dependencies, for the formation of hostile rivalries between brothers and sisters, and for the development of a sense of inadequacy on the part of all children as they measure themselves against the father—particularly on the part of those who are close to the dominated mother. The alignments in such a family will tend to be well defined and sometimes they are rigid, that is, fixed for all time. They tend also to become the focal points of rivalries and antagonisms, and the family is frequently divided into two camps, one against the other. This is likely to be true when the mother has been in conflict over her place in the relationship.

These families are often encountered in public assistance programs at a time when this parental relationship also is thrown out of balance. It might be thought that the change would inevitably be for the better, but this is not necessarily so; in fact, the members of such a family may have a difficult time not only in meeting adverse circumstance but also in their relationships with one another. Again the significant factor to observe is how the remaining parent or the parent with a changed status is adapting to his or her new part and how others are responding to the change that has occurred. For example, is the widowed mother quite lost and confused because of the necessity to assume a leadership role? Does she instead show considerable gratification in her freedom with, however, some resultant anxiety that leads her to idealize her husband and dramatize her loss? Is the wife of a now handicapped man unable to assume more responsibility than formerly and fearful of taking any initiative because it seems like a gesture of hostility against him? This was the plight of Mrs. D, who could only say, "I cannot put him out of the house," and "What would the neighbors think?"—Does the suddenly dethroned man cling to his former status or does he regress into infantile dependency, asserting his will in a new way? Are the children, with the sudden loss of an authoritative hand, in open revolt against a father who has lost his power or oblivious to the controls set by an ineffectual mother? Because a relationship in which the outstanding characteristic has been an unequal distribution of authority and dependency often has had as its base the relatively immature development of one or both parents, we frequently find that the imposed change is causing a reaction of marked anxiety and some breakdown of what formerly seemed to be family solidarity. Actually, these families sometimes typify the house that is divided against itself, so that when adversity comes its schisms are widened and the relationships are maintained with great difficulty. These families may present many problems in their use of assistance, and it is important that the worker recognize the need for supportive help at certain points in a period of adjustment to change that is fraught with deeply disturbing emotional conflicts for the individuals concerned.

3. A third pattern is that of the family in which the mother carries the major responsibility and occupies first place in the affairs of the family. She manages the money and carries the burden of planning for and managing the children. It is her ambition and her efforts that keep things going, with or without the co-operation of a father who may be passive and dependent or ineffectually protesting and dependent. Social workers have encountered many such families and have learned the importance of knowing whether the woman is playing the dominant part out of a deep need to dominate the man or because this role has been forced on her through circumstance. Some women with a capacity and desire to share responsibility have been forced into carrying the major burden by their concern for the welfare of the children. This has occurred in instances when the husband has been deeply dependent and ineffectual or has been rendered ineffectual and demoralized through circumstances outside his control.

Many relatively mature women who have no marked need for dominance fall readily into the part of providing for and protecting their families. They may readily assume a maternal role toward the father if he is basically helpless or rendered so through circumstance. The primacy of the maternal impulse makes them vulnerable to this part, to an extent that may undermine the husband's adequacy and have destructive import for the children. Sometimes, however, when the husband has a deep dependency this response is not only gratifying but also sustaining and may help him carry on after a fashion. It has also been commonly observed that the man gains his sense of adequacy and feeling of status insofar as he is able to cope with the world. He measures himself as a man by what he attains as provider for his family. When he meets defeat outside the home, he not merely suffers loss of status there but may not bring much to the role of husband and father. Instead, discouraged and defeated, he may become dependent and look to his wife not only to comfort and reassure him but also to take the leadership in the home.[12]

Public assistance workers encounter many fathers who have been defeated, often through force of circumstance and not necessarily through basic inadequacy.

As a result, many mothers are found in a role of dominance that may or may not be wholly gratifying to them but which they are striving to carry for the sake of their families. In these instances the family life may or may not be harmonious. When the mother wants the major responsibility and the husband is satisfied in his dependency, there may be a certain serenity and solidarity in the situation. When the husband's dependency is imposed from without and when the woman is carrying the major responsibility against her inclination, there may be many conflicts for both parents and for the children. As problems arise that bring these families to public assistance agencies, the significant factor to observe is, again, how the remaining parent, or the parent with changed status, is adapting to his or her new part and how others are responding to the change. Is the social problem reinforcing the family pattern through giving the mother an even greater place than she formerly held and through further undermining the father? If so, is the reaction one of gratification or discomfort? In cases when there is discomfort, both parties may be receptive to assistance that strengthens the husband's position, such as employment opportunities or greater participation with the agency in planning for the family.

Whether or not this parental relationship is harmonious, it theoretically presents certain problems for the development of children. While they may receive the protective care during infancy and early childhood essential for basic security in life, they may experience deprivation, insecurity, and feelings of inadequacy in their relationship with the father. The importance of the father relationship in the life of a child, as affording a medium that enables him to move away from dependency on the mother and to find his place in the world outside the home, is well recognized. These children have a problem in growing up, either because the father is basically dependent or because he has been forced into dependency through finding the world too much for him. Alignments in these families, particularly when there is parental conflict and discomfort, are well defined, and again one may find a house divided, in that the children are strongly aligned with the mother against the father, who is a rival for her affections, or some of them may be identified defensively with the inadequate father while the others take on the strong mother's more aggressive patterns. These alignments, again, may become the focal points around which rivalries and antagonisms are centered.[13] These families may present many problems in their use of assistance. One frequently noted is the tendency of the mother to carry undue responsibility for the family in handling its affairs with the agency. Unless she has an inherent need to subordinate the father, she may welcome opportunities to include him in plans. Furthermore, he may be receptive to recognition, so that his active use of assistance may prove to be a step toward rehabilitation.

4. In still another family pattern, neither parent wants or assumes a responsible role and each resists being head of the family. Each charges the other with irresponsibility or laxity and each nags the other to take more responsibility. "They are your children too," may be an oft-reiterated charge. Theoretically, this

is the least favorable configuration for the development of children. Home life is frankly discordant and there is marked insecurity in relationships with both parents. This situation creates a maximum of hostile rivalry among brothers and sisters, who compete anxiously for the fragments of care they can elicit from either or both parents. The alignments within the family may be weak and wavering, for the children shift from one parent to the other in an endless quest for security.

In public assistance agencies, these families are encountered when the relationship between the parents often has been rendered even more precarious than formerly. Again, however, it is important to observe how the remaining parent, or the parent with changed status, is adapting to the new situation. In one case a young mother, in the early days of conscription for military service, was applying for ADC, her husband having enlisted in the navy. Her response throughout the stage of establishing her eligibility was apathetic and flighty. Her final decision was to withdraw her application and to place her children and go to work, saying, "Why should I stay at home and scrimp along on relief to care for *his* children? If he does not care for them enough to stay with them, why should I?" These families present many problems as they use public assistance services. The parents obviously bring few strengths to the experience and are likely to relegate to the agency as many of their parental responsibilities as a willing worker interested in the welfare of the children will take over. Understanding what they want, need, and can use is important for effective service, and these cases often present the problem of protective measures in behalf of the children.

Every aspect of family life reflects family relationships

Since it is important that public assistance workers understand family interplay in order to safeguard the welfare of this group in the interests of the individual and society, it might be asked how we may achieve this understanding since it is not within our province to explore marital relationships and family interrelationships. *The nature of these relationships is reflected in every aspect of family life.* Everything that is revealed sheds light on the family patterns. The applicant's response in establishing eligibility—the information revealed as to financial management, household planning, care of the children, attitudes toward employment, attitudes toward asking for assistance—becomes meaningful to a worker who is trying to gather something more than unrelated facts. If the worker knows something of common family patterns and their significance for his work, the information that has immediate relevance for determination of eligibility and need will form the groundwork for an understanding of the family as a whole. As the contact continues, this understanding will be supplemented gradually and naturally without infringement of the applicant's rights if the worker's efforts to understand stem from a genuine interest in the individual's right to whatever assistance we have to offer.

Recognition of the importance of certain insights into family life should influence favorably not only the worker's inquiry into the family situation but also his use of agency procedures and practices. For example, when he recognizes the importance of learning the place formerly held by the father in a family receiving ADC he will appreciate the changes that often are imposed on him through illness and unemployment. He will see the import of agency practice for the father when the mother now not only receives the money from someone else but controls it herself and turns to the worker as someone who can better share her responsibilities than the now useless father. Seeing this, the worker may alter his current relationship with the family. For future reference, agency administrative staff may use many such cases as a basis for objective questioning, not only of casework practice but also of any existent statutory provisions or policies that rigidly define one parent as against the other to receive and sign for the payment.

When a worker not only knows the relationship needs of the infant and young child but also sees in the specific case the meaning parenthood has for each parent concerned, he may be more helpful to the woman who turns to him for advice as she struggles with the question of whether she should work. When the worker knows something of family relationships, he may bring to parents who seek his help in difficulties with an aged grandparent sound counsel based not only on his understanding of the needs of the aged but also on his understanding of what this particular person means to the family group as a whole. When administrators know something of the import of relationships within a family, policies will reflect this understanding. Workers with conviction in this area will be better able to apply these policies with regard for their intent.

Respect for family life entails changes in assistance policies and laws

It has been possible to present only sketchily a few common examples of interplay in family life and to suggest briefly how recognition of significant meanings may be used in our work. Perhaps this may stimulate us to draw on our past observations and experience, to look inquiringly into the meanings of the responses between individuals we are encountering in our present experience, and to read elsewhere for further insight into family life. In all aspects of our work in which we try to help people establish their right to financial assistance and other services, we encounter many reflections and vestiges of family life. The child in man is there, modified but at moments amazingly intact, the past urgently active in the present. These needs must be taken into account if we are to help people maintain their adulthood. The ways of growth and the present family relationships deserve of our consideration, both at the administrative level, where statutory provisions are amended and policies formulated, and in the day-to-day contacts of the worker who administers the program. The latter may be able only to work within the rigid framework of restrictive regulations that belie man's right to assistance on the basis of need. In these instances, understanding what adherence to agency demands may mean to the recipient in the light of his sometimes contradictory need for dependence and for self-identity may enable the worker to help him clarify and work through feelings so that the agency experience will be more constructive. It must be recognized, however, that unsound administrative practices based on unsound eligibility requirements cannot be remedied adequately through casework skills.[14]

Notes

1. For further study of family life and its contribution to individual difference in development, see Norman W. Bell and Ezra F. Vogel, eds., *A Modern Introduction to the Family* (Glencoe, Ill.: Free Press, 1960); Evelyn Millis Duvall, *Family Development* (2d ed.; Philadelphia: J. B. Lippincott Co., 1957); Frances Lomas Feldman, *The Family in a Money World* (New York: Family Service Association of America, 1957); Dorothy Aikin, "A Project on Family Diagnosis and Treatment," *Social Work Practice, 1963* (New York: Columbia University Press, 1963); Frances L. Beatman, "Family Interaction: Its Significance for Diagnosis and Treatment," *Social Casework*, Vol. 38, No. 3 (March 1957), pp. 111–118; Felix P. Biestek, *The Casework Relationship* (Chicago: Loyola University Press, 1957); Ludwig L. Geismar and Beverly Ayres, "A Method for Evaluating the Social Functioning of Families Under Treatment," *Social Work*, Vol. 4, No. 1 (January 1959), pp. 102–108; Howard J. Parad and Gerald Caplan, MD, "A Framework for Studying Families in Crisis," *Social Work*, Vol.5, No. 3 (July 1960), pp. 3–15; Lydia Rapoport, "Working with Families in Crises: An Exploration in Preventive Interaction, Social Work, Vol. 7, No. 3 (July 1962), pp. 86–91; and Kermit T. Wiltse, "The Hopeless Family," *Social Work*, Vol. 3, No. 4 (October 1958), pp. 12–22.

2. Willa Cather, *Not Under Forty* (New York: Alfred A. Knopf, 1936).

3. Dorothy G. Bird, "How Relief Affects Parent–Child Relationships," *The Family*, Vol. 22, No. 4 (June 1941), pp. 117–122.

4. For further discussion, see Charlotte Towle, "The Individual in Relation to Social Change," *Social Service Review*, Vol. 13, No. 1 (March 1939), pp. 1–31.

5. *See* Chapter 2, p. 14.

6. *See* Chapter 3, pp. 55–56.

7. For an example of family alignments, see William Maxwell, *They Came Like Swallows* (New York: Harper & Brothers, 1937).

8. *See* Chapter 2, pp. 28–30.

9. For an example of a family in which the effect of the father's autrocratic role is modified by the mother's adaptation, *see* Clarence Day, *Life With Father* (New York: Alfred A. Knopf, 1937).

10. For an example of family life in which the father is autocratic and the mother frustrated and hostile though submissive, see Mildred Jordan, *Apple in the Attic* (New York: Alfred A. Knopf, 1942).

11. *See* Chapter 2, p. 14.

12. For an example of a family in which the wife assumed this maternal role without destructive import for the children and perhaps with sustaining values for a dependent husband, see Betty Smith, *A Tree Grows in Brooklyn* (New York: Harper & Brothers, 1943). For an example in which the traditional role of the father as head of the house weakens and breaks down through the impact of adversity in the outside world, while at the same time the mother's position grows increasingly strong and her impulse to protect waxes rather than wanes, note the Joad family in John Steinbeck, *Grapes of Wrath* (New York: Macmillan Co., 1941).

13. For an example of the importance to a boy growing up of the father's status in the eyes of the mother and in the eyes of the world, see Edwin Bjorkman, *The Soul of a Child* (New York: Alfred A. Knopf, 1922).

14. *See* Edith Abbott, "Social Work After the War," in Helen R. Wright, ed., *Social Service in Wartime* (Chicago: University of Chicago Press, June 1944), pp. 169–196; Swithun Bowers, "Human Values and Public Welfare," *The Social Worker*, Vol. 23 (December 1954), pp. 1–7; M. Elaine Burgess and Daniel O. Price, *An American Dependency Challenge* (Chicago: American Public Welfare Association, 1963); Harry L. Hopkins, *Spending to Save: The Complete Story* (New York: W. W. Norton, 1936); Theodore W. Schultz, "Investment in Man: An Economist's View," *Social Service Review*, Vol. 33, No. 2 (June 1959), pp. 109–117; Charlotte Towle, "Social Casework in Modern Society," *Social Service Review*, Vol. 20, No. 2 (June 1946), pp. 165–179; Towle, "Social Work: Cause and Function," *Social Casework*, Vol. 42, No. 10 (October 1961), pp. 385–397; Benjamin E. Youngdahl, "What We Believe," *The Social Welfare Forum, 1952* (New York: Columbia University Press, 1952), pp. 29–45; and Gordon Hamilton, "The Underlying Philosophy of Social Casework Today," *The Family*, Vol. 22 (July 1941), pp. 139–147.

PART THREE

Supervision

7

Some general principles in the light of human needs and behavior motivations

Insight into basic motivations in human behavior and common human needs has great significance for supervision of public assistance staff. The present brief and general discussion cannot attempt to make a direct contribution to supervisory methods except as the reader uses the references for further study.

Supervision in public assistance programs has been defined as an administrative process that has as one of its purposes contribution to staff development. Every staff member in a position of responsibility for the work of other staff members has an obligation to give *leadership that develops the abilities of the staff* under his immediate direction in the useful application of knowledge and skills on the job. It has been emphasized that

> the adequacy of agency function in terms of service to people in need occurs in direct relation to the growth of individual staff members in their capacity to render these services. Accordingly, supervision, in addition to having the derivative meaning, "to have a general oversight of," must focus upon the development of knowledge, the use of that knowledge, and the application of skills by staff in their day-to-day activities on the job.

Supervision in public assistance, therefore, has been envisaged as a teaching-learning situation, that is, as an educational rather than a purely administrative process.[1]

Attitudes of the worker

It has been said for workers in public programs:
Liking and concern for people as individuals should be deep enough to hold

103

even when its object presents himself under disadvantageous circumstances, and should be of such a quality as to enable its possessor to see each person, in a succession of persons, as an individual human being, and to feel a quick and vivid interest in him. What is involved is not a detached or abstract interest but an attitude and a feeling that can be the basis of a disciplined skill....[2]

Insofar as these qualities are requisite in public programs, there is need for workers who have considerable capacity to live beyond absorption in self and who are inclined toward creative activity.[3] To be sure, here, as in other fields, one may encounter individuals who are conspicuously unready for professional development. There may be workers whose excessive need still to be given to compels them to choose and pursue work with people for purposes of self-gratification. They may need to be served by the people whom presumably they are there to serve, and they may use the client as an outlet for their hostile impulses or frustrated wishes. By and large, however, it is probable that in these times of wide and varied opportunity many workers choosing this field of activity have done so out of their readiness to live beyond themselves, out of their liking and concern for people as individuals, and out of their impulse to participate in and to contribute to the life of the community. If this is so, we can assume considerable readiness to learn and considerable stamina to resist regression when the demands of the job are not nicely timed to the worker's acquisition of knowledge and skill.[4] This assumption does not imply an absence of personal need to be realized in their work, but instead readiness to understand and some capacity to deal with such need. The supervisor's understanding of behavior motives and principles of personality growth may throw light on the worker's learning response and thus enable him to convey knowledge and impart skills more competently.

Emotions influence use of supervision and learning response

Since emotions largely determine our thinking and action, it is important to recognize that workers bring strong feelings into this experience of helping people and that these feelings will influence what they think and do.[5] Feelings will also operate significantly in the worker's use of supervision and in his learning response. The important part played by the worker's feelings and emotional convictions has been suggested repeatedly throughout this discussion.[6] First, in helping people in time of trouble, the public assistance worker encounters them when they are disturbed, sometimes when they are their least rational selves. Insofar as he feels *with* them, which he must do to relate himself to them sympathetically and with understanding, he runs the risk of coming to feel *like* them. It is unfortunate when this occurs, for when we feel the same way about a person's problem as he feels, we cannot help him cope with it. Instead, our emotional response may reinforce his, thus adding to his confusion and ineptitude. Second, the public assistance worker brings an ever varying array of so-called "lay attitudes"—the deep convictions, prejudices, and biases to which every human is heir in his thinking about social problems, human behavior, and the social order, particularly in terms of economic and racial groupings. As he actually encounters certain social problems, he may be deeply moved; as he comes up against behavior that violates his personal standards, he may be shocked or fearful; as he derives knowledge and gains experience, some of his deepest and most cherished convictions may be challenged. Thus, day in and day out, he is subject to considerable emotional wear and tear. Third, he works within the framework of an agency that is accountable to a community of persons who likewise have pronounced convictions and cherished feelings about individuals who apply for public assistance. He is subject to the pressure of these attitudes, often literally subject to them, for they are imbedded in agency policies and in statutory regulations that so govern his activity that he may fearfully withdraw from any critical evaluation of them. In blind frustration, he may fail to use these policies and regulations intelligently or resourcefully, or to work within them productively.[7]

"Lay attitudes" brought into social work

A few of the "lay attitudes" commonly brought into social work that may influence the worker's way of extending help in establishing eligibility as well as his handling of financial assistance have been noted as follows.

A conviction that people do not want to work has prompted workers to mistrust the applicant's statements regarding unemployment and his efforts to find employment. This mistrust is often reflected in the nature of the worker's interpretation of the agency's need for proof of these facts and in his conduct of the investigation. In such instances, workers have been known to take affairs out the applicant's hands—that is, to gather evidence the applicant himself could well submit and to check evidence needlessly. The posssible demoralizing effect of this activity on an applicant seems obvious.

Closely related to this idea is the belief that if one meets dependency freely or economic need adequately, the person will be pauperized. It is a common conviction in this country that adult responsibility will be assumed by the poor only as adverse circumstance forces them into it. If irresponsibility is more prevalent among the poor than other groups, it can well be a product of too much rather than too little harsh circumstance. In work colored by this conviction, we fail to face the fact that adult responsibility is always escapable if one basically needs to escape it, that is, if one has not the strength to assume it. We overlook also the now well-recognized psychological fact that, in the last analysis, those of us who readily assume the responsibilities of adulthood have been enabled to do so largely through a total experience in which our emotional needs have been met freely while our circumstances have been sufficiently advantageous to have given us something to give in relationships with others. Workers who give begrudgingly, that is, fearfully, may undermine rather than strengthen the capacities for personality growth the individual brings to the public assistance experience. Many workers have been reared in sufficiently comfortable economic circumstances so that they have been able to accept unquestioningly the idea cherished by their thrifty parents that a man who is "worthwhile," that is, thrifty, stable, and responsible, will somehow save money for "a rainy day" regardless of the size of his family or the meagerness of his income. This belief may lead them to minimize strengths the applicant brings to his time of economic need and to treat him in general as a much less responsible, ambitious, and self-respecting person than he is.[8]

Prejudiced attitudes on the part of workers are not confined wholly to the need for financial assistance but may be encountered in any and all aspects of life. Only a few can be cited to illustrate how they may dominate our work. Frequently, workers bring the conviction that certain racial or national groups are innately inferior intellectually and morally to other groups. This may lead them to accept unquestioningly a lower standard of living for these people and to withhold needed and desired help with problems other than financial assistance, on the assumption that these problems are inherent and that the individuals concerned would not make productive use of help. Or considering these people inadequate and less well-endowed to assume responsibility, the worker may take over the management of their affairs in ways that constitute an infringement on their rights.

Workers may have strong feelings about certain human relationships, such as a conviction that all mothers should love their children and that it is abnormal or immoral when they do not love them. In such an instance, a worker with these feelings may decide that these parents should be made to assume responsibility for their children. When a mother's desire to work seems to stem from a wish to escape from her children, a worker may make her feel obligated to continue to receive assistance rather than permit her freedom of choice as she weighs the pros and cons of an employment and child-placement plan. Or the worker may express disapproval and condemnation through coercive attitudes in various other ways.[9] On the other hand, workers sometimes have worshipful attitudes toward self-support. Financial independence may be so enthroned in their thinking that they are not responsive to a mother's desire to remain with her children and thus discourage her as she applies for assistance.

Attitudes change with new experience

What of the attitudes that limit the worker's ability to help the recipient in terms of his need and that drive him to meet his own needs rather than the client's? Are these attitudes subject to change and can workers be helped to think and feel differently about people? May they gain some capacity to withhold their own feelings so that the recipient is treated as an individual in his own right rather than as an extension of the worker's self? It is probable that many of these lay attitudes *gradually* will undergo marked change as the worker's experience widens. Gradually they may change also as the worker encounters new ideas and thinking on social problems in his professional relationships with colleagues and supervisors as well as through reading. Reading is productive when it is done with the purpose of learning. It is unfortunate that workers sometimes read out of fear of others who know more; it may not be helpful if it serves primarily as a defense against one's colleagues and one's supervisor who values reading. Insofar as prejudices stem from ignorance, misinformation, and lack of experience or a narrow one-sided experience they will give way as new knowledge is attained and as the worker's range of identifications with people widens. Until we know the poor, the rich, the black, the white, the Jew, the Gentile, the Pole, the Greek, the Norwegian, and so on, we may set any one of these groups apart and react to them in terms of misconceptions based on inadequate knowledge and inexperience.

It should be noted that in most instances lay attitudes and prejudices will give way *gradually* rather than suddenly. Here we encounter the previously described response of resistance to sudden change that operates throughout the learning process. We may see this in the instance of the worker who has been reared to believe that all people can save money if they are sufficiently planful. This idea gradually will be modified in determining need as the worker explores resources of applicants. He may be helped to gain a more realistic view if he is referred to certain studies which show that, below a certain economic level, a family of a given size cannot save while maintaining minimum standards of safety and decency. As he comes to know the so-called "improvident" J family and thus to experience their uncomplaining resourcefulness in coming somewhere near making ends meet on resources which make that goal all but unattainable, he "gets the feel" of strength rather than weakness, of fortitude rather than self-indulgence. The J family become, in his mind, people of parts, responsible and conscientious—not irresponsible—members of the community.

Likewise, in a case when a worker has entered several situations with a pessimistic outlook based on racial prejudice, these attitudes may undergo gradual change as he is inescapably confronted with some of the reality factors that may well serve as a basis for the "group's ineptitude," such as bad housing, discriminatory employment practices, low wages, high rentals, restricted and meager community resources, and the like. Again an attitude of deprecation may change to one of respect for the capacity of these people to manage as well as they do within the rigid limits of their lives. The worker's reorientation to minority groups may be facilitated further through professional association with members of the group, through knowing leaders in the group, and through reading that will give valid information on their history and customs, as well as on the social and economic problems that have been their particular lot.

The worker's attitude will undergo such change in response to enlarged experience and new knowledge provided: (1) The worker does not have a deep need to think in the old ways because the ideas have been satisfying and useful. For example, a basic feeling of inferiority against which he reacts with a need to feel superior. Minority groups are useful to many of us as a way of easing our discomfort over our own ineptitudes and frustrations. (2) The worker's conviction does not derive from a relationship to which he is still closely tied and on which he depends for gratification and safety. For example, a worker who retains a deep dependence on his parents may not be emotionally free to think independently. As they thought, so he must think, because he still needs them too much to endanger the relationship through departures even in thinking. (3) His old thinking has not been the tradition of his *entire social group*. In such an instance, change may come more slowly because it involves many relationships and his total life situation. (4) The new orientation does not come from an individual or an authority the worker mistrusts or toward whom he feels deeply hostile or resentful. It is important to note here that, conversely, new concepts may be quickly influential when they are imparted in a relationship in which the worker feels secure because he feels respected and adequate in the eyes of the supervisor and the agency.

In supervision, which is essentially a teaching-learning situation—that is, an educative process—*we rely heavily on the principle that a new intellectual orientation may influence feeling and hence action.*[10] Conditions are especially favorable for this outcome when the intellectual orientation is largely gained through or accompanied by experience that affords opportunity for the immediate demonstration and use of the ideas. For this reason, *the teaching aspects of supervision within a social agency afford a challenging opportunity for the realization of educational aims.* When the worker is unable to utilize experience and knowledge because of some of the emotional involvements described, he may be uneducable in areas of prejudice insofar as his performance on the job is concerned. His need for self-understanding, for help in working through old conflicts, and for help in emancipating himself from old entangling relationships may constitute a problem that is beyond the scope of an agency supervisor. If the worker has many prejudices that remain intact in spite of new experience and exposure to new thinking within a helpful supervisory relationship, he will be limited in capacity for development as a professional person, and one can well question his ability to offer a constructive helping relationship to people in need.

In supervision there is a content of knowledge and skills to be imparted, the assimilation of which will depend in large measure on certain conditions that facilitate rather than obstruct learning. What are some of these conditions?

The new worker has a dual anxiety

As a worker enters a new field of professional endeavor, the most basic impulse, the impulse to survive, is in operation in modified form. *Here we do not have a struggle to come through alive, but we do have a struggle for life on satisfying terms.* Workers and students new to the field of social work commonly express a dual desire and, since our desires beget anxieties, a dual fear.

1. The desire to serve people competently, to help them rather than to harm them. On the positive side, this desire stems from the worker's concern and liking for people and his capacity to live beyond narrow absorption in self. From the negative standpoint, it may be motivated by a fear of hurting or failing people that derives from personal experience in having been hurt or having failed in some of his own relationships. Or this fear of not doing the right thing for people may stem from a repressed impulse to hurt them or let them down. This negative motivation has been recognized and its implications for professional education have rightly been given great emphasis. It is important, however, when confronted with the educational problems created by anxiety and aggressive interest in helping people, that we not overlook the positive motivation. Among individuals who choose work that involves helping people, positive motivation occurs frequently and in many instances may predominate over the negative motivation.

2. The desire to perform his work competently for his own satisfaction. This desire likewise stems from a combination of needs: the need to feel secure, safe in competition with others in that area of life in which his livelihood is at stake; the need to fulfill his ideal of himself as an adequate person. Through self-respect he feels secure in commanding the respect of others and more confident of gaining status in the group. These desires commonly are expressed in terms of fear and uncertainty: "I am afraid I have done the wrong thing in advising Mr. X." "I am worried that I am not contributing to the welfare of my clients in this or that respect." "I am afraid I am not making good." This fear may be expressed in anxious comparisons with others as to productivity, size of case load, promptness, and so on. It may be expressed also in a compelling quest for praise or criticism, or in avoidance of evaluation.

In relation to these desires and fears the supervisor becomes an important person. He is the measuring stick who measures the worker's competence and against whom he measures himself. The supervisor has other values also that will be mentioned shortly. *Normally we encounter these anxieties in workers new to the agency or to the field.* Since fear of the unkown normally creates feelings of helplessness, dependency responses of varying degrees will be a common manifestation in new workers.[11]

Learning eases fears

How may these fears be eased? *They are eased primarily through learning about the strange situation so that it is no longer strange and through learning to cope with it, that is, to carry out the agency's function within the framework of its statutory regulations, its policies, and its procedures.* In recent years much has been said about the anxieties workers bring into this learning experience and about the importance of our understanding and knowing how to help them with these anxieties. Some of us may have grown a bit anxious about workers' anxieties and feel that their resistance to learning will be insurmountable or at least beyond our ability to deal with in the agency. One supervisor expressed his fear of the responsibility involved in this, *to him,* new area of activity in words to the effect that if workers "really do" get "so upset" over a new experience and over learning new things, it would seem that every supervisor should be a psychiatrist. Perhaps it will be reassuring to bear in mind the following factors:

1. Every worker has throughout life experienced new situations. He knows, even though the knowledge may not be conscious, that the feelings of helplessness and anxiety will subside in due time. Throughout life, the impulse to learn—that is, the impulse to gain self-sufficiency in order to feel safe—has served him in some measure; therefore, in this situation he will reach out almost automatically to relieve his own tension through efforts to learn.[12] *At the start, therefore, when first we encounter new workers, they, with exceptions, will have a natural bent toward learning.*[13] Likewise, all workers have experienced the disturbed feelings that accompany new knowledge. More than once they have resisted change and repeatedly, in the long run, they have accepted it in some measure. They have, therefore, built up a certain foreknowledge of the discomfort involved and its transitoriness, together with a certain stamina for bearing that "pain" as well as ways of dealing with their own discomfort. Furthermore, some of them have been conditioned positively to the pleasures of learning. The very process may have in it the thrill of an adventure in which, though foreknowledge, they ease the momentary pain through anticipation of pleasure. *Therefore, unless conditions for learning are adverse, or sometimes even in spite of unfavorable conditions, workers will learn out of their own need for learning.*

2. Supervisors, in their efforts to teach and to help workers learn, have long been dealing with these emotional responses. Sometimes our efforts have been helpful and sometimes, because we have not understood the import of these responses, they have not. With awareness of the emotional response factor in learning, we will continue to use many of the same teaching and supervisory devices, but we may come to use them differently. We may now place greater emphasis on some than on others. We may discard some of them because they obstruct, rather than facilitate, learning. This knowledge, however, will not demand a total change in our professional activity.

Supervisory measures can aid learning

Out of past experience, workers will bring varying patterns of response into the present learning experience, patterns supervisors can learn to recognize and deal with differentially.[14] This discussion can present only some supervisory measures and educational principles that commonly are helpful and that, in general, may tend to facilitate the learning process for many workers. As we watch differences in the responses of workers to these measures, we may learn something of individual learning patterns and of ways of individualizing our supervision appropriately.

Carefully planned orientation periods are important

It is general practice in public assistance agencies to give careful consideration to the orientation period of staff.[15] This concern about the initial phase of the worker's learning experience is in accord with sound educational principles. It has long been realized that the first steps in a learning process may set a pattern and determine the subsequent response in the continuous educational process it is hoped the agency experience will be for every worker. Immediate attempts to orient the worker for adequate performance utilize the compelling need to learn that workers tend to have in the initial stages when they are feeling anxious and somewhat helpless; neglect to provide well-selected introductory content for workers new to the agency repeatedly has put workers in the position of groping aimlessly to find what they need to know; needless errors of omission and commission then destine them to learning the hard way and may increase their discouragement. Since this result prolongs the period of helplessness and increases anxiety, not only over not knowing "what and how" but also through needless errors in practice, it frequently has intensified the worker's dependency. Accordingly, the worker may be driven into greater dependency on his supervisor than would otherwise occur. The failure of the agency staff voluntarily to give him essential knowledge at the start is sometimes interpreted by workers to mean that they are expected to know more than they do. This may make them fearful of supervision and drive them to seek knowledge from their co-workers. The relationship with the supervisor may thereby become confused and the natural lines of agency organization entangled.

Inadequate orientation may lessen creativity

In general, postponement of adequate orientation tends to delay productive effort, produce confusion, and encourage undue absorption in routine activity rather than stimulating creative effort. Why the absorption in routine activity? We refer to a previously described behavior adaptation.[16] When the individual is insecure, when he is unable to master his environment, when he is not equipped to meet the changing demands of a situation, he falls back on automatic behavior as a source of security. Therefore, as the individual gains basic security in a work situation, he will have less dependence on habitual ways and should be more flexible in meeting the varying aspects of the complex total of his job.

Routines, regulations, and fixed procedures constitute the medium for automatic behavior in the social agency setting. It has been observed repeatedly in many agencies that workers, not only in the period of orientation but also subsequently, may revert to absorption in agency mechanics when the pressures of their work are too great or when the demands of the job carry them beyond their depth. Perhaps some of us have known the supervisor or administrator who likewise, when he is insecure in his leadership or has little to bring to his staff in knowledge and certain professional skills, becomes anxiously engaged in drafting and redrafting forms, procedures, and regulations and in checking up on his staff in relation to them. In this way we falsely reassure ourselves that we are able to function or we avoid meeting more threatening responsibilities through an escape into activity that, when carried far enough, can become purposeless.

In discussing dependence on agency mechanics from this standpoint, it is not meant to discount the importance of careful adherence to agency routines and procedures. Their purpose is to make our work go smoothly and efficiently. Knowing them well, so well that we are able to use them almost unconsciously, should free us to focus on the people we are serving and to give intelligent consideration to their needs in relation to the agency's and the community's resources. *We may become enslaved by agency mechanics when we do not know them well and understand their purpose or when we need to use them as a defense against other activity.* It is generally agreed by experienced administrators that failure to give new workers an adequate orientation to the work of the agency at the start may set the pattern for absorption in routine activity as an end in itself and thus block creative effort.

Guiding principles for orientation content

Detailed statements of essential content and effective methods to be used in orientation have been presented elsewhere and will not be repeated here.[17] Rather, in the light of our understanding of the needs and ways of responding that workers commonly bring to this educational experience, an attempt will be made to present a few principles to serve as a guide in the use of orientation content. Study of various carefully prepared programs that cover the work of public assistance agencies thoroughly shows that content may be grouped as follows:

1. *Insight into the broad purpose of the agency's work.* This includes some understanding of the historical background of the agency and its relation to

other government units and services. It includes also an attempt to convey the principles and philosophy underlying the administration of public assistance.

2. *Understanding staff functions and relationships.* Here content commonly includes (a) familiarity with the legal basis and administrative structure, including source of funds, policies, rules, regulations, and procedures of the agency as a whole, as well as the respective functions of the several divisions, (b) definition of the worker's own responsibilities and precise information about what is expected of him in relation to responsibilities of other staff members, (c) understanding of his relationship with the supervisor and resources for staff development, (d) acquaintance with personnel policies, including interpretations of the purpose of the merit system and its significance for him, and information on service ratings as they relate to the continuing supervision given the worker.

3. *Understanding the services rendered individual applicants.* Here content includes (a) precise information on the specific services offered and the conditions under which applicants are eligible, (b) precise information on the facts required in establishing eligibility, (c) efforts to ensure understanding of agency policies on determining need, (d) information on agency and community resources available for the use of applicants and recipients, and (e) discussion of professional ethics—for example, the confidential nature of information given by the applicant, political prohibitions, and so on.

Before commenting on this comprehensive content, it might be well to restate the purpose of the orientation program. The broad purpose is to enable workers as quickly as possible to administer effectively the agency's service to applicants and recipients. Such administration postulates resourceful use of the agency's policies and procedures. It is hoped that content of the orientation programs and the method of presentation will be such as to use to the utmost that natural bent for learning workers commonly bring to a new work experience and that as an introduction to learning the programs will set in operation a positive response to a continuing educational process. This hope, in turn, entails choice of content and use of methods that tend to ease, rather than promote, anxiety and resistance.

Insofar as orientation programs defeat this purpose, the failure may be owing to two weaknesses commonly observed: (1) They may attempt to cover too much in too great detail, thus confusing the worker by overwhelming him with a sense of the great complexity of the program. (2) They have sometimes been regarded as an entity. Once the program is ended, it is assumed that the worker is now trained and should know for all time the content it has conveyed. Actually, this content will be only gradually assimilated as it is put to use. It will need to be recapitulated and worked on repeatedly in group and individual conferences with the supervisor as the worker struggles to apply it in practice, case by case.[18]

Purpose of content areas

The general purpose of orientation programs has been stated. It would seem that each of the three areas of content given has a specific purpose in this educational process. It would seem also, at this introductory stage, that some contents might have greater importance than others. In helping students to assimilate knowledge quickly *there must always be a dominant emphasis*.[19] Orientation programs may have a disorienting effect when workers are introduced to a great mass of material all of which seemingly is equally emphatic or unemphatic. They may be left at sea and, furthermore, there will be a dulling of interest. There can be no real learning without interest. Interest is absolutely essential for attention and comprehension. It is essential, then, to decide what shall be emphasized, and this involves consideration of the purposes of specific contents.

Understanding the whole incites eagerness to explore the parts

The first content area is "insight into the broad purpose of the agency's work." Aside from giving certain information the worker should have, what other educational purpose may this content serve? Here the worker is given an idea of the whole. Always, in envisaging the whole, we have an opportunity to stimulate interest, to capture the imagination, to enlist eagerness for the adventure of exploring its parts. Sometimes we fail to use this opportunity in this way because we attempt an exhaustive, detailed, unfocused recital of everything. For example, we all know that the historical background of an agency can be a sterile narrative of its dead past or it can be a stirring account that stimulates imaginative consideration of its present program and future objectives. When historical information is presented dynamically, it is more than a series of events. Events are related to major social trends and to the changing purposes of the program as brought about by a changing point of view on the importance of the individual. Workers then get a sense of onward movement in which they are to participate. The past is important insofar as it has significance in the present and import for the future. It is this significance that must come alive for them if historical information is to serve our educational aim. Likewise, the specific content on the principles and philosophy underlying the administration of public assistance can be a stereotyped recital of platitudes that leaves the listener apathetic. On the other hand, this area of content can be conveyed in such a way as to strengthen the worker's creative impulse to make those principles and that philosophy real.

Administrators and supervisors who help workers envisage the import of the Social Security Act and public assistance programs in the evolution of man's social conscience and their significance for democracy stimulate identification with and participation in the administration of the agency's function. It is through this first area of content that we have the opportunity to impart the ideals of our program. Ideals can be empty words on high, or they can become meaningful and close at hand, an ever ready opponent to aimless toil and frustration. It has been said, "When ideals have sunk to the level of practice, the result is stagnation."[20] We all grow less weary when we can see the larger meaning of the daily grind and when we can consciously exert effort toward well-defined goals. Because our ideals at any given time always will be beyond practice, workers may need help in relating their practice to them. As this help is given, the frustration common to the beginner may be allayed in some measure.

In summary, it may be said that it is through this area of content, which attempts to impart insight into the broad purpose of the agency's work, that we have an opportunity to stimulate the interest that is essential for attention and comprehension. This content may enable us to engage at the start that natural inclination toward learning workers commonly bring to a new work situation. Thus their fears of the unknown may subside more quickly. Through this area of content we may affirm also the adult inclination for creative activity that has been described as an individual's impulse to give and live beyond himself. The mature strivings of the worker may operate more fully when he is not blindly absorbed in a struggle for self-survival in his own specific job. When he is not walled in but instead can see and feel his part in relation to the whole, growth through the educational process may be facilitated.

Understanding staff functions helps the worker to be a part of the program

The second area of content, sometimes termed "understanding staff functions and relationships," continues the worker's orientation to the agency as a whole. In addition, it offers him the opportunity to see and feel in a more personal way the relationship of his own function to that of other workers, as well as the relationship of his particular service to the total program. Here he must come to grips with his own dependency needs and responses as well as with his feelings in relation to authority. This area involves relating what he learns of the content of his own job to what he learns about the agency as a whole. In a sense, it represents an outgrowth of the fusion of the content in the third area, "understanding the services rendered individual applicants," with that of the first area, "insight into the broad purpose of the agency's work."

Briefly, in this area he is exposed to the agency's complexity, which is not only a complexity of a routine but also one of human relationships. At the introductory stage it is possible only to impart a certain limited understanding of this area of content. Much of it must be gained bit by bit as the worker experiences the agency. Insofar as the limited understanding is imparted in ways that are helpful, the learning experience can be greatly facilitated at the start. It is in this area that frequently we have erred in giving too detailed a picture of the administrative structure, policies, rules, regulations, and procedures as a whole, as well as of the respective functions of the several divisions. A worker new to a complex agency has a vague awareness that all these elements surround him. Some of his initial fear stems from the fact that he does not know in what ways other divisions and a whole network of policies, procedures, rules, and regulations are going to involve him. Do they concern him at every point or only at certain points in his immediate tasks? This is the anxious inquiry uppermost in his mind. It is well that he be given a general idea of other divisions within the agency and more explicit information only about those functions that will be of immediate concern to him in his own work.

The same might be said of policies, procedures, rules, and regulations that by their very names and nature tend to arouse anxiety and resistance. Early in life many individuals have built up a resistance to learning because it has been tied in with obedience to the dictates of parents.[21] Educators have become familiar with the problems presented through the fact that learning patterns have been established on the basis that to learn is to obey—that is, to submit—instead of on the basis that to learn is to gain greater powers within oneself—that is, to attain freedom. When the former pattern has been established, learning is motivated more largely through fear of not knowing—that is, of suffering consequences—than through assurance of the values of knowing— that is, advantages to be gained.

It is probable that adults commonly bring these motives simultaneously into a learning experience. Their response is facilitated when the positive, rather than the negative, impulses are affirmed. A body of knowledge that is comprised of rules, regulations, and procedures is peculiarly constituted to awaken any vestiges of negative conditioning to learning that are present. It is therefore important that workers find this knowledge immediately useful, that they have the opportunity to experience its advantages to them in their work, and that they receive immediate explicit information on the contents they must have in order to function. Detailed discussion of contents that will not be of immediate use should be avoided. The worker may then find security in the protection afforded by a framework of well-defined policies, procedures, and regulations that not only guide him in his work but also limit the demands placed on him for highly individualized judgments and decisions.

In conclusion, it might be said that at the introductory stage this whole area of content should for the most part be general. It should be detailed in the portions the worker will need to know in order to begin activity. There should be explicit information as to the presence of two resources within the agency: (1) material such as manuals and statements of policy and procedure to which he may turn independently for guidance, and (2) staff to whom he may turn for help in understanding and using the agency as a whole. To this end definite arrangements for supervision and some clarification of his relationship with the supervisor are necessary. Emphasis on the importance of his use of these resources may in itself be reassuring, for we thereby imply that we do not expect him to know everything at the start. We also make clear that he has a responsibility *to find out* and *to seek help.* Thus we convey acceptance of his need for help, while charging him with responsibility for his own development.

Understanding services promotes worker's self-dependence

The third area of content, "understanding the services rendered individual applicants," should be greatly emphasized in the introductory stage. This material constitutes the content of the worker's own job. The first area of content should have served to incite his interest and to fire imaginative consideration of the total program in which he is to play an important part. It is to be hoped that the second area, in giving him a background of the workings of the agency, has served to give him some security, through establishing his identity with the agency and through putting him into relationship with those who will share his responsibility. This third area is the one of *primary* concern to him *at the start,* and unless he moves quickly into gaining some competence here, the inspiration and the sense of belonging to the agency afforded through the other orientations will not be maintained. He must gain some self-dependence before he can enter fully and freely into the interdependent relationships that the agency comprises. In the area of his own responsibility he will need precise knowledge, given at as rapid a tempo as effective service to applicants demands and as fast as he can assimilate it. Frequently there is a discrepancy here. He cannot take it in as rapidly as he should in order to give competent service. When this occurs, a sense of failure may impede progress. It is important, therefore, that administrative and supervisory staffs decide what the worker needs to know first and that there be a definite focus on these areas. A helpful supervisor is one who has formulated quite clearly in his own mind what the worker has to know in precise fashion. He conveys this knowledge to the worker or directs him to it. He places emphasis on the quick use of it, knowing that if the worker uses it, it will take on meaning and be retained.

What portions of the total content of this area should come first? We utilize the worker's initial anxious eagerness to survive in his work on satisfying terms when we help him achieve a sense of competence in doing some aspect of the work. Best taught at once are the routine parts of the job that are standardized and laid down by authority. At this point the worker is naturally and normally more dependent on the supervisor than he will be later, and therefore the things he can and should be told to do, the performance of which will give him a feeling of safety in the group, are appropriate contents.

If he can master procedures at an early point, he will be free to give his attention and creative capacities to more indefinite skills at a later time, when he is more ready to assume responsibility and to work differentially.

This immediate mastery of routines has the advantage of giving the worker mechanical facility in handling his job. He thus attains a sense of competence. Furthermore, the fact that he is leaning on established procedures (dictates) meets his initial dependency needs, which eases anxiety. Anxiety is eased also through the limits set on his responsibility. As dependency is thus freely met, so that he feels secure, he should gain freedom to enter into those parts of his work that permit more independent thinking and that call for judgment and initiative. Here it is important to recall a previously stated concept: the advantage of automatic behavior is that it is effortless; its disadvantage is that it is adapted to definite situations and is not easily modified when changed conditions or new sets of circumstances require it. As the individual masters his environment, as he gains experience to function on his own both physically and psychologically, automatic behavior plays a less important role and he meets changing circumstances more readily.[22] It has been the observation of experienced supervisors that he will spontaneously move in this direction provided: (1) He does not bring a deep dependency to his work, so that he finds this stage of learning so gratifying that he tends to cling to it. (2) The lack of too great pressure of work in the agency makes possible something other than mechanical activity. The development of some public assistance workers has been arrested at this stage of energy-saving automatic performance of routine. Heavy case loads and a hectic pressure doubtless have been important factors, but frequently they have not been the sole reason for this fixation at a rudimentary level of performance. (3) The supervisor has not been wholly absorbed in the worker's mechanical performance so that he has been able to give some content to supervision other than checking on routines.

Other content to be imparted

In public assistance programs that have emphasized workers' use of the agency positively, flexibly, and resourcefully in the light of varying needs of individuals from the initial service of helping the applicant establish eligibility to other casework services, there is other knowledge content to be imparted *gradually* but in some measure from the very start. This content includes directing the worker to consider the individual's needs and the significance of some of his responses both to the agency service and to his life circumstances. Such content we have attempted to present in the preceding chapters. This material can best be used as a springboard to further learning, and for this reason footnotes have been given.[23]

Service must be individualized

In general, it might be said that as the worker gains facility in administering agency services through careful adherence to policies and procedures, gradually he may be directed to consider what the individual needs beyond financial assistance and what factors and forces in the client's life have created his economic and other needs. What does his way of managing his affairs up to now tell us about him? What does his use of our help tell us about him? In the light of his needs and response, how may we best help him within the framework of our agency and through utilizing community resources? How, in a framework of routines, may we individualize our service? How may we use and conserve the strengths the person brings into this experience? At an early point, we must help the worker begin to see, feel, and think of the individual as a human being, rather than as a depersonalized applicant or recipient inserting his evidence of eligibility as a coin in a kind of automat. This individualization will occur as the worker gains experience with many people and as his natural responses to their problems and troubles are brought into individual conferences with the supervisor and into group case conferences.

Self-knowledge content should not loom large

There has been considerable reference throughout this material to the part the worker plays in determining the applicant's response. The worker can be helped to attain some self-understanding as there is exploration of the applicant's attitudes toward help, the worker's ways of rendering services, and the applicant's use of help. Because workers new to an agency and new to this field of work frequently are self-conscious at the start, direct focus on this important factor should be timed to the worker's readiness for scrutiny of his own prejudices, needs, and responses. In general, we wait until he has gained some sense of belonging within the agency and has attained at least superficial competence in helping people. The supervisor is guided also by the nature of his relationship with the worker. In general, content bearing on self-knowledge should not loom large in the introductory stage of learning.[24]

Three basic principles

Throughout the orientation period, as in subsequent days and in relation to content of all kinds, supervisors are guided by three basic principles that educators long have recognized:[25] (1) Begin where the learner is. This admonition implies knowing the worker, which involves finding out something of what he knows and what he does not know in relation to his work. In an agency situation this principle must be qualified to some extent: Begin *insofar as possible* where the worker is. The demands of the job sometimes make it necessary to advance information and to exert guidance that in another situation might await his greater readiness. This reality creates a need for help from the supervisor, a point that will be discussed shortly. (2) Use whatever past experience the individual brings to the situation as a foundation for more learning. New content that can be related to past experience enables the worker to feel more competent and to be in many instances less fearful and less resistive. (3) Convey new learning as it can be assimilated. This implies imparting knowledge at points when it can be used immediately in case situations. Almost inevitably there will be some lag between intellectual grasp of subject matter and ability to use it. Time and additional experience may take care of this descrepancy, but sometimes here again there is need for special help focused on the worker's learning problem.

Guiding principles in the helping aspect of supervision

Supervisors have a dual function—teaching certain contents of knowledge and skill and helping workers to learn.[26] This helping relationship may facilitate or obstruct the learning process, depending on its nature. It is generally recognized as one of the important elements in staff development. Brief consideration will therefore be given to some general principles that may serve as guides in the helping aspects of the supervisory function.[27]

Worker's normal dependency will subside

With reference to the worker's "natural dependency" when he first enters an agency—a dependency that stems from lack of knowledge, insecurity in a strange situation, and the anxiety provoked by the change involved in learning—the supervisor can give freely. This is a normal dependency that will subside in large measure as the worker gains knowledge and becomes secure in the agency and insofar as his resistance to and fear of new ideas are understood. The supervisor *gives* in varied ways—information, knowledge, and direction to other sources of knowledge and information. He also shares his experience and conveys understanding of the worker's prejudices and the ideas he brings to the situation. The supervisor can understand even through differing in thinking and feeling from the worker. Sometimes supervisors have feared that if they give freely they will make workers dependent. In this connection it is well to recall two concepts:

1. The impulse to learn is strong; it survives against much discouragement. Why does it persist? Probably because in the last analysis there is no real security, no deep assurance of survival, in being wholly dependent on others. In the interest of survival, the individual reaches out to learn in order to become self-sufficient. In the interest of survival, he struggles against dependency.

2. When an individual's impulses toward independence are strong a
patterns of self-dependence are will-entrenched, the resistance to becoming
wholly dependent is also strong. In such an instance, it is as difficult to induce
comfortable dependency as it is to stumulate self-responsibility in a chronically
dependent individual.

Reasons for continuing or increased dependency

We therefore may assume that if the worker's natural and inevitable
dependency in a learning situation is met freely, he will move spontaneously
toward independence as he gains knowledge and skills that enable him to be
self-dependent. It is indicated that help is given freely when, for example, the
demands of the job are excessive in relation to the worker's experience. It is
likewise indicated that helpful suggestions on applying theory in practice are
conveyed when there is a lag between grasp of theory and ability to utilize
it. It is reasonable to assume that, by and large, the majority of young adults
who enter this field have a normal development in terms of readiness for growth
toward greater self-sufficiency. One would, therefore, assume that if the worker
uses the supervisor's freely given help in a regressive way, that is, continues
to be dependent or to grow increasingly dependent, his response may be owing to one or more of several factors:

1. A deep and well-entrenched dependency need that finds gratification
in leaning on the supervisor and in submitting to authority—the authority
of ideas or the authority implied in the supervisor's direction of his work and
check on his production.

2. A worker who has marked anxiety about, and resistance to, his own
normal dependency needs may develop so much hostility toward a supervisor
who gives freely that he is unable to emancipate himself from that very
dependence which he fears and hates. This curious reaction has baffled many
supervisors. We have come to understand that it is an exaggeration or distor-
tion of a potentially constructive impulse. While all individuals in the interests
of survival react against remaining dependent, some who have not built up
enough self-sufficiency continue to need to be quite dependent. Frustrated by
their inability to be self-dependent, they become enraged. The rage, particularly
when directed toward those whom they need and to whom they are obligated,
arouses guilt and fear. These feelings operate against their becoming independent for several reasons. Out of anxiety, they feel all the more helpless and
must cling to the supervisor for support. Out of their anger, they fear emancipation because the wish for it expresses their rejection of the supervisor and
they dare not enact their rejection for fear of retaliative treatment. In the life
of adult, some of the most tenacious dependency ties we encounter stem from
these feelings of fear and hostility. Experienced supervisors long have noted
that workers who have a marked authority-dependency problem tend to remain

in the introductory stage of learning. These workers require special help, sometimes of a kind beyond the scope of their supervisors.[28]

3. The supervisor's gratification in a worker's dependency is sometimes a factor operating against the worker's development. This gratification may have led the supervisor to impose help, to be authoritative, and to show approval of a worker's submissive response. Supervisors sometimes strive for self-realization through workers who in turn become dependent in their effort to get along with their supervisors or to meet their supervisors' needs.

One of the chief aims of the educational effort is to help workers become increasingly self-dependent. As has been brought out, meeting natural dependency needs promptly and freely is one measure for doing this. While meeting initial dependency—and increasingly as the worker shows readiness for it—supervisors may affirm the strengths and the adult impulses to carry responsibility that the worker brings to the situation. In social agencies a teaching situation exists that is for the most part favorable to this, in that it affords opportunity for "learning by doing" and in that the very nature of our work calls both for the assumption of responsibility and for living beyond narrow absorption in self. Our work calls forth concern for the welfare of others and makes continuous use of our impulses to give to and to serve others. Its almost boundless appeal constitutes a problem that it is well to recognize. When demands for assumption of responsibility and for giving beyond self, in terms of meeting the needs of others, exceed the worker's capacities, temporary regression to dependency may occur. It is important that we be continuously aware of the need to help workers maintain the strengths they bring to this experience as well as to help them attain further growth. In this connection, we must work *with* the individual in such a way as both to use what he has to give and to avoid undermining his sense of adequacy.

Start where the worker is

It is important to start where the worker is. This involves eliciting his ideas and using them whenever possible. It involves helping him to relate the present experience to his past experience so that he may get a sense of having something to use and to give, rather than a feeling that he can only be a recipient of what the supervisor has to offer. All this entails mutual discussion of the work to be done rather than wholly telling and instructing. It contraindicates also giving undue prominence to one's "check-up" function. If we are not to undermine the worker's adequacy, it is important that we respond to lay attitudes, prejudices, and erroneous ideas in such a way that he does not feel ridiculed, condemned, or unacceptable as a person. We can show interest in and understanding of what he thinks and feels, then lead him to consider his standpoint in relation to what the applicant needs, thinks, and feels. Insofar as the worker, in spite of the supervisor's difference in point of view, has felt understood by him, he may move more readily into understanding others who see and feel differently.

Worker's participation in evaluation is important

Mutual discussion of the work to be done should be extended also into evaluation of the worker's activity. In evaluation, the worker's participation is highly important. A co-operative discussion in which the worker can take stock of his work with respect to both strengths and progress and weaknesses and difficulties will help him become less dependent on others both for approval and disapproval. Many workers find it hard to acknowledge their own good points. Perhaps this difficulty derives from the social custom in which many of us have been reared, to conceal our powers and triumphs modestly. Perhaps because we have had to do this, we have become more protective of our weak points. Certainly it has been noted that as workers feel free to evaluate themselves positively, they are less defensive about the negative aspects of their work.

Supervisors help workers become free to criticize themselves when they are as interested in discovering and in acknowledging what the workers do well as in finding the flaws and commenting on sins of omission and commission. A traditional weakness of administrators and supervisors has been this tendency to take for granted or to pass unnoticed the worker's production other than in areas of failure. In giving the worker an opportunity to become self-critical, we are helping him become more self-sufficient. In sharing evaluation with him from the start, we help him maintain his adequacy, for it is less humiliating to criticize oneself than to be criticized. Insofar as the supervisor can make the evaluation mutual—that is, help the worker bring out his criticism of supervision—and can, without reserve or humiliation, acknowledge limitations, oversights, and errors, he has the opportunity to realize that criticism and humiliation need not go hand in hand. Evaluations so conducted become mutual learning experiences and in time reassure rather than threaten both worker and supervisor.[29]

Direct the worker to other sources of information

In helping workers to become increasingly self-dependent, supervisors have come to know that it is important that they not be the sole medium through which the worker learns. Accordingly, from the start a supervisor can well direct a worker to other sources of information and knowledge. We can place on him the responsibility of using office manuals, of being informed on policies and procedures through careful study of them. At certain points this will mean withholding information that we could give quickly while he less quickly explores and digs for himself. Group conferences in which cases are discussed, common problems are thought through, or the application of policies and procedures is considered constitute a measure that, among many other values, will help the worker find his place in the group and thus make the supervisory relationship less self-centered. We can encourage workers to use available resources for staff development at appropriate points. We can direct the worker to appropriate readings as an additional way in which he can learn through his own efforts. These suggestions will be most productive when given in response to questions raised, at times when the worker is reaching out for enlightenment on particular problems with which he is confronted.

The client is the primary source of learning

Finally, we need to help the worker focus on his clients as the primary source from which he will be learning throughout his activity in the field of social work. Supervisors can stimulate intellectual curiosity, help him attain a questioning attitude, convey certain knowledge and skills that may make him a more intelligent observer and give greater significance to what he sees. During a learning period we may afford him the security he needs as a facilitating factor in the educational process and, insofar as we give constructive help as well as teach, we may contribute to his personality growth in such a way as to enable him to work more effectively and thereby to learn more productively.[30] We must avoid the danger, however, of standing between the worker and the client as the primary fount of learning. This implies a continual direction of the worker's thinking toward an analytic consideration of what case developments are telling him. Insofar as supervisors look to the client's response for orientation to the worker's activity and the import of administrative practices, workers will tend to do likewise.

Resistance to change must be lowered

The individual's common tendency to resist change has great significance in the learning process throughout life, and the educational situation in which we attempt to teach workers is no exception. Workers often are confronted and suddenly overtaken by new customs, new ideas, new demands, new situations that call for new ways of thinking and acting. Many elements in such changes are commonly decried and struggled against. Some of the anxiety and some of the resistance directed toward our helping efforts may, therefore, stem from the element of change in the worker's life, and may not mean that he literally does not want or gradually may not be able to use the supervisory help he momentarily rejects, protests, or to which he submits protectively without full participation. Since growth occurs through change, however, marked and prolonged resistances to change will interfere with growth. We facilitate the learning process and promote more effective agency service as we are able to understand the individual's resistance and to know some ways whereby it may be lowered and its time span shortened. In public assistance agencies, one area in which this common reaction to change stands forth in bold relief is in staff responses to changing policies and procedures. One discussion of this subject describes clearly typical responses to new policies suddenly imposed. It describes also some ways of helping staff members take over and use the policies constructively rather than destructively.[31] Any new concept the adoption of which would reregulate one's activity may be responded to in similar ways and may call for the use of educational principles stated or implied in the aforementioned discussion. These responses are summarized, and at points elaborated, as follows:

1. Asking questions about a new idea is one way in which the worker will find out whether it is useful or acceptable. What does it mean? Here is a case situation—these are the facts—how could you appply *this idea* to it? What would be the result? Is this idea generally applicable? Could I use it in the same way in the X case as in the A case? Inquiries may be accompanied by protests, expressed or unexpressed. If this idea is valid...but it cannot be valid. If it is, then I have *always* been wrong. Others from whom I derived it have been wrong—that cannot be. But perhaps *they* are right and *we* have been wrong. And so the mental struggle proceeds as the individual wavers from doubt of the idea to self-doubt and doubt of others to tentative and experimental trial. In this process he tries to recall the usefulness of his old thinking as proof of its validity, while at the same time he may be reaching out to test the new thinking in the present work experience. He will be convinced only if it works well for him.

2. In the midst of this struggle he may at some point plunge into *too great* dependence on the new idea. He uses it blindly, unquestioningly, routinely, and without discrimination. He may prove it wrong through unconscious misuse, and this can be an effective way to resist it. He can then justify his rejection of it. "I tried it out thoroughly and it did not work" would be his argument. If the individual brings to the new content certain convictions for which he is seeking support in the ideas themselves, he may unconsciously use them to serve his own ends.

Another way of denying an unacceptable new idea is to place the responsibility for it wholly on others. "Supervisors think this or social workers in general think that; therefore, even though I do not agree with the thinking, I must use it if I am a worker here." In such an instance the idea will be used without conviction, and if the worker must interpret this idea to others, his interpretations will be colored by his lack of conviction. If, for example, the worker does not actually believe that the applicant has a right to public assistance, his ways of helping the applicant establish eligibility will reflect this disbelief.[32]

In relation to these responses, several educational measures and principles have been useful:

1. The supervisor's response to a worker who is in a questioning phase about much that is new to him is of decisive importance. We can make a worker feel stupid and inadequate as he questions, or we can convey respect for his intelligence. It is important that he be given the feeling that we regard all ideas and methods new to him as being open to his questioning. This may be difficult to do in relation to contents of knowledge and ideas now old to us and obvious in their import from our standpoint of wide experience in their use. If we can see questioning as a healthy response, signifying the worker's interest and curiosity as his first step toward taking on what he needs to know, then we will be gratified to have questions emerge, rather that wearied at the thought of considering them with him. There is much repetition in teaching, repetition from worker to worker, and it is only as we are inspired by appreciation of the movement that is occurring that we do not grow impatient. In general, we try to avoid closing up or blocking the tendency to question. Instead, we show interest in and understanding of his questions. Often we can grant him that some ideas are difficult to accept—they have baffled and confused many of us. We can avoid too much pressure to win his consent by acknowledging with him that he may or may not find some of the thinking here acceptable. We can direct him toward trying out our thinking, still with the idea that he can thereby prove or disprove it. We can sometimes offer him the reassurance that his doubts are valid and can be dissipated only through trial.

2. It is important that workers have opportunity to discuss controversial issues freely, both in individual conferences with the supervisor and in discussion groups. Of workers' activity in discussing a proposed policy it has been said, "The harder it is hauled around, the tougher the use, the better."[33] The same might be said, for example, of a concept regarding human behavior that a worker finds disturbing. The more he challenges it, repudiates it, or even ridicules it, the more he may come to accept it in the long run. The principle here is that we offer an opportunity for discharge of feeling. When disturbed feelings are expressed, the individual may be free of their pressure and better able to give rational consideration to ideas, methods, and policies. For the present, the worker must accept existing policies and work with them, a demand he will be likely to meet resourcefully, rather than submissively, insofar as he is given a right to be heard and has every opportunity to contribute his ideas for the betterment of the program.

3. It is important that supervisors help workers see the significance of new procedures, new policies, new ideas, new contents of knowledge, in their work. He should be helped to evaluate their purpose. When a worker envisages experiences and evaluates the usefulness of new thinking and new ways of

doing, he becomes aware of the extension of his powers. Fear of the new because it is strange and makes him feel helpless tends to disappear when this occurs.

4. Insofar as supervisors have been able to accept workers' questioning responses without irritation or a defensive attitude, insofar as they have been able to permit free discussion and to give workers help in seeing the import of their initial use of new material, it is probable that a reassuring relationship will have developed. In such a relationship, workers commonly will have derived a sense of security. This should lessen anxiety about and resistance to the new elements in the learning experience. The supervisor's different thinking and way of doing is no longer so frightening. At this point there may develop a progressively positive attitude toward the learning with which the supervisor is identified.

5. When supervisors recognize that the worker's subjective involvement is interfering with his meeting the needs of the client, discussion of this involvement should focus on its implications *for the client*. If the worker is not helped by this measure, it is highly probable that his personal needs call for help of a special kind, beyond the scope of agency supervision. Concern for the client's welfare and for his own professional competence, otherwise, would motivate change.

Summary

It has been possible to discuss only a few measures that are useful in making the most of the natural bent for learning workers commonly bring to the new work experience of a public assistance program, and to present only sketchily some of the learning problems involved in work that commonly demands much change in the worker's thinking and in his way of helping people. It is believed that these measures and educational principles will be helpful to a great majority of workers. It has not been possible to discuss the special help needed by those who present marked educational problems by reason of their need to cling to routines, hang on to prejudices, continue to think and act in old ways out of some marked resistance to change. In many of these instances would be found deep personality problems that are beyond the helping and teaching responsibility of the supervisor. Workers who are able to use productively the teaching methods and ways of helping described here are the educable workers who would profit most by opportunity for professional education. It is these workers whom supervisors may well encourage to remain in this field of work and to seek education beyond that which can be given within a social agency.[34]

Notes

1. For elaboration of the educational and administrative aspects and their interplay, *see* Social Security Board, "Supervision as an Administrative Process Contributing to Staff Development," Bureau of Public Assistance Circular No. 6 (Washington, D.C.: U.S. Government Printing Office, 1940) (processed); Lydia Rapoport, *The Role of Supervision in Professional Education*, Health Education Monographs No. 15 (Rye, N.Y.: Society of Public Health Education, 1963); Charlotte Towle, "The Place of Help in Supervision," *Social Service Review*, Vol. 37, No. 4 (December 1963), pp. 403–415; Sydney J. Berkowitz, "The Administrative Process in Casework Supervision," *Social Casework*, Vol. 33, No. 10 (December 1952), pp. 419–423; Alton A. Linford, "Education and In-Service Training for the Public Family and Children's Services" (New York: Council on Social Work Education, 1963), pp. 81–92; Lydia Rapoport, "Consultation: An Overview," in Rapoport, ed., *Consultation in Social Work Practice* (New York: National Association of Social Workers, 1963), pp. 7–21; and Corinne H. Wolfe, "Basic Components in Supervision," *The Social Welfare Forum, 1958* (New York: Columbia University Press, 1958), pp. 177–189.

2. Karl de Schweinitz, "Education for Social Security," *The Educational Record*, Vol. 25, No. 2 (April 1944), pp. 142–153.

3. For import of this in the growth process, *see* Chapter 2, pp. 35–36.

4. For elaboration of the concept of regression, *see* Chapter 2, pp. 33–35.

5. *See* Chapter 2, pp. 25–26.

6. For study of the part emotions have in the educative process and hence in the use of knowledge and skill, *see* Charlotte Towle, *The Learner in Education for the Professions* (Chicago: University of Chicago Press, 1954), pp. 86–174, 266–270, 334–336, 347–354, 402–403; Anita Faatz, *The Nature of Policy in the Administration of Public Assistance* (Philadelphia: University of Pennsylvania Press, 1943); Florence Hollis, "The Emotional Growth of the Worker Through Supervision," *Proceedings of the National Conference of Social Work, 1936* (Chicago: University of Chicago Press, 1936), pp. 167–178; and David Kevin, "Use of the Group Method in Consultation," in Rapoport, ed., *Consultation in Social Work Practice*, pp. 69–85.

7. *See* Chapter 2, pp. 24–25; Herman Grossbard, "Methodology for Developing Self-Awareness," *Social Casework*, Vol. 35, No. 9 (November 1954), pp. 380–386; and Gordon Hamilton, "Self-Awareness in Professional Education," *Social Casework*, Vol. 35, No. 9 (November 1954), pp. 371–379. For discussion of attitudes and their change, *see* Mary Louise Somers, "The Small Group in Learning and Teaching," *Learning and Teaching in Public Welfare I* (Washington, D.C.: U.S. Department of Health, Education, and Welfare, 1963), pp. 158–175; Towle, *The Learner in Education for the Professions*, pp. 23–133; Muriel W. Pumphrey, *The Teaching of Values and Ethics in Social Work Education*, Vol. XIII of the Curriculum Study (New York: Council on Social Work Education, 1959); Arthur Abrahamson, *Group Methods in Supervision and Staff Development* (New York: Harper and Brothers, 1959); Arlien Johnson, "Educating Social Workers for Ethical Practice," *Social Service Review*, Vol. 24, No. 2 (June 1955), pp. 125–136; and Virginia P. Robinson, *The Dynamics of Supervision Under Functional Controls* (Philadelphia: University of Pennsylvania Press, 1949).

8. *See* Chapter 2, pp. 23–25. *See also* references cited in n. 7.

9. *See* Chapter 4, pp. 69–70, for further discussion of this problem. *See also* references cited in n. 7.

10. For further discussion, *see* Charlotte Towle, "Underlying Skills of Case Work Today," *Social Service Review*, Vol. 15, No. 3 (September 1941), pp. 456–471.

11. For further study of anxiety and of how it may operate in the learning process in education for the profession of social work, *see* Towle, *The Learner in Education for the Professions*, index on Anxiety.

12. For further discussion of this point, *see* Chapter 3, pp. 42–43.

13. The exceptions are persons in whom anxiety provokes marked opposition or has a paralyzing effect. These individuals do not reach out to learn. They will require more time in which to find themselves in a new situation and in relation to new knowledge. They will require more help at the start. In sketching "usual" and "exceptional" attitudes toward learning, one must remember that there will not be a complete absence of so-called "exceptional attitudes" in the group that reaches out to learn. Here one will find fragmentary resistance, momentary retreats, and inhibitions, but they will be *predominantly* eager and ready to learn in contrast to others who are *predominantly* troubled and unready to learn. *See* Towle, *The Learner in Education for the Professions*, index on Anxiety and pp. 334–336, 347–354.

14. For further study of the variety of learners and differential supervision, *see Widening Horizons in Medical Education: A Study of the Teaching of Social and Environmental Factors in Medicine* (New York: Commonwealth Fund, 1948); Lola Selby, "Helping Students in Field Practice Modify Blocks in Learning," *Social Service Review*, Vol. 29, No. 1 (Marcy 1955), pp. 53–63; Towle, "The Place of Help in Supervision"; and Margaret Golton, "The Beginning Casework Practitioner: A Categorical Delineation," *Social Service Review*, Vol. 33, No. 3 (September 1959), pp. 245–252.

15. Social Security Board, "The Orientation Period for Public Assistance Staffs as Part of a Total Staff Development Program," Bureau of Public Assistance Circular No. 11 (Washington, D.C.: U.S. Government Printing Office, August 1941). (Processed.)

16. *See* Chapter 2, p. 31.

17. Social Security Board, "The Orientation Period for Public Assistance Staffs is Part of a Total Staff Development Program"; Social Security Board, "Effective Use of Supplementary Resources in a Staff Development Program," Bureau of Public Assistance Circular No. 15 (Washington, D.C.: U.S. Government Printing Office, 1942) (processed); and Social Security Board, "Supervision as an Administrative Process Contributing to Staff Development."

18. For discussion of the purposes served by various staff-development methods such as the individual conference, group discussion, institutes, and the like, *see* Social Security Board, "Effective Use of Supplementary Resources in a Staff Development Program"; Somers, *op. cit.*; Abrahamson, *op. cit.*; Eileen A. Blackey, *Group Leadership in Staff Training*, Bureau of Public Assistance Report No. 29, Children's Bureau Publication No. 361 (Washington, D.C.: U.S. Department of Health, Education, and Welfare, 1957); Linford, *op. cit.*; and Rapoport, "Consultation: An Overview," in Rapoport, ed., *op. cit.*

19. Alfred North Whitehead, *Aims of Education and Other Essays* (New York: Macmillan Co., 1929).

20. *Ibid.*, p. 45.

21. *See* Chapter 3, p. 42.

22. For a statement on automatic behavior in the learning process, *see* Chapter 2, p. 31.

23. For study of certain principles in the use of readings in student training and staff development, *see* Towle, *The Learner in Education for the Professions*, pp. 324–330.

24. Bertha C. Reynolds, *Learning and Teaching in the Practice of Social Work* (New York: Farrar and Rinehart, 1942), pp. 230–252.

25. *Ibid.*, pp. 202–203.

26. Virginia P. Robinson, "Education Processes in Supervision," *Worker and Supervisor* (New York: Family Welfare Association of America, 1936), pp. 7–15.

27. It will not be possible to discuss specific methods of helping, for which the reader is referred to Reynolds, *op. cit.*, pp. 214–316.

28. Reynolds, *op. cit.*, pp. 66, 297–305.

29. Vivian Johnson and Margaret Windau, "The Supervisor–Worker Relationship as an Element in Training: I. Mutual Activity as a Way of Development; II. Mutual Evaluation," *The Family*, Vol. 15, No. 6 (October 1934), pp. 184–188.

30. For further discussion of the use of readings in teaching social casework, *see* Fern Lowry, "Teaching Social Case Work," *The Family*, Vol. 21, No. 5 (July 1940), pp. 159–165.

31. Anita J. Faatz, *The Nature of Policy in the Administratio of Public Assistance* (Philadelphia: University of Pennsylvania Press, 1943), pp. 40–52.

32. *See* Chapter 2, pp. 24–26.

33. Faatz, *op. cit.*, p. 50.

34. Edith Abbott, *Social Welfare and Professional Education* (rev. ed.; Chicago: University of Chicago Press, 1942). *See also* Leah Feder, "Why the Professional?" *The Family*, Vol. 13, No. 8 (December 1932), pp. 275–279; Somers, *op. cit.*; and Robinson, *op. cit.*

APPENDIXES

Foreword to the 1945 edition

The Social Security Act establishes a framework for the partnership of the Federal Government and the States in providing financial assistance to large groups of individuals who temporarily or permanently lack the means of livelihood. This is an expression of a democracy's concern that its human resources be conserved, that opportunities for self-development and contribution to family and community life be safeguarded. It is a recognition of the destructive effects of economic deprivation upon human achievement. The objective of meeting need in a way which will be acceptable, and therefore most helpful, to the individual requires a staff with conviction regarding the social purpose of this government service based on human rights and an expanding recognition of common human needs.

Providing assistance sympathetically and using the agency's and other community resources fully to meet the individual's needs in his social situation require that staff understand the effect of economic need on other areas of an individual's normal life. In a money economy, loss of the usual financial resources and application for assistance can immediately affect the individual's capacity to deal effectively with everyday affairs of his life and can modify his opportunities for physical, intellectual, emotional, and spiritual development. Changes associated with his need for assistance may alter his status and role in the family group. A public assistance program, therefore, must understand and deal with the whole gamut of different reactions of people to a situation which threatens their basic independence and the normal pattern of their family and community relationships.

It is, therefore, essential that public assistance staff have a general understanding of common human needs and behavior as well as of economic and social factors in the community which affect the individual. Supervisors and training consultants in State agencies have emphasized the need for training materials which would widen and deepen the staff's understanding of individuals and would form the basis for developing skill in administering services which intimately touch people's lives. To meet these urgent requests, the present discussion of common human needs has been prepared by Charlotte Towle in consultation with the staff of the Bureau. The document was developed in Technical Training Service of the Bureau of Public Assistance as a part of its regular services to States in promoting the training of staff. Supervisory personnel and persons with special responsibility for staff training will find the material of particular value in planning and conducting training sessions as well as in the less formal day-to-day individual and group conferences. Only as this content stimulates study, becomes a basis for discussion, and is thoughtfully applied, will it fully realize its educational aim.

JANE M. HOEY, *Director*
April 1945   *Bureau of Public Assistance*

Acknowledgments

Grateful acknowledgment is made to Jane M. Hoey, Director, Bureau of Public Assistance, who read this discussion and gave thoughtful criticism. I wish to express deep appreciation to Agnes Van Driel, Chief of the Technical Training Service, and to the members of her staff, Cordelia Trimble, Dorothy Lally, and Thomasine Hendricks, for clarifying discussions in our many consultations. I am particularly indebted to Miss Hendricks who has given much time and thoughtful help in the final assembling of the material and in the preparation of the bibliography. I am indebted also to Martha Phillips, Helen Dart, and other members of the regional public assistance staff in Chicago, as well as to staff members of the several divisions of the Bureau in Washington who made very helpful suggestions. I acknowledge also the invaluable help of Mary Ross, Chief, Division of Publications and Review.

I am under obligation to Karl de Schweinitz, American Council on Education, as well as to several colleagues outside the Social Security Board for careful reading and thoughtful comments: Jeanette Hanford and Mary E. Rall of the Family Service Bureau, United Charities, Chicago; Helen R. Wright, Dean of the School of Social Service Administration, University of Chicago; and to Dr. Thomas M. French, Associate Director of the Institute of Psychoanalysis and Instructor in the School of Social Service Administration.

CHARLOTTE TOWLE
April 1945   *University of Chicago*

Foreword to the 1957 edition

The National Association of Social Workers is pleased to publish this new edition of *Common Human Needs* by Charlotte Towle. Since it was first issued by the Federal Security Agency in 1945, it has been extensively used by social work educators and practitioners in the United States and in other countries. Permission has been granted to translate it into the Dutch, French, German, Japanese, and Arabic languages.

When the Federal Security Agency decided to withdraw this publication from circulation, the National Board of the American Association of Social Workers assumed responsibility for its publication because of its deep conviction that this book presents a valuable exposition of basic social work concepts, practice, and philosophy. As in the case with any professional publication, there is not complete agreement among social workers with every idea or with every concept which is expressed. The Board of Directors of the National Association of Social Workers is of the opinion that this volume is a professionally sound and thoughtful presentation and that the principles enunciated have general acceptance among social workers in both public and voluntary agencies.

For the sake of accuracy in interpretation, and in order that the material may more accurately reflect recent amendments to the Social Security Act, some minor editorial changes have been made by Miss Towle in this edition of the book.

This new edition of *Common Human Needs* is dedicated to the students, educators, and practitioners in social work who are constantly striving to improve the quality of service which they are giving to the people who are in need of them, and to the society of which they are a part.

JOSEPH P. ANDERSON, *Executive Director*
National Association of Social Workers

Preface to the 1965 edition

This book was written twenty years ago. You who open it now may have been a toddler then—exploring, on uncertain legs, the world of tables and chairs and doorways that led to new vistas and corners that contained both mystery and security. Or you may have been beginning at school— exploring, big eyes and ears open, the world of words and numbers that brought new meanings to your astonished mind, and the world of new people who, you found, were like but also different from the people you knew at home. And if you found your childhood explorations bewildering and curious but also interesting and exciting you have come to this day—and to this book—still eager to explore, to know more, particularly to know more about human beings and the mysteries of their everyday lives.

There was never a more telling title than *Common Human Needs*. It says precisely what the book is about, for it tells of the needs, wants, and desires of every one of us, and further, of the behavior—sometimes foolish, sometimes wise; sometimes rash, sometimes thoughtful—by which human beings try to get those needs and wants met. Because the book was written specifically to help social workers in their transactions with all the hurt, inarticulate, fenced-in people with whom they deal, especially those long-poor or long-sick who are the recipients of public assistance—because of that purpose, the author has taken the next step beyond helping the reader "to understand": she has pointed to ways by which that understanding may be put to use.

Common Human Needs was written originally for social workers in public agencies, in particular for those who shouldered the tough jobs in mass programs for alleviating economic need and promoting family and personal well-being. But it was not long before the uncommon common sense that is its mark and its lucid explanations of human behavior leaped across professional and geographic boundaries. The book was discovered and read and used by social workers in every field, and then by sectors of the nursing, medical, teaching, and other helping professions. It has been translated into eight languages.[1] It has, in short, become a classic.

Make no mistake. The insights and implications in this book are as fresh and true today as they were twenty years ago. There are, it is true, examples that make reference to circumstances that may be unknown to the young social worker ("What is the WPA?"), but only these fragments are time-bound. The basic facts of life, the psychological import of such mandane matters as money, three meals a day, going to school, getting sick—all these are in an all but timeless presentation here. The fact is that Charlotte Towle is one of those rare, sage teachers who has always been ahead of her time as well as with it. Foresights are the natural consequence of her insights, and the implications she suggests or that leap to mind from her explorations of human behavior hold for social work practice today as surely as they did when the book was written. The psychological reactions of both relief-recipient and relief-giver, the relation of policy and procedures to humane practice, the relation between emotion and motivation and between these and rational behavior, the recognition of the caseworker himself as a person with human needs and feelings— all these and more are set down here with economy and simplicity.

Simplicity is different from simple-mindedness. Simplicity is the unpretentious, forthright, wholeness of exposition that bespeaks complete grasp and integration. It is possible only when a writer understands something so thoroughly that he can extract its very essence and translate it into common human terms. This is what Charlotte Towle has done in this book: her clear thinking results in clear writing. Sometimes we tend, all of us, to equate obscurity with profundity. But there is no such inevitable relationship. Sometimes, too, we hold the obvious to be trivial. Yet what is obvious, what may be seen as ordinary, everyday, may hold in it great meaning both for the human being who experiences it and for him who takes the trouble to look into it. Charlotte Towle takes just such trouble. That is why this is a book not alone for beginners in social work. It bears rereading, even by those who are sophisticated and long experienced in practice. Perhaps one should say "especially by those." They are likely to find new meanings in it, new levels of understanding, just beause they can illuminate it with their experience and knowledge.

There is another set of factors that makes *Common Human Needs* most timely. We are embarked on a War on Poverty. The poor, once almost the exclusive concern of social work, have now become the concern of our whole society. Not only public assistance programs but public educational, vocational, youth and family rehabilitation programs are being furthered or newly devised. The success of any of these efforts to raise the living standards and the self-realization and aspirations of the economically and culturally poor will depend not only on the money and inventiveness poured into these programs but, at base, on the understanding—from the direct service worker all the way up to the line to the blueprint-maker—of common human needs and the common human ways by which they may be met.

This is why it is of such special importance that the National Association of Social Workers has set out to present this fresh edition of this small but vital book, and why it gives me such pleasure, at once humble and proud, to write its preface.

HELEN HARRIS PERLMAN

Chicago, Illinois

February 10, 1965

Notes

1. At present, *Common Human Needs* has been published in Arabic, Dutch, German, Greek, Hebrew, Italian, Japanese, and Spanish (in a Mexican edition). Permissions now granted with translations pending are Bengali, Egyptian, French, Indonesian, Indonesian-Malay, Korean, Persian, Turkish, and Urdu.

Resolution on
Common Human Needs adopted
at meeting of National Board—
October 18–20, 1951

WHEREAS *Common Human Needs*, a publication prepared at the initiation of the Bureau of Public Assistance by Miss Charlotte Towle, has become a widely accepted exposition of basic social work concepts, practice and philosophy in relation to the common needs of people, and

WHEREAS in April, 1951 Mr. Oscar Ewing, Federal Security Administrator, announced that the book would no longer be issued or published by the Government Printing Office, and

WHEREAS this action is so out of keeping with the general position of the Federal Security Agency in its advocacy and support of sound social welfare programs and effective administration, and

WHEREAS we believe that there is, and will continue to be, great demand for this book by agencies, schools of social work, professional practitioners, and many others for the purpose of professional training, inservice training, and individual enlightenment and stimulation, and

WHEREAS we believe that it is of the utmost importance that *Common Human Needs* be available to persons and agencies on a continuing basis,

BE IT THEREFORE RESOLVED that the National Board of AASW express its deep regret that the Administrator of the Federal Security Agency acted to terminate government sponsorship, publication and distribution of *Common*

Human Needs, and that the Board record its belief that such action by the Administrator represents a yielding to unjustified and unfounded criticisms of the book, and

BE IT FURTHER RESOLVED that the AASW take steps to make certain that *Common Human Needs* is made available to the reading public in future on a continuing basis by offering to undertake its publication, and

BE IT FURTHER RESOLVED that copies of this resolution be sent to Mr. Oscar Ewing, Administrator of the Federal Security Agency and to Miss Charlotte Towle, and that it be published in the SOCIAL WORK JOURNAL.

Selected reading references

This volume originally was written for use by supervisors in the in-service training of public assistance staffs. It has, however, been used beyond these confines. The following references, therefore, are suggested for use by teachers, supervisors, workers, and students studying various aspects of the subject matter presented. Supervisors will direct the worker's attention to the references deemed useful in the problems of daily work or that give a background for group discussion. Weight has been given to references that provide an easily understood interpretation of major areas of knowledge required by the public assistance worker in understanding human needs and behavior. Each section, however, contains references of a more advanced or technical character for selected use in in-service training programs and for progressively more comprehensive use in preprofessional courses of study and in the beginning courses in schools of social work.

In agencies these references will be supplemented by readily available publications of the Social Security Board and the Children's Bureau of the U.S. Department of Health, Education, and Welfare. In schools they will in addition be supplemented by course bibliographies. Many agency libraries and probably all school libraries contain such compilations as the *Social Work Year Book*, published triennally 1929–1960, and the *Proceedings of the National Conference of Social Work*. These are invaluable in identifying trends in the context of the times and in over-all coverage of items in Section I. For the current scene, see the *Encyclopedia of Social Work* (New York: National Association of Social Workers, 1965), which now replaces the *Social Work Year Book*.

I am indebted to colleagues on the faculty of the School of Social Service Administration of the University of Chicago for their assistance in their selection, namely, Dorothy Aikin, Helen Harris Perlman, Edward E. Schwartz, Mary Louise Somers, Irving H. Spergel, and Alan D. Wade.

April 1965 CHARLOTTE TOWLE

I. Social work as a profession

Function in society; philosophy, ethics, and values; social conditions and social change; historical perspectives

Abbott, Edith. *Public Assistance: American Principles and Policies.* Chicago: University of Chicago Press, 1940.

Abbott, Grace. *From Relief to Social Security.* Chicago: University of Chicago Press, 1941.

Addams, Jane. *Twenty Years at Hull House.* New York: Macmillan Co., 1919.

_____. *The Second Twenty Years at Hull House.* New York: Macmillan Co., 1930.

Bisno, Herbert. *The Philosophy of Social Work.* Washington, D.C.: Public Affairs Press, 1952.

Boehm, Werner W. "The Nature of Social Work," *Social Work,* Vol. 3, No. 2 (April 1958), pp. 10–18.

_____. "The Role of Values in Social Work," *Jewish Social Service Quarterly,* Vol. 26 (June 1950), pp. 429–438.

Bowers, Swithun. "Human Values and Public Welfare," *The Social Worker,* Vol. 23 (December 1954), pp. 1–7.

Bremner, Robert H. *American Philanthropy.* Chicago: University of Chicago Press, 1960.

_____. *From the Depths: The Discovery of Poverty in the United States.* New York: New York University Press, 1956.

Bruno, Frank J. *Trends in Social Work, 1874–1946.* New York: Columbia University Press, 1948. Chap. 19, pp. 183–191.

Burgess, M. Elaine, and Price, Daniel O. *An American Dependency Challenge.* Chicago: American Public Welfare Association, 1963.

Cohen, Nathan E. "A Changing Profession in a Changing World," *Social Work,* Vol. 1, No. 4 (October 1956), pp. 12–19.

_____. "Future Welfare Policy, Program and Structure," *The Social Welfare Forum, 1964.* New York: Columbia University Press, 1964. Pp. 3–19.

de Jongh, J. F. "Self-Help in Modern Society," *Social Work Journal,* Vol. 35, No. 4 (October 1954), pp. 139–144, 166–168.

de Schweinitz, Karl. *England's Road to Social Security.* Philadelphia: University of Pennsylvania Press, 1943.

_____. "Social Values and Social Action: The Intellectual Base as Illustrated in the Study of History," *Social Service Review,* Vol. 30, No. 2 (June 1956), pp. 119–131.

Epstein, Lenore A. "Unmet Need in a Land of Abundance," *Social Security Bulletin,* Vol. 26, No. 5 (May 1963), pp. 3–11.

Garrett, Annette. "Historical Survey of the Evolution of Case Work," *Social Casework,* Vol. 30, No. 6 (June 1949), pp. 219–229. Reprinted in Cora Kasius, ed., *Principles and Techniques in Social Casework.* New York: Family Service Association of America, 1950. Pp. 393–411.

Hamilton, Gordon. "Helping People: The Growth of a Profession," *Social Casework,* Vol. 29, No. 8 (October 1948), pp. 291–299.

_____. *Theory and Practice of Social Work.* 2d ed., rev.; New York: Columbia University Press, 1951.

Hellenbrand, Shirley C. "Client Value Orientations: Implications for Diagnosis and Treatment," *Social Casework*, Vol. 42, No. 4 (April 1961), pp. 163–169.

Hofstadter, Richard. *Social Darwinism in American Thought.* Philadelphia: University of Pennsylvania Press, 1944.

Hopkins, Harry L. *Spending to Save: The Complete Story of Relief.* New York: W. W. Norton and Co., 1936.

Konopka, Gisela. "Attention Must Be Paid," *American Journal of Orthopsychiatry*, Vol. 34, No. 5 (October 1964), pp. 805–817.

Lampman, Robert J. "The Low Income Population and Economic Growth." Study Paper No. 12 prepared for The Study of Economic Growth and Price Levels for the Joint Committee, Eighty-sixth Congress, 1st Session. (Joint Committee Print.)

Lee, Porter R. "Social Work: Cause and Function," *Proceedings of the National Conference of Social Work, 1929.* Chicago: University of Chicago Press, 1930. Pp. 3–20. Also in Fern Lowry, ed., *Readings in Social Casework: 1920–1938.* New York: Columbia University Press, 1939. Pp. 22–37.

Lurie, Harry L. "The Responsibilities of a Socially Oriented Profession," in Cora Kasius, ed., *New Directions in Social Work.* New York: Harper & Brothers, 1954. Pp. 31–53.

———. "The Development of Social Welfare Programs in the United States," in Russell H. Kurtz, ed., *Social Work Year Book, 1957.* New York: National Association of Social Workers, 1957. Pp. 19–45.

NASW Personnel Standards and Adjudication Procedures. New York: National Association of Social Workers, 1963. *See* "NASW Code of Ethics" and "Standards for Social Work Personnel Practices."

Orlansky, Mollie. "Children of the Poor," *Social Security Bulletin*, Vol. 26, No. 7 (July 1963), pp. 3–13.

Perlman, Helen Harris. "The Caseworker's Use of Collateral Information," *Social Casework*, Vol. 32, No. 8 (October 1951), pp. 325–333.

———. "Freud's Contribution to Social Welfare," *Social Service Review*, Vol. 31, No. 2 (June 1957), pp. 192–202.

Pray, Kenneth L. M. *Social Work in a Revolutionary Age and Other Papers.* Philadelphia: University of Pennsylvania Press, 1949.

Pumphrey, Muriel W. "Mary E. Richmond—The Practitioner," *Social Casework*, Vol. 42, No. 8 (October 1961), pp. 375–385.

Pumphrey, Ralph E., and Pumphrey, Muriel W. (eds.). *The Heritage of American Social Work: Readings on Its Philosophical and Institutional Development.* New York: Columbia University Press, 1961.

Reynolds, Bertha C. *An Uncharted Journey.* New York: Citadel Press, 1963.

———. "The Social Casework of an Uncharted Journey," *Social Work*, Vol. 9, No. 4 (October 1964), pp. 13–17.

Rich, Margaret E. "Mary E. Richmond: Social Worker," *Social Casework*, Vol. 33, No. 9 (November 1952), pp. 363–370.

Richmond, Mary E. *What Is Social Casework?* New York: Russell Sage Foundation, 1922.

Robinson, Virginia P. *A Changing Psychology in Social Casework.* Chapel Hill: University of North Carolina Press, 1930.

——— (ed.). *Jessie Taft, Therapist and Social Work Educator.* Philadelphia: University of Pennsylvania Press, 1962.

Schlesinger, Arthur M., Jr. *The Crisis of the Old Order, 1919–1933*. 3 vols.; Boston: Houghton-Mifflin Co., 1959–60.

Schultz, Theodore W. "Investment in Man: An Economist's View," *Social Service Review*, Vol. 33, No. 2 (June 1959), pp. 109–117.

"Social Casework—Generic and Specific," *An Outline. A Report of the Milford Conference*. New York: American Association of Social Workers, 1929.

Therkildsen, Paul T. *Public Assistance and American Values*. Albuquerque, N.M.: University of New Mexico Press, 1964.

Towle, Charlotte. "The Client's Rights and the Use of the Social Service Exchange," *Social Service Review*, Vol. 23, No. 1 (March 1949), pp. 15–20.

_____. "Social Casework in Modern Society," *Social Service Review*, Vol. 20, No. 2 (June 1946), pp. 165–179.

_____. "Social Work: Cause and Function," *Social Casework*, Vol. 42, No. 8 (October 1961), pp. 385–397.

Wade, Alan D. "Social Work and Political Action," *Social Work*, Vol. 8, No. 4 (October 1963), pp. 3–10.

Weber, Arnold R. "The Rich and the Poor: Employment in an Age of Automation," *Social Service Review*, Vol. 37, No. 3 (September 1963), pp. 249–262.

Wecter, Dixon. *The Age of the Great Depression, 1929–1941*. New York: Macmillan Co., 1948.

Youngdahl, Benjamin E. "What We Believe," *The Social Welfare Forum, 1952*. New York: Columbia University Press, 1952. Pp. 29–45.

Younghusband, Eileen. "The Social Services and Social Work," *Social Work and Social Change*. (National Institute for Social Work Training Series, No. 1.) London: George Allen and Unwin, Ltd., 1964. Part I, pp. 15–52.

_____. "International Aspects of Social Work," *Social Work and Social Change*. (National Institute for Social Work Training Series, No. 1.) London: George Allen and Unwin, Ltd., 1964. Part II, pp. 103–166.

Methods, defined and delineated: administration, casework, community organization, group work, and research

Blau, Peter, and Scott, W. Richard. *Formal Organizations: A Comparative Approach*. San Francisco: Chandler Publishers, 1962.

Boehm, Werner W. *The Social Casework Method in Social Work Education*. (Vol. X of the Curriculum Study.) New York: Council on Social Work Education, 1959. Pp. 13–49.

Bowers, Swithun. "The Nature and Definition of Social Casework," *Social Casework*, Vol 30, Nos. 8, 9, and 10 (October, November, and December 1959), pp. 311–317, 369–375, and 412–417. Reprinted in Cora Kasius, ed., *Principles and Techniques in Social Casework*. New York: Family Service Association of America, 1950. Pp. 97–127.

"Defining Community Organization Practice." New York: National Association of Social Workers, 1962. Mimeographed.

Dumpson, James E. "Community Organization in Public Administration," *Community Organization*. New York: Columbia University Press, 1958. Pp. 50–59.

Hamilton, Gordon. "The Underlying Philosophy of Social Casework Today," *The Family*, Vol. 22 (July 1941), pp. 139–147. Also in *Proceedings of the National Conference of Social Work, 1941*. Chicago: University of Chicago Press, 1941. Pp. 237–253.

————. "The Role of Social Casework in Social Policy," *Social Casework*, Vol. 33, No. 8 (October 1952), pp. 316–324.

Homans, George. *The Human Group*. New York: Harcourt, Brace, and Company, 1950.

Kidneigh, John C. "Administration of Social Agencies," in Russell H. Kurtz, ed., *Social Work Year Book, 1957*. New York: National Association of Social Workers, 1957. Pp. 75–82.

Konopka, Gisela. *Social Group Work: Generic Treatment Form—A Helping Process*. Englewood Cliffs, N.J.: Prentice-Hall, 1963.

Kruse, Arthur H. "The Psychodynamics of Administration," *The Social Welfare Forum, 1958*. New York: Columbia University Press, 1958. Pp. 166–176.

Lowry, Fern. "Current Concepts in Social Casework Practice," *Social Service Review*, Vol. 12, Nos. 3 and 4 (September and December 1938), pp. 365–373 and 571–597.

Millett, John D. *Management in the Public Service: The Quest for Effective Performance*. New York: McGraw-Hill Book Co., 1954.

Perlman, Helen Harris. "Social Casework," in Harry L. Lurie, ed., *Encyclopedia of Social Work*. New York: National Association of Social Workers, 1965. Pp. 704–714.

Potentials for Service Through Group in Public Welfare. Chicago: American Public Welfare Association, 1962.

Ross, Murray G. *Community Organization: Theory and Principles*. New York: Harper & Brothers, 1955.

Tead, Ordway. *Democratic Administration*. New York: Association Press, 1945.

White, Reuel. *Administration of Public Welfare*. New York: American Book Co., 1950.

Wilensky, Harold L., and Lebeaux, Charles M. *Industrial Society and Social Welfare*. New York: Russell Sage Foundation, 1958.

Legal provisions, policies, and services in health welfare programs

Caplovitz, David. *The Poor Pay More: Consumer Practices of Low Income Families*. New York: Free Press of Glencoe, 1963.

Clarke, Helen I. *Social Legislation*. 2d ed., New York: Appleton-Century-Crofts, 1957.

Burns, Eveline M. *The American Social Security System*. Boston: Houghton-Mifflin Co., 1951.

————. *Social Security and Public Policy*. New York: McGraw-Hill Book Co., 1956.

Maas, Henry S., and Engler, Richard E., Jr. *Children in Need of Parents*. New York: Columbia University Press, 1959.

Perkins, Ellen J. "A.F.D.C. in Review, 1936–1962," *Welfare in Review*, Vol. 1, No. 5 (November 1963), pp. 1–15.

Reich, Charles A. "Searching Homes of Public Assistance Recipients. The Issues Under the Social Security Act," *Social Service Review*, Vol. 37, No. 3 (September 1963), pp. 328–339.

Rosenheim, Margaret K. (ed.). *Justice for the Child.* New York: Free Press of Glencoe, 1962.

Schwartz, Edward E. "A Way to End the Means Test," *Social Work,* Vol. 9, No. 3 (July 1964), pp. 3–12, 97.

Ten Broek, Jacobus. *The Constitution and the Right of Free Movement.* New York: National Travelers Aid Association, 1955.

U.S. Bureau of Public Assistance. *The Application Process in Public Assistance Administration.* (Public Assistance Report No. 14.) Washington, D.C.: Bureau of Public Assistance, Social Security Administration, Federal Security Agency, May 1, 1948.

U.S. Children's Bureau. *Five Decades of Action for Children: A Short History of the Children's Bureau.* (Children's Bureau Publication No. 358.) Rev. ed.; Washington, D.C.: U.S. Department of Health, Education, and Welfare, 1962.

Wade, Alan D. "Social Work and Political Action," *Social Work,* Vol. 8, No. 4 (October 1963), pp. 3–10.

Younghusband, Eileen. "The Juvenile Court and the Child," "The Dilemma of the Juvenile Court," "Juvenile Court Reform," *Social Work and Social Change.* (National Institute for Social Work Training Series, No. 1.) London: George Allen and Unwin, Ltd., 1964. Pp. 62, 78, and 92.

II. Human development: maturation stages (norms and variations)

Addams, Jane. *The Spirit of Youth and the City Streets.* New York: Macmillan Co., 1912.

"Adolescent Problems Related to Somatic Variations in Adolescence." *43d Yearbook of the National Society for Study of Education, Part I.* Chicago: University of Chicago Press, 1943. Pp. 80–99.

Agee, James, and Evans, Walker. *Let Us Now Praise Famous Men.* Boston: Houghton-Mifflin Co., 1939.

Aldrich, C. A., and Aldrich, M. M. *Babies Are Human Beings: An Interpretation of Growth.* New York: Macmillan Co., 1938.

Benedik, Therese, MD. "Personality Development," in Franz Alexander and Helen Ross, eds., *Dynamic Psychiatry.* Chicago: University of Chicago Press, 1952. Pp. 63–111.

Bettelheim, Bruno. *The Informed Heart: Autonomy in a Mass Age.* Glencoe, Ill.: Free Press, 1960.

Blos, Peter. *The Adolescent Personality.* New York: D. Appleton-Century Co., 1941.

Bornstein, Berta. "On Latency," *Psychoanalytic Study of the Child,* Vol. VI. New York: International Universities Press, 1951. Pp. 79–285.

Busbaum, Edith. "A Contribution to the Psychoanalytic Knowledge of the Latency Period," *American Journal of Orthopsychiatry,* Vol. 21, No. 2 (March 1951), pp. 182–198.

Caplan, Gerald H., MD, DPM. "Emotional Implications of Pregnancy," "Mother-Child Relationships: Origin and Development of," "During the First Year of Life," *Concepts of Mental Health and Consultation.* (Children's Bureau Publication No. 373.) Washington, D.C.: U.S. Department of Health, Education, and Welfare, 1959. Pp. 44–109.

Cavan, Ruth S., Burgess, E. W., Havighurst, Robert J., and Goldhamer, Herbert. *Personal Adjustment in Old Age.* Chicago: Social Science Research Association, 1949.

Cottrell, Leonard S. "The Adjustment of the Individual to His Age and Sex Roles," *American Sociological Review,* Vol. 7, No. 5 (October 1942), pp. 370–382.

Ephron, Beulah Kanter. *Emotional Difficulties in Reading.* New York: Julian Press, 1953.

Fraiberg, Selma H. *The Magic Years.* New York: Charles Scribner's Sons, 1959.

Freud, Anna, and Burlingham, Dorothy T. *Infants Without Families.* New York: International Universities Press, 1944.

Friedman, E. H., and Havighurst, Robert J. *The Meaning of Work and Retirement.* Chicago: University of Chicago Press, 1954.

Gardner, George E., MD. "Present Day Society and the Adolescent," *American Journal of Orthopsychiatry,* Vol. 27 (July 1957).

Gesell, Arnold, and Ilg, Frances L. *Infant and Child in the Culture of Today.* 6th ed.; New York: Harper & Brothers, 1943.

———. *The Child from Five to Ten.* New York: Harper & Brothers, 1946.

Greenleigh, Lawrence. "Some Psychological Aspects of Aging," *Social Casework,* Vol. 36, No. 3 (March 1955), pp. 99–106.

Hart, Henry H. "Work as Integration," *Medical Record,* Vol. 160, No. 12 (1947), pp. 735–739.

Havighurst, Robert J. *Middle Age: The New Prime of Life.* Ann Arbor: University of Michigan Press, 1956.

Hendricks, Ives. "Work and the Pleasure Principle," *Psychoanalytic Quarterly,* Vol. 12, No. 3 (1943), pp. 311–329.

Josselyn, Irene, MD. *The Happy Child.* New York: Random House, 1955.

———. *The Adolescent and His World.* New York: Family Service Assocation of America, 1952.

Lawton, George. *New Goals in Old Age.* New York: Columbia University Press, 1943.

Levine, Maurice. *Psychotherapy in Medical Practice.* New York: Macmillan Co., 1942. *See* pp. 283–302.

Lichter, Solomon A., Rapien, Elise B., Seibert, Frances M., and Sklansky, Morris O., MD. *The Drop-Outs.* New York: Free Press of Glencoe, 1962.

Mohr, George, MD, and Depres, Marian. *The Stormy Decade.* New York: Random House, 1958.

Palmer, Francis H. "Critical Periods of Development," *Social Science Research Council,* Vol. 15, No. 2 (June 1961), pp. 13–18.

Rall, Mary E. "Dependency and the Adolescent." *Social Casework,* Vol. 28, No. 4 (April 1947), pp. 123–130.

Saul, Leon J., MD. *Emotional Maturity.* Philadelphia: J. B. Lippincott Co., 1947.

Sklansky, Morris O., MD, and Lichter, Solomon A. "Some Observations on the Character of the Adolescent Ego," *Social Service Review,* Vol. 31, No. 3 (September 1957), pp. 271–276.

Spock, Benjamin, MD. *Baby and Child Care.* Rev. ed.; New York: Pocket Books, 1957.

Tyler, Edward A., MD. "The Process of Humanizing Physiological Man," *Family Process,* Vol. 3, No. 2 (September 1964), p. 280.

Washburn, Alfred. "Human Growth, Development and Adaptation," *American Journal of Diseases of Children,* No. 90 (July 1955), pp. 2–5.

White, Robert W. *Lives in Progress. A Study of the Natural Growth of Personality.* New York: Dryden Press, 1952.

III. Personality (structure, function, and dynamics in relation to the family, culture, social conditions, stress, and crisis)

Alexander, Franz, MD. *Our Age of Unreason. A Study of the Irrational Forces in Social Life.* Rev. ed.; Philadelphia: J. B. Lippincott Co., 1951.

————. "Development of the Fundamental Concepts of Psychoanalysis," in Alexander and Helen Ross, eds., *Dynamic Psychiatry.* Chicago: University of Chicago Press, 1952. Pp. 3–34.

Allen, Frederick H. *Psychotherapy with Children.* New York: W. W. Norton and Co., 1942. *See* chaps. 1 and 2, pp. 13–36.

Allport, Gordon W. *Pattern and Growth in Personality.* New York: Holt, Rinehart, and Winston, 1961.

————. *Becoming: Basic Considerations for a Psychology of Personality.* New Haven: Yale University Press, 1955.

Ausubee, David P., MD. "Ego Development Among Segregated Negro Children," *Mental Hygiene,* Vol. 42, No. 3 (July 1958), pp. 362–369.

Babcock, Charlotte G., MD. "Food and Its Emotional Significance," *Journal of the American Dietetic Association,* Vol. 24 (May 1948), pp. 390–393.

Bell, Daniel. *Work and Its Discontents.* Boston: Beacon Press, 1956.

Bell, Norman W., and Vogel, Ezra F. (eds.). *A Modern Introduction to the Family.* Glencoe, Ill.: Free Press, 1960.

Berelson, Bernard, and Steiner, Gary A. *Human Behavior—An Inventory of Scientific Findings.* New York: Harcourt, Brace, and World, 1964.

Blake, Florence G. *The Child, The Parent and The Nurse.* Philadelphia: J. B. Lippincott Co., 1954.

Bowlby, John, MD. "Childhood Mourning and Its Implications for Psychiatry," *American Journal of Psychiatry,* Vol. 117 (December 1961), pp. 481–498.

Brenner, Charles, MD. *An Elementary Textbook of Psychoanalytic Theory.* New York: International Universities Press, 1955.

Caplan, Gerald, MD, DPM. "Ingredients of Personality and Personality Development," *Concepts of Mental Health and Consultation.* (Children's Bureau Publication No. 373.) Washington, D.C.: U.S. Department of Health, Education, and Welfare, 1959. Pp. 8–36.

Cartwright, Dorwin, and Lander, Alvin. *Group Dynamics—Research and Theory.* Evanston, Ill.: Row, Peterson, and Co., 1960.

Cohen, Pauline C. "Impact of the Handicapped Child on the Family," *Social Casework,* Vol. 43, No. 3 (March 1962), pp. 137–142.

Dai, Bingham. "Some Problems of Personality Development Among Negro Children," in Clyde Kluckhohn, Henry A. Murray, and David Schneider, eds., *Personality in Nature, Society and Culture.* 2d ed. rev.; New York: A. A. Knopf, 1953. Pp. 437–458.

Duvall, Evelyn Millis. *Family Development.* 2d ed.; Philadelphia: J. B. Lippincott Co., 1957.

English, O. Spurgeon, MD. "The Psychological Role of the Father in the Family," *Social Casework,* Vol. 35, No. 8 (October 1954), pp. 323–329.

Erikson, Erik H. *Childhood and Society.* New York: W. W. Norton and Co., 1950.

Feldman, Frances Lomas. *The Family in a Money World.* New York: Family Service Association of America, 1957.

Grinker, Roy R., MD, and Spiegel, John, MD. *Men Under Stress.* Philadelphia: Blakiston Co., 1945.

Hill, Rueben. *Families Under Stress.* New York: Harper & Bros., 1949.

_____. "Generic Features of Families Under Stress," *Social Casework,* Vol. 39, Nos. 2–3 (February–March 1958), pp. 139–150.

Hollis, Florence. *Women in Marital Conflict: A Casework Study.* New York: Family Service Association of America, 1949.

Jahoda, Marie. "The Meaning of Psychological Health." *The Social Welfare Forum, 1953.* New York: Columbia University Press, 1953. Pp. 197–204.

Josselyn, Irene M. *Psychosocial Development of Children.* New York: Family Service Association of America, 1948.

Kubie, Lawrence S. "Social Forces and the Neurotic Process," in Alexander H. Leighton *et al.*, eds., *Explorations in Social Psychiatry.* New York: Basic Books, 1957. Pp. 77–104.

Langner, Thomas S., and Michael, Stanley, T. *Life Stress and Mental Health: The Midtown Manhattan Study.* New York: Free Press of Glencoe, 1963.

Leighton, Alexander, MD. "Individuals Under Stress," *The Governing of Men.* Princeton, N.J.: Princeton University Press, 1945.

_____. *My Name is Legion: Foundation for a Theory of Man in Relation to Culture.* New York: Basic Books, 1959.

Levy, David M. *Maternal Overprotection.* New York: Columbia University Press, 1943.

Lewis, Hylan. "Child Rearing Practices Among Low Income Families," *Casework Papers, 1961.* New York: Family Service Association of America, 1961. Pp. 79–92.

Lewis, Oscar. *Five Families.* New York: Basic Books, 1959.

Littner, Ner, MD. "Some Traumatic Effects of Separation and Placement." New York: Child Welfare League of America, 1956. Pp. 5–32. Also in *Casework Papers, 1956.* New York: Family Service Association of America, 1956. Pp. 121–140.

Mead, Margaret. "The Contemporary American Family as an Anthropologist Sees It," in Herman D. Stein and Richard A. Cloward, eds., *Social Perspectives on Behavior.* Glencoe, Ill.: Free Press, 1958. Pp. 20–26.

_____, and Wolfenstein, Martha (eds.). *Childhood in Contemporary Cultures.* Chicago: University of Chicago Press, 1955.

Olmstead, Michael. *The Small Group.* New York: Random House, 1959.

Plant, James. *Family Living Space and Personality. Personality and the Culture Pattern.* Washington, D.C.: Howard University Press, 1937.

Sprott, W.J.H. *Human Groups.* New York: Pelican Books, 1958.

Thelen, Herbert A. *Dynamics of Groups at Work.* Chicago: University of Chicago Press, 1963.

IV. Illness and handicaps (physical, mental, emotional, and social)

Babcock, Charlotte G., MD. "Inner Stress in Illness and Disability," in Howard J. Parad and Roger R. Miller, eds., *Ego-Oriented Casework: Problems and Perspectives.* New York: Family Service Association of America, 1963. Pp. 45–64.

Bloch, Herbert, and Flynn, Frank T. *Delinquency.* New York: Random House, 1956.

Cannon, Walter B. *The Wisdom of the Body.* 2d ed.; New York: W. W. Norton and Co., 1939.

Cloward, Richard A., and Ohlin, Lloyd E. *Delinquency and Opportunity: A Theory of Delinquent Gangs.* Glencoe, Ill.: Free Press, 1960.

Deutsch, Albert. *The Mentally Ill in America.* 2d ed.; New York: Columbia University Press, 1949.

Engle, George L. "Is Grief a Disease? A Challenge for Medical Research," *Psychosomatic Medicine,* Vol. 33 (January and February 1961), pp. 18–22.

Finch, Stuart M., MD. *Fundamentals of Child Psychiatry.* New York: W. W. Norton and Co., 1960.

Garrett, James F. (ed.). *Psychological Aspects of Physical Disability.* (Rehabilitation Service Series No. 210.) Washington, D.C.: U.S. Office of Vocational Rehabilitation, 1952.

Gerard, Margaret W., MD. *The Emotionally Disturbed Child.* New York: Child Welfare League of America, 1957.

Hollingshead, August B., and Redlich, Frederick C. *Social Class and Mental Illness— A Community Study.* New York: John Wiley and Sons, 1958.

Interview Guide for Specific Disabilities. 7 vols.; Washington, D.C.: U.S. Employment Security Bureau, 1954–57.

Kanner, Leo, MD. *Child Psychiatry.* 3d ed.; Springfield, Ill.: Charles C Thomas, 1962.

Kanner, Leon F. "Parent Counseling," in Jerome H. Rothstein, ed., *Mental Retardation.* New York: Holt, Rinehart, and Winston, 1961. Pp. 453–461.

Keyserling, Leon. *Poverty and Deprivation in the United States.* Washington, D.C.: Conference on Economic Progress, 1962.

Kruse, N. D. (ed.). *Alcoholism as a Medical Problem.* New York: Paul B. Hoeber, 1956.

Lindemann, Eric. "Symptomatology and Management of Acute Grief," *American Journal of Psychiatry,* Vol. 101 (September 1944), pp. 141–148.

Mandelbaum, Arthur, and Wheeler, Mary E. "The Meaning of a Defective Child to Parents," *Social Casework,* Vol. 41, No. 7 (July 1960), pp. 360–367.

Masland, Richard L., Sarason, Seymour B., and Gladwin, Thomas. *Mental Subnormality. Biological, Psychological, and Cultural Factors.* New York: Basic Books, 1958.

May, Edgar. *The Wasted Americans.* New York: Harper and Row, 1964.

Nelson, Waldo E. *Textbook of Pediatrics.* 6th ed.; Philadelphia: W. B. Saunders, 1954.

Noyes, Arthur C., and Kolb, Lawrence C. *Modern Clinical Psychiatry.* 6th ed.; Philadelphia: W. B. Saunders, 1963.

Olshansky, Simon. "Chronic Sorrow: A Response to Having a Mentally Defective Child," *Social Casework,* Vol. 43, No. 4 (April 1962), pp. 190–193.

Passamaneck, Benjamin, and Knoblock, Hilda. "Epidemiologic Studies on the Complications of Pregnancy and the Birth Process," in Gerald Caplan, ed., *Prevention of Mental Disorders in Children—Initial Explorations.* New York: Basic Books, 1961. Pp. 77–94.

Rose, Arnold M. *The Negro in America.* New York: Harper & Brothers, 1948.

———. *Mental Health and Mental Disorders.* New York: W. W. Norton and Co., 1955.

Srole, Leo, *et al. Mental Health in the Metropolis. The Midtown Manhattan Study.* New York: Blakiston Division, McGraw-Hill Book Co., 1962.

Selye, Hans, MD. *The Stress of Life.* New York: McGraw-Hill Book Co., 1956.

Smith, Michael (ed.). *Management of the Handicapped Child.* New York: Grune and Stratton, 1957.

Thurston, Henry W. *The Dependent Child.* New York: Columbia University Press, 1930.

Thurston, John R. "Counseling the Parents of the Severely Handicapped," in Jerome H. Rothstein, ed., *Mental Retardation*. New York: Holt, Rinehart, and Winston, 1961. Pp. 461–467.

U.S. Children's Bureau. *Emotional Problems Associated with Handicapping Conditions in Children*. (Children's Bureau Publication No. 336.) Washington, D.C.: U.S. Department of Health, Education, and Welfare, 1952.

Vincent, Clark. *Unmarried Mothers*. New York: Free Press of Glencoe, 1961.

White, William A. *The Meaning of Disease: An Inquiry in the Field of Medical Psychology*. Baltimore: Williams and Wilkins, 1926.

V. Social work practice with individuals and groups

Social casework—general

Aikin, Dorothy. "A Project on Family Diagnosis and Treatment," *Social Work Practice, 1963*. New York: Columbia University Press, 1963. Pp. 111–118.

Beatman, Frances L. "Family Interaction: Its Significance for Diagnosis and Treatment," *Social Casework*, Vol. 38, No. 3 (March 1957), pp. 111–118.

Biestek, Felix P. *The Casework Relationship*. Chicago: Loyola University Press, 1957.

Briar, Joseph Scott. "The Family as an Organization: An Approach to Family Diagnosis and Treatment," *Social Service Review*, Vol. 38, No. 3 (September 1964), pp. 247–255.

de Schweinitz, Karl, and de Schweinitz, Elizabeth. "Interviewing in the Social Services." (NCSS Reference No. 636.) London, England: National Council of Social Service for the National Institute for Social Work Training, September 1962. Distributed in North America by the Council on Social Work Education, New York.

Garrett, Annette. *Interviewing: Its Principles and Methods*. New York: Family Service Association of America, 1942.

Geismar, Ludwig L., and Ayres, Beverly. "A Method for Evaluating the Social Functioning of Families Under Treatment," *Social Work*, Vol. 4, No. 1 (January 1959), pp. 102–108.

Hamilton, Gordon. *Theory and Practice of Social Casework*. 2d ed., rev.; New York: Columbia University Press, 1951.

Hamilton, Kenneth W. *Counselling the Handicapped in the Rehabilitation Process*. New York: Ronald Press, 1950.

Hollis, Florence. "The Relationship Between Psychosocial Diagnosis and Treatment," *Social Casework*, Vol. 32, No. 2 (February 1951), pp. 67–74.

———. *Casework: A Psychosocial Therapy*. New York: Random House, 1964.

Landy, David. "Problems of the Person Seeking Help in Our Culture," *The Social Welfare Forum, 1960*. New York: Columbia University Press, 1960. Pp. 127–145.

Overton, Alice. "Taking Help from Our Clients," *Social Work*, Vol. 5, No. 2 (April 1960), pp. 42–50.

Parad, Howard J., and Caplan, Gerald, MD. "A Framework for Studying Families in Crisis," *Social Work*, Vol. 5, No. 3 (July 1960), pp. 3–15.

Perlman, Helen Harris. "Social Components of Casework Practice," *The Social Welfare Forum, 1953*. New York: Columbia University Press, 1953. Pp. 124–136.

_____. *Social Casework: A Problem-Solving Process*. Chicago: University of Chicago Press, 1957.

_____. "Family Diagnosis: Some Problems," *The Social Welfare Forum, 1958*. New York: Columbia University Press, 1958. Pp. 122–134.

Rapoport, Lydia. "Working with Families in Crises: An Exploration in Preventive Interaction," *Social Work*, Vol. 7, No. 3 (July 1962), pp. 86–91.

_____. "The State of Crisis: Some Theoretical Considerations," *Social Service Review*, Vol. 36, No. 2 (June 1962), pp. 211–217.

Richmond, Mary E. *Social Diagnosis*. New York: Russell Sage Foundation, 1947.

Ripple, Lilian, with Alexander, Ernestina, and Polemis, Bernice W. "Motivation, Capacity and Opportunity." (Social Service Monographs, Second Series.) Chicago: School of Social Service Administration, University of Chicago, 1964. Pp. 19–39.

"Scope and Methods of the Family Service Agency." New York: Family Service Association of America, 1953.

Selby, Lola G. "Supportive Treatment—The Development of a Concept and a Helping Method," *Social Service Review*, Vol. 30, No. 4 (December 1956), pp. 400–414.

_____. "Social Work and Crisis Theory," *Social Work Papers, X*. Los Angeles: University of Southern California, 1963. Pp. 1–11.

Towle, Charlotte. "Factors in Treatment," *Proceedings of the National Conference of Social Work, 1936*. Chicago: University of Chicago Press, 1936. Pp. 179–191.

_____. "Underlying Skills in Social Casework Today," *Social Service Review*, Vol. 15, No. 3 (September 1941), pp. 456–471. Also in *Proceedings of the National Conference of Social Work, 1941*. Chicago: University of Chicago Press, 1941. Pp. 254–266.

_____. "Casework Methods of Helping the Client to Make Maximum Use of His Capacities and Resources," *Social Service Review*, Vol. 22, No. 4 (December 1948), pp. 469–480.

_____. "Client Centered Casework," *Social Service Review*, Vol. 24, No. 4 (December 1950), pp. 451–458.

Social casework—specific (settings, needs, and problems)

Bernstein, Rose. "Unmarried Parents," in Harry L. Lurie, ed., *Encyclopedia of Social Work*. New York: National Association of Social Workers, 1965. Pp. 797–801.

"Casework with the Aging," *Social Casework*, Vol. 42, Nos. 5–6 (May–June 1961), pp. 219–290.

Daly, Dorothy Bird. *Casework Practice in Public Assistance Administration*. Chicago: American Public Welfare Association, 1942.

Foster, Helen B. "Family Centered Services Through Aid to Dependent Children," *The Social Welfare Forum, 1958*. New York: Columbia University Press, 1958. Pp. 154–165.

Hersh, Alexander. "Casework with Parents of Retarded Children," *Social Work*, Vol. 6, No. 2 (April 1961), pp. 61–66.

Leach, Jean M. "The Intergenerational Approach in Casework with the Aging," *Social Casework*, Vol. 45, No. 3 (March 1964), pp. 144–149.

Lokshin, Helen. "Critical Issues in Serving an Aging Population," *Social Casework*, Vol. 42, No. 1 (January 1961), pp. 21–27.

Mitchell, Celia Brody. "The Use of Family Sessions in the Diagnosis and Treatment of Disturbances in Children," *Social Casework*, Vol. 41, No. 6 (June 1960), pp. 283–290.

Perlman, Helen Harris. "Family Diagnosis in Cases of Illness and Disability," *Family-Centered Social Work in Illness and Disability: A Preventive Approach*. (Monograph VI in the series "Social Work Practice in Medical Care and Rehabilitation Settings.") New York: National Association of Social Workers, 1961. Pp. 7–20.

_____. "Mental Health Planning for Children," *Child Welfare* (June 1949), pp. 8f, 16–18.

_____. "Casework Services in Public Welfare," *Proceedings of the National Conference of Social Work, 1947*. Chicago: University of Chicago Press, 1947. Pp. 261–269.

_____. "Identity Problems, Role and Casework Treatment," *Social Service Review*, Vol. 37, No. 3 (September 1963), pp. 307–318.

Rall, Mary E. "The Effective Use of Casework Principles in the Family Agency," *Social Service Review*, Vol. 24, No. 3 (September 1950), pp. 327–333.

_____. "Casework with the Minor Unmarried Mother and Her Family," *Social Casework*, Vol. 39, No. 9 (November 1958), pp. 494–502.

Wasser, Edna. "Responsibility, Self-Determination and Authority in Casework Protection of Older Persons," *Social Casework*, Vol. 42, Nos. 5–6 (May–June 1961), pp. 258–266.

Wiltse, Kermit T. "Social Casework Services in the Aid to Dependent Children's Program," *Social Service Review*, Vol. 28, No. 2 (June 1954), pp. 173–185.

_____. "Social Casework and Public Assistance," *Social Service Review*, Vol. 32, No. 1 (March 1958), pp. 41–50.

_____. "The Hopeless Family," *Social Work*, Vol. 3, No. 4 (October 1958), pp. 12–22. Also in *The Social Welfare Forum, 1958*. New York: Columbia University Press, 1958. Pp. 135–153.

Younghusband, Eileen. "Adoption and the Unmarried Mother," *Social Work and Social Change*. (National Institute for Social Work Training series, No. 1.) London: George Allen and Unwin, Ltd., 1964. Part I, pp. 53–61.

Social group work—general

Coyle, Grace L. "Concepts Relevant to Helping the Family as a Group," *Social Casework*, Vol. 43, No. 7 (July 1962), pp. 347–354.

Falck, Hans. "The Use of Groups in the Practice of Social Work," *Social Casework*, Vol. 44, No. 2 (February 1963), pp. 63–67.

Frey, Louise A. "Support and the Group: Generic Treatment Form," *Social Work*, Vol. 7, No. 4 (October 1962), pp. 35–42.

Phillips, Helen H. *Essentials of Group Work Skill*. New York: Association Press, 1957.

_____. "Group Services to Clients: Purpose and Process," *Child Welfare*, Vol. 42, No. 6 (June 1963), pp. 265–272.

Vinter, Robert. "New Evidence for Restructuring Group Services," *New Perspectives on Services to Groups*. New York: National Association of Social Workers, 1961. Pp. 48–69.

Social group work—specific

Bell, Courtenay, and Kaplan, Harvey. "Public Voluntary Sponsorship of a Mothers' Group," *Social Casework*, Vol. 45, No. 1 (January 1964), pp. 21–25.

Falck, Hans. "Helping Caseworkers Use the Social Group Method," *Public Welfare*, Vol. 22, No. 2 (April 1964), pp. 125–129.

Fenton, Norman, and Wiltse, Kermit (eds.). *Group Methods in the Public Welfare Programs*. Palo Alto, Calif.: Pacific Books, 1963.

Group Treatment in Family Service Agencies. New York: Family Service Association of America, 1964.

Klein, Alan. "Exploring Family Group Counseling," *Social Work*, Vol. 8, No. 1 (January 1963), pp. 23–29.

Shoemaker, Louise. "Social Group Work in the ADC Program," *Social Work*, Vol. 8, No. 1 (January 1963), pp. 30–36.

Trecker, Harleigh B. *Group Services in Public Welfare*. Washington, D.C.: U.S. Department of Health, Education, and Welfare, Bureau of Family Services, 1964.

VI. Social work education (administering, teaching, and helping)

Within schools (classroom and field)

Berengarten, Sidney. "Identifying Learning Patterns of Individual Students: An Exploratory Study," *Social Service Review*, Vol. 31, No. 4 (December 1957), pp. 407–417.

The Case Method in Teaching Social Work. New York: National Association of Social Workers, 1959.

Heywood, Jean. *An Introduction to Teaching Casework Skills*. New York: Humanities Press, 1964.

Joint Committee of the Association of American Medical Colleges and the American Association of Medical Social Workers. *Widening Horizons in Medical Education: A Study of the Teaching of Social and Environmental Factors in Medicine*. New York: Commonwealth Fund, 1948.

Large, Dorothy. "Four Processes of Field Instruction in Casework," *Social Service Review*, Vol. 37, No. 3 (September 1963), pp. 263–282.

Lehrman, Louis J. "The Integration of Class and Field in Professional Education," *Social Casework*, Vol. 33, No. 6 (June 1952), pp. 250–255.

———. "Field Work Training in a Public Assistance Setting," in Cora Kasius, ed., *Principles and Techniques in Social Casework: Selected Articles, 1940– 1950*. New York: Family Service Association of America, 1950. Pp. 213–221.

Lindenberg, Ruth Ellen. "Changing Traditional Patterns of Supervision," *Social Work*, Vol. 2, No. 2 (April 1957), pp. 42–46.

Lloyd, Katherine A. "Field Work as Part of Undergraduate Preparation for Professional Education," *Social Service Review*, Vol. 30, No. 1 (March 1956), pp. 55–64.

Merrifield, Aleanor. "Changing Patterns and Programs in Field Instruction," *Social Service Review*, Vol. 37, No. 3 (September 1963), pp. 274–282.

Neustaedter, Eleanor. "The Field Supervisor as Educator," in Cora Kasius, ed., *Principles and Techniques in Social Case Work*. New York: Family Service Association of America, 1950. Pp. 200–212.

Pumphrey, Muriel W. *The Teaching of Values and Ethics in Social Work Education.* (Vol. XIII of the Curriculum Study.) New York: Council on Social Work Education, 1959.

Rapoport, Lydia. *The Role of Supervision in Professional Education.* (Health Education Monographs No. 15.) Rye, N.Y.: Society of Public Health Education, 1963.

Reynolds, Rosemary. "Evaluating the Field Work of Students." New York: Family Service Association of America, 1946.

————. "Relationship of Fieldwork to Classroom Teaching," *Social Casework*, Vol. 33, No. 3 (March 1952), pp. 99–105.

Selby, Lola. "Helping Students in Field Practice Modify Blocks in Learning," *Social Service Review*, Vol. 29, No. 1 (March 1955), pp. 53–63.

Somers, Mary Louise. "The Small Group in Learning and Teaching," *Learning and Teaching in Public Welfare I*. Washington, D.C.: U.S. Department of Health, Education, and Welfare, 1963. Pp. 158–175.

Towle, Charlotte. *The Learner in Education for the Professions.* Chicago: University of Chicago Press, 1954.

————. "The Place of Help in Supervision," *Social Service Review*, Vol. 37, No. 4 (December 1963), pp. 403–415.

Wessel, Rosa, and Faith, Goldie. *Professional Education Based in Practice*. Philadelphia: University of Pennsylvania School of Social Work, 1953.

Within agencies and institutions (supervision and consultation)

Abrahamson, Arthur. *Group Methods in Supervision and Staff Development*. New York: Harper & Brothers, 1959.

Austin, Lucille. "Basic Principles in Supervision," *Social Casework*, Vol. 33, No. 10 (December 1952), pp. 411–419.

Berkowitz, Sydney J. "The Administrative Process in Casework Supervision," *Social Casework*, Vol. 33, No. 10 (December 1952), pp. 419–423.

Black, Bertram J. "Tools and Techniques of Administration," *Social Casework*, Vol. 31, No. 6 (June 1950), pp. 223–229.

Blackey, Eileen A. *Group Leadership in Staff Training.* (Bureau of Public Assistance Report No. 29, Children's Bureau Publication No. 361.) Washington, D.C.: U.S. Department of Health, Education, and Welfare, 1957.

Faatz, Anita. *The Nature of Policy in the Administration of Public Assistance.* Philadelphia: University of Pennsylvania Press, 1943.

Feldman, Yonata. "The Teaching Aspect of Casework Supervision," in Cora Kasius, ed., *Principles and Techniques in Social Casework*. New York: Family Service Association of America, 1950. Pp. 222–232.

Gilmore, Mary Holmes. "Consultation as Social Work Activity," in Lydia Rapoport, ed., *Consultation in Social Work Practice*. New York: National Association of Social Workers, 1963. Pp. 33–51.

Golton, Margaret. "The Beginning Casework Practitioner: A Categorical Delineation," *Social Service Review*, Vol. 33, No. 3 (September 1959), pp. 245–252.

Gorman, Joanna F. "Some Characteristics of Consultation," in Lydia Rapoport, ed., *Consultation in Social Work Practice*. New York: National Association of Social Workers, 1963. Pp. 21–33.

Grossbard, Herman. "Methodology for Developing Self-Awareness," *Social Casework*, Vol. 35, No. 9 (November 1954), pp. 380–386.

Hamilton, Gordon. "Self-Awareness in Professional Education," *Social Casework*, Vol. 35, No. 9 (November 1954), pp. 371–379.

Hollis, Florence. "The Emotional Growth of the Worker Through Supervision," *Proceedings of the National Conference of Social Work, 1936*. Chicago: University of Chicago Press, 1936. Pp. 167–178.

Introduction to a Social Worker. (National Institute for Social Work Training Series, No. 2.) London: George Allen and Unwin, Ltd., 1964.

Johnson, Arlien. "Educating Social Workers for Ethical Practice," *Social Service Review*, Vol. 24, No. 2 (June 1955), pp. 125–136.

Kevin, David. "Use of the Group Method in Consultation," in Lydia Rapoport, ed., *Consultation in Social Work Practice*. New York: National Association of Social Workers, 1963. Pp. 69–85.

Linford, Alton A. "Education and In-Service Training for the Public Family and Children's Services." New York: Council on Social Work Education, 1963.

Perlman, Helen Harris. *So You Want to be a Social Worker?* New York: Harper and Row, 1962.

Rapoport, Lydia. "Consultation: An Overview," in Rapoport, ed., *Consultation in Social Work Practice*. New York: National Association of Social Workers, 1963. Pp. 7–21.

Robinson, Virginia P. *The Dynamics of Supervision Under Functional Controls*. Philadelphia: University of Pennsylvania Press, 1949.

Schour, Esther. "Helping Social Workers Handle Work Stresses," *Socal Casework*, Vol. 35, No. 10 (December 1953), pp. 423–428.

Spencer, Esther C., and Croley, H. T. "Administrative Consultation," in Lydia Rapoport, ed., *Consultation in Social Work Practice*. New York: National Association of Social Workers, 1963. Pp. 51–69.

Stiles, Evelyn. "Supervision in Perspective," *Social Casework*, Vol. 44, No. 1 (January 1963), pp. 19–25.

Techniques of Student and Staff Supervision. New York: Family Service Association of America, 1953.

Towle, Charlotte. "The Contribution of Education for Social Casework to Practice," in Cora Kasius, ed., *Principles and Techniques in Social Casework*. New York: Family Service Association of America, 1950. Pp. 260–274.

———. "The Role of Supervision in the Union of Cause and Function in Social Work," *Social Service Review*, Vol. 36, No. 4 (December 1962), pp. 396–411.

Williamson, Margaret. *Supervision—New Patterns and Processes*. New York: Association Press, 1961.

Wolfe, Corinne H. "Basic Components in Supervision," *The Social Welfare Forum, 1958*. New York: Columbia University Press, 1958. Pp. 177–189.

82M/65–81/P.D.

3M/3/85